WHAT ARE THE ODDS?

FROM CRACK ADDICT TO CEO

WHAT ARE THE ODDS?
FROM CRACK ADDICT TO CEO

BY MIKE LINDELL

For more information:
343 E. 82nd Street, Suite 102, Chaska, Minnesota 55318

Library of Congress Cataloging-in-Publication Data is available.
ISBN 978-1-7342834-0-2 (HC)
ISBN 978-1-7342834-1-9 (PB)

1 3 5 7 9 10 8 6 4 2

Book Design: GLS / NEXT Precision Marketing

PRINTED IN THE UNITED STATES OF AMERICA

Lindell Publishing, LLC

In this life we all experience moments,
sometimes so unique or unusual that we pause and say,
Wow...what are the odds that could happen?
And if something like that happens again,
maybe we say it's just coincidence.

How many once-in-a-lifetime events do we
attribute to simple chance before we believe that
perhaps it's something more? At what point
do you ask yourself, is it all just luck
or have I experienced a miracle?

I dedicate this book to anyone looking for hope.

FOREWORD

BY DR. BEN CARSON

The first time I met Mike Lindell was at a National Prayer Breakfast event, and it was his voice that I recognized. His "MyPillow" commercials were everywhere—you couldn't turn on the TV without seeing him. In fact, after I bowed out of the 2016 presidential race and endorsed Donald Trump, I mentioned Mike and his pillow company to then-candidate Trump.

"That guy is on television more than anyone I've ever seen," Trump said, "including me."

MyPillow is the most successful direct marketing product in the history of America. You don't have to know its inventor very long to see why. Mike Lindell is a natural marketer and entrepreneur. God gives everyone special gifts, but He also places challenges in our way to make us stronger. Some people meet these challenges head-on, right away, inspiring us all. Others take a "broken road," inspiring us all the more by overcoming not only external challenges, but perhaps the greatest obstacle of all—themselves.

Mike's is that kind of story. Gambling addiction seized him while he was still a teenager. In his 20s, he became a frequent cocaine user and then an addict. When crack cocaine came on the scene in the late 1990s, Mike swore he would never use it. But he broke that vow and when he did, crack took him down fast.

Together, Mike's cocaine, crack, and gambling addictions would drive him into the darkest corners of America, bankrupt his family, ruin his marriage, and nearly take his life. But even as he was in the depths of despair, God inspired a dream, and MyPillow was born. At first, Mike thought his company would be a way to support his family. But over time, God showed him that the company was really a tool Mike could use to share his own story of hope and recovery.

What Are the Odds? is a testimonial about the power of a dream. It is about a man who went about as far down as a human being can go, but came out clean and sober on the other side. It's a story about failure, success, humility, courage—and ultimately, hope.

Benjamin S. Carson, Sr., MD
Professor Emeritus of Neurosurgery
Johns Hopkins Children's Center

PROLOGUE

I remember the moment, the exact scene. My wife and teenage son sat on the living room floor, cheerfully at work on the family business, boxes and labels scattered around. They were yakking away about this and that as they hand-labeled MyPillow shipping boxes with Magic Markers.

Yet what I saw before me was not a happy family scene, but a world about to collapse.

It was February 2007. Our little family business—which I was running out of a rented bus shed—was on the verge of a hostile takeover. We were about to lose our house. Our bank accounts had dwindled to almost nothing. So had my marriage to Karen.

And then there was all the hidden stuff. Alcohol and drugs were taking their toll. I was heavily into gambling. I owed my bookie $45,000. Everything was about to come crashing down.

My family just didn't know it yet.

I'd walked the razor's edge for years, blessed with a lifelong lucky streak. I would back myself into one hopeless corner after another and then, at the last possible minute, pull off a miraculous escape. Which is why I found myself wondering: *What if—somehow—the odds again fell in my favor? What if I could somehow squeak by…again?* That's just the way my mind worked.

Which is why I didn't cancel our annual trip to Mexico.

Well, that and the fact that a Mexican drug dealer had promised me an unlimited supply of cocaine.

Yes. I was an addict. Part of my story is about addiction. But not the kind where the user winds up living in the streets. I'm an ordinary guy from Minnesota. I had owned businesses and raised a family. Coached our kids in Little League. Taken them hunting and fishing. All that small-town America stuff.

You see, not all addicts live under a bridge somewhere, lonely and broke.

In fact, our house was the house where all our kids' friends wanted to hang out. Neither our kids nor their friends knew that the Lindell adults were addicts. This is the hidden world of addiction that most people don't see. Men and women with families—people functioning in the community, serving on committees, owning businesses, holding down jobs. At least for a while. Addiction affects everyone, no matter how many forks they eat with.

That spring of 2007, as my self-destruction gained speed, I did what addicts do: I tried to escape my problems. Karen and I, with our close friends Paul (nicknamed Skelly) and Jenny, flew down to a Mexican beach town. The flight seemed to take forever. Looking down on passing clouds, all I could think about was that first line of cocaine.

I fidgeted in my seat, looking at the satellite map on the seat in front of me, counting down the southbound miles until we got there. Time dragged as the animated airplane seemed to barely move. Once we landed, it would be an hour ride to the resort and maybe even longer until I could meet up with my coke-promising dealer, a Mexican we called "the Greek." I didn't want to wait that long.

Finally, we landed and boarded the shuttle to our resort. As we rolled toward the beach, Skelly, Jenny, and Karen relaxed with beers and watched the sights through the window like normal tourists. But for me, the miles ticked by with agonizing slowness. The bus driver droned on about the sights, and I couldn't have cared less. I just want to get there—a place where there were no governors on my addiction. No work, no family obligations, not even the police. Even more importantly, I wouldn't have to worry about where to get my coke, because down here, it was *everywhere*. It was an addict's dream.

With my life and business crumbling around me, I wanted to get high and stay high. In fact, whenever we went to Mexico, I never slept. Literally never. Skelly joked that for me, a week in Mexico was like a 14-day vacation.

As soon as we got to the coast, we checked into our favorite resort. The guest rooms were inside a pair of tall, white, modern buildings that overlooked a giant sapphire pool. From our balcony, we could see past the pool to a small group of islands not far from shore. The whole place was spa-like and beautiful. But in my mind, I was already out the door. As soon as we dropped our bags, I left the hotel to track down the Greek. The others knew I wouldn't be back until I found him.

I found the Greek on the beach, as usual. The previous year, I'd blundered into a situation that pitted rival dealers against each other. I barely escaped with my life, but the incident turned out well for the Greek. Now, in return, he handed over a few baggies of coke. It wasn't the huge supply he'd promised, but then again, drug dealers aren't known for keeping their promises. Shouldering through crowds of tourists who blurred as I passed them, I rushed back to the hotel, clutching my drugs.

Finally, my vacation had begun.

For the next couple of days, Karen, Skelly, and Jenny did touristy things—club-hopping, sitting by the pool, buying trinkets at the local markets. I tagged along for some of that stuff, but then around midnight on the fifth day, I ran into a problem. The Greek had given me four "teeners," little packets of coke that weighed just under two grams each. We had finished two and had a little left in a third. The four of us were hanging out in my hotel room when I realized I couldn't find the fourth and final packet.

I began a casual search that quickly escalated into a frantic tossing of our entire room. I pawed through all the crap that had by now exited our suitcases and was lying all over the place—clothes, shoes, toiletries. I turned out the pockets of all the shorts I'd brought. Rifled in and around leftover room service items.

Had I left the teener in the bathroom? I went to look. No.

Had I put it under the mattress for safekeeping? No.

Had I given it to Skelly, Jenny, or Karen to hold? No, no, and no.

It hit me that before I could see the Greek around 7 or 8 a.m. the next morning, we were going to run out of coke. I looked at Jenny. "This is going to be a disaster," I said.

Looking back, I can see that I was blind to my obsession. Blind to the crazy logic that to have to wait just a few hours for a fresh supply of drugs would ruin the whole evening.

Back home in Minnesota, my mind was always working on the problem of supply even while I was doing other things. I had once been a professional card counter in Vegas—I'll tell you more about that later—so I tended to think in terms of percentages, probability, and odds. Always, I would see the supply issue in my mind like "the count" in a casino, me against the house: How much coke or crack I had, which dealers were available, how much money I needed, or if I didn't have any money, which dealers would give me drugs on credit, and what I needed to say to persuade them.

No matter what, I never, ever wanted a gap.

And it wasn't just about me, or at least that's what I thought. In my own twisted thinking, I was the guy who could get things done when others couldn't and show people things they'd never seen before. I'd played the role since childhood.

Now, I stood in the middle of the hotel room worried that Karen, Skelly, and Jenny's night would be ruined. I can't run out, I thought. I *can't*. This was my fourth trip to Mexico, so I knew where to find coke. From the charter-fishing guys to the beach chair rental guys to the taxi drivers, there was always someone ready and willing to sell.

My first plan was to find a taxi. In this town, taxis were basically rolling drug stores. I was a smoker then, so I tucked my cigarettes in my t-shirt pocket, noticing that I was almost out of those, too. I made a mental note to buy another pack, then stepped out of the resort lobby into the warm summer night.

Even though it was almost 1 a.m., the air felt warm and humid, and I was comfortable in a t-shirt, shorts, and flip-flops. I walked down a street crowded with tourists spilling out of the cantinas, laughing over bottles of Corona and Dos Equis, still partying into the wee hours of the morning. But after about three blocks, the foot traffic thinned out, and I hadn't seen a single cab. By the fourth block, I was walking alone through the dark.

It wasn't long before I arrived at a little store on the edge of town. Just a wooden shack, really, maybe 10-by-10. They sold convenience store stuff—beer, soda, cigarettes. I had been there the year before, in connection with that favor I had done for the Greek. The street was quiet now and deserted except for four Mexican guys out front. One man was standing and the other three sat on a long, wooden bench.

"Hello! How are you doing?" the standing man said. He spoke very good English. He was casually dressed and clean cut, with short, dark hair.

"Do you have any cocaine?" I said it straight out. I had done this before.

"Sure! Sure, *señor*!" Clean Cut said, smiling. "No problem. Do you want a beer?"

To be polite, I accepted. He seemed friendly, but I knew an act when I saw one. I had earned a lot of money on Vegas blackjack tables by then. Great card counters disguise their mental calculations by putting on an act. They also "read the room." Clean Cut was schmoozing me, but I knew his smooth words covered a hard edge.

I gave him a $100 bill, and when he went to grab the beer from somewhere in the shack, I took the opportunity to read his companions. They were all slouched on the bench smoking cigarettes. Even though they were sitting, I could tell all three were shorter than me, 5-foot-9 or 5-foot-10.

Nothing remarkable about the one closest to me. The third guy—the one farthest from me—I knew immediately that he had a gun. I thought that was weird. Buying drugs in Mexico was usually pretty casual, and dealers down here wore board shorts and straw hats, not nine-millimeter pistols.

Strangely, it was the man in the middle who worried me more. He had angry eyes, like the eyes of a young gang member who is just burning up inside because of some awful pain in his past. I'd seen eyes like that in some pretty bad places. Glancing down, I noticed that Eyes had something leaning against the bench next to his leg. Some long, slim object wrapped in a white cloth. I didn't know what it was, but I decided right then that he was the kind of guy I didn't want to upset. You never know what a man with eyes like that will do.

Clean Cut came back with the beer. "Here you go, *amigo*. Sit! Sit! I called my friend. The *coca* will be here in a little while."

I took a seat on the bench next to the three others, pulled out a cigarette and lit it. Again, I noticed how lonely this place was. Not even a block away, I could hear late-night party sounds. But here, nothing.

"What are you doing way out here, *amigo*?" Clean Cut said.

"I told you," I said. "Looking for some cocaine."

"You don't like taxi cabs? Plenty of *coca* in taxis."

I laughed a little. "I was actually looking for a taxi, and I couldn't find one." He looked at me suspiciously. "Where are you staying?"

Hmm. An uncomfortable question from a drug dealer. I lied and gave him the name of a resort down the street.

Clean Cut glanced down at my arms. "Where's your wristband?"

Now I knew something was up. He was talking about the wristband that tourists wear when they're booked into an all-inclusive resort. Clean Cut was trying to catch me in a lie.

"We didn't get the all-inclusive package," I said.

"You don't like the police, do you?" he said.

The schmoozing was over. The back of my neck tingled, but otherwise I felt no fear. Maybe it was the line I did before I left the hotel, maybe it was instinct, but I eyeballed Clean Cut and gave it right back to him. "Police? What are you talking about?" I pointed to my nose and the little white flecks caught in my mustache. "Do I look like a cop to you?"

He held up his hands in a *whoa* motion. "Okay, okay. Do you want another beer?"

"Sure."

I didn't really, but I needed to buy time. It seemed Clean Cut thought I was some kind of undercover cop or spy or something. By now about 20 minutes had passed. As he headed into the shack, I looked around. The other three were still seated on the bench to my right, the long, cloth-wrapped object still leaning against the bench at Eyes' feet.

Even though I could still hear bar music and chatter not far off, not a single car had passed by the shack. It was eerie. I felt shut off from the world, trapped in a dark bubble where bad things could happen.

But where was that cocaine?

When Clean Cut brought me the second beer, I kept up the casino act I'd chosen for the occasion: Slightly Offended Customer.

I jumped up. "Look, we've been waiting a long time," I said. "My wife is going to be worried. I need to call her." I reached into my shorts pocket for my cell phone.

"Sit down," Clean Cut said evenly. "You don't need to call your wife." The coke would arrive soon, he assured me. But he wasn't smiling anymore. Then he said something that swung the needle on my danger meter all the way to the right: "You look very familiar. Have you ever been here before?"

"No, never." Another lie.

"Really? You look like a gringo from last year. He was with some enemies of ours."

Time froze. I know it sounds like a cliché, but some things are clichés for a reason. Remember that incident I mentioned with the Greek from the previous year? It involved rival drug gangs, and that time, the Greek's gang came out on top. I had never seen Clean Cut in my life, but I suddenly realized he must have been part of the other gang. Worse, he suspected that I had been involved.

I kept up my act, which I had sharpened in earlier gambling escapes in Vegas, Milwaukee, and Kansas City: Deflect. Divert. Act as though the other person hadn't said what he said.

"You know what?" I said angrily. "Why don't you just keep the cocaine? My wife is really going to be upset that I'm not back yet." I pulled out my phone.

Clean Cut's stare got harder. "No, *amigo*, you don't need to call her. It will be here soon."

"Really?" I said impatiently. "The coke will be here soon? You keep saying that."

I thought of Karen. Suddenly, the financial mess I'd been hiding from her seemed trivial compared with this immediate danger. My mind ran like a hamster on a wheel, calculating what I needed to say to get out of this. I was usually very good at tight scenarios like this, but it was very late, and I'd been up for days. Maybe that was why I said exactly the wrong thing.

"Where is the coke coming from?" I asked, then blurted out the name of a nearby town.

That was a huge mistake. The name of the town wasn't something I would have known if I had never been there before. The three men on the bench leapt to their feet, surrounding me. In one motion, Eyes unsheathed the mysterious object and pressed it against my throat. It was a machete, and its blade gleamed dully in the light from the shack. I felt electrified, but not scared, if you know what I mean—like when you almost get in a car wreck but somehow steer clear, *then* break into the shakes and cold sweat when the danger is past.

In that moment, a normal person would have started begging for his life. But I was not normal. I grabbed the machete blade with both hands and looked Eyes square in the face.

"What's the matter with you? I'm not buying this sword! I'm here to buy cocaine, and you keep saying it's coming, but it's still not here!"

I wasn't showing anger or resistance. If I had shown either, it would have been over. Instead, I treated Eyes' sudden threat like a misguided sales demo. I shoved the blade away and looked down at my hand. I noticed drops of blood.

"I'm not buying this sword," I said again, showing them my hand. "It's not even very sharp!"

Clean Cut's mouth fell open. Then he recovered and chuckled in disbelief. "You seem a little *loco, señor*. He doesn't want to sell you his machete. He wants to cut off your head."

"Cut off my head? My wife would be really upset if you did that. Come on, you guys. You know I'm here to buy cocaine." My tone was a patient scolding, as if we were all friends. I held out my bloody hand, waiting.

But Clean Cut wasn't stupid. "If you have never been here before, how did you know the name of the town?"

"Look, I do a lot of cocaine, okay? That's the whole reason I came here in the first place. The whole time I was flying here, all I did was look at the little map on the back of the seat in front of me and count down how many towns were left before we got here." That part was actually true.

With that, Clean Cut relaxed a little, but all four men still surrounded me. Maybe Clean Cut believed me. Or maybe he was tired and just didn't feel like going to all the trouble of burying a dead guy that night. Whatever it was, he looked at me and said, "Okay."

Relieved but still on guard, I decided to rant a little more, the innocent man feeling put out after being falsely accused. "I'm out of coke and I come all the way out here to buy from you guys, and this is how you treat me?"

"Okay, okay, calm down. It's almost here," Clean Cut said. "Can I have a cigarette?"

"Yeah," I said, annoyed, glancing around at the group. With my right hand, I reached into my t-shirt pocket, pulled out my last cigarette, and immediately froze.

As I pulled it out, the missing teener came with it. I must have slipped it down inside my cigarette pack for safekeeping and forgotten about it. Now, it came up from my pocket in full view of Clean Cut and his machete enforcer. My blood turned to ice in my veins.

I had told them I was out of coke. There was not a person in the world who was going to be out alone in the Mexican 'hood buying coke in the wee hours of the morning when he already had a pile of it in his pocket. Anybody who would do that was a cop, an informant, or a spy from a rival gang. Clean Cut had already suspected I was the tourist from the year before. If he saw the teener, he'd decide I had set him up, 100 percent.

Did he see it? Did any of them see it?

I hadn't been afraid before, but the fear I felt now—nothing in my life even compared. I felt the blood drain from my face and chest, heading south to my legs, which were being told by my brain, *"Run!"*

But I didn't dare move. I was rooted in place, the faces of all the important people in my life flashing through my head like a slideshow—my wife, my kids, my parents, the grandkids I would now never meet. In that moment, death became a reality for the first time, and my future turned to ashes.

I felt a sudden sadness. This was where my addictions and bad decisions had led me. It was ridiculous when I thought about it. All my decades of scheming and groveling to get that white powder, only to lose everything to it in the end. All that time thinking I was so smart I would beat the odds.

But now the game was over. The house had won. I was going to die right here on this dark, deserted street, a small item in the news: "American tourist goes missing in Mexico."

BOOK

1

COCAINE
Minnesota, USA
1990–1999

CHAPTER

1

Schmitty's

SUMMER 1993

S tanding behind the bar at Schmitty's Tavern in the summer of 1993, I poured a generous stream of Jack Daniels into a highball glass for Petey, one of my Regulars. Even though it was 80 degrees outside, Elvis was pining for Christmas on the jukebox. On the far side of the room, a construction worker waved his arms like a symphony conductor as the whole bar sang along:

> *Oh, why can't every da-a-ay be like Christmas?*
> *Why can't that feeling go on endlessly-y-y-y?*
> *For if every day could be ju-u-u-st like Christmas?*
> *What a won-der-ful world this would be-e-e.*

When the song ended, my customers broke out in cheers. I grabbed a big stack of bar napkins and tossed them up into a giant ceiling fan, and they fluttered down around us in a curtain of white.

We may have been in the middle of a Minnesota summer, but inside Schmitty's, it was snowing.

That's the way it was at my bar, which sat across the street from Stieger Lake in Victoria, a town of about 2,000. There was always something unusual going on, always something to get folks talking. People dancing on the bar, spraying each other with Super Soakers, hanging upside down from the rafters, or playing three-on-three basketball. Someone setting off a brick of firecrackers.

The main thing I set out to do when I bought the place three years before was to create a place where anyone from anywhere from any background—whether they wore tool belts or motorcycle leathers or business suits—could feel like they belonged.

Schmitty's came with a colorful crew of Regulars. Take Petey, for example. He was—and is—a long-haired, dedicated Deadhead who was just devastated when Jerry Garcia died. He came in at the same time every day, sat on the same barstool, and drank the same drink—Jack and Coke. The only thing that changed was his shirt, which alternated between a tie-dyed tee and a Grateful Dead concert tee. And every day at exactly 4:30 p.m., he would make me change the channel on the big screen TV to *Jeopardy!* This always triggered groans from everyone else, but they put up with it because it was only for half an hour—and after all, it was Petey.

Most of the Regulars had grown up together in Victoria. Skelly, Petey, Pokey, Fly Man, Mohawk, Sibby. There was Toad and Tom, too, and Tom's older cousin Tony. They came from good German stock with names like Schmieg, Vogel, Schrempp, Notermann, and Schneider, along with the Diethelms, who had descended from the man believed to have settled the area in 1851. The whole town was a mash-up of brothers and sisters and cousins and in-laws from big Catholic families. I loved them all.

Victoria had two gas stations and two churches, but three bars. I had been running LeeMichaels, another bar I owned a few miles away in Chaska, Minnesota, when my friend Wayne Hilk went down to check out Schmitty's for possible purchase.

After sitting in the bar all night, he called me the next morning with the results of his reconnaissance. "Mike, you wouldn't believe this place! People are falling-down drunk. They're rowdy and throwing stuff. It's a nut house!"

Wayne finished by telling me he didn't want to have anything to do with Schmitty's. Meanwhile, I was thinking, *This sounds like my kind of place.*

So I bought it—or more accurately, gambled for it. That was in 1990, and since then, with help from my Regulars, I had built Schmitty's into a bar like no other. A daily escape from reality. A place that carried amazement on tap.

It wasn't an accident that Elvis was playing on the jukebox in the middle of summer. Whether you showed up for a Monday lunch or a Friday night outing, Schmitty's would pump out the same holiday vibe. Music was crucial to the mood, so I handpicked every song in the jukebox. Instead of loading up on the hits of the day, I made sure we had plenty of hits from the 70s and earlier—the songs our parents would listen to. In addition to my favorites, Bob Seger, the Eagles, and Prince (whose home, Paisley Park, was just a few miles down the road), I stocked up on sing-along classics, like Johnny Cash's "Ring Of Fire," Lynn Anderson's "(I Never Promised You a) Rose Garden," and "I Think I Love You" by the Partridge Family.

Whenever anyone played that one, you'd hear someone groaning about why they had to endure such a corny song. But next thing you knew, you'd see a whole table of bikers singing along with David Cassidy at the top of their lungs:

> *I think I love you!*
> *So what am I so afraid of?*
> *I'm afraid that I'm not sure of,*
> *A love there is no cure for…*

The old songs made people happy. They took us back to simpler times. That's what I wanted Schmitty's to be—a place that made you forget your troubles for a while. A place you would go to see things you don't see every day. People seemed drawn to that atmosphere, and Schmitty's quickly developed a loyal following. I was selling alcohol, but I wasn't *selling alcohol*, if you know what I mean. I was selling fun. Family. *Belonging*.

Maybe that was because, beginning in childhood, I never felt like I belonged.

CHAPTER

2

Crazy Things
1968

In my mind, my childhood is divided into Before and After. It's funny what I remember about the last day of Before. I remember that I had attended exactly nine days of second grade. I don't know why I remember that, but I do. Nine days.

On the last day of Before, we were living in a big house on a lake in southern Minnesota. I was sitting at the kitchen table, one of those with the bright Formica top and aluminum legs, in a home full of 1960s Brady Bunch colors: yellow, orange, and avocado green. I was pouring milk into a bowl of cereal. Those were the glory days of sugary breakfast cereals: Lucky Charms, Cap'n Crunch, Frosted Flakes. Even if your mom got on a health kick with Cheerios or something, you could dump in as much sugar as you wanted. In those days, there was smoking and there was sugar and nobody cared.

I had a couple of Matchbox cars near my cereal bowl and was about to dip in my spoon when my mom walked into the kitchen. "Grab your things. We're leaving," she said. My mother, Barbara Booth, was and is a strong-willed, caring woman. Born in 1941, she was the kind of mom who became what some call a matriarch.

What did she mean by "leaving," I wondered. Did it have something to do with the house? The neighborhood? My father, who sold Allstate Insurance out in front of Sears? I had no idea. In any case, she wanted us to hurry.

I remember going to my bedroom and throwing a few clothes and toys in a box. And I remember being very concerned about my Matchbox cars. My younger sister Cindy and I played cars all the time, and I had built up a pretty good collection. I scrambled to hunt down as many of the tiny cars as I could before Mom hurried Cindy and me, along with our sister, Robin, into the car. It was already running. As Mom tossed last-minute belongings into the car and slammed the doors, I knelt in the back seat and turned around to look out the rear window.

I gazed at my house. When I woke up that day and sat down to pour milk over my cereal, our home had been a comfortable, familiar place backed up against a lake. Already it felt like it belonged to someone else.

Mom backed out of the driveway and pulled away. From my spot in the back seat, I watched my home, on the left side of the street, growing smaller and smaller.

At the corner, Mom turned right and my house was gone. I turned around face-forward and sat down, my stomach fluttering with nerves over the sudden change. This was big. I don't know if Cindy and Robin felt it, but at seven, I knew things were never going to be the same.

I began counting my Matchbox cars—and kept counting them over and over again.

On the two-hour drive northeast to Chaska, my mom explained that we were going to live in a new town, in a new house, and go to a new school.

Our new home turned out to be in a trailer park.

Clutching my cars, I got out and looked around. There were maybe 45 trailers, lined up in rows four deep and organized around a gravel playground with monkey bars and a merry-go-round. Directly across the street was the Gedney pickle factory and to the west of that, a sugar factory. Inside, the trailer was tiny, the hallway so narrow that I could put one hand and one foot on each wall and climb to the ceiling.

The next day at my new school surrounded by new kids, I kept very quiet. I felt awkward and different. That's normal, of course. What wasn't normal was that feeling never went away. Ever.

I suppose you could say it was a step down, moving from a suburban home on a lake to a trailer court across from a pickle factory. But I didn't really see it that way. Our life there reminds me now of that movie, *The Sandlot*. Kids everywhere and ball games in an open field that was really just a sticker patch. We didn't have a giant, slobbering dog terrorizing us from the other side of a fence, but we did have one of those classic scary neighbors whose trailer we rushed past with a chill. (He was probably just a grouch.) Those were the days when kids could leave home after breakfast and not come home until sunset, and we had lots of places to seek adventure.

Like *The Sandlot's* Scotty Smalls, I was the kid from the broken family trying to fit in. I always had a weird feeling that I was different from the other kids, but soon I learned a technique that made up for it, a new habit that would become a pattern that lasted well into adulthood: showing off.

"I'll bet you I can jump out this window," I said to Dean and Tim, pointing at the school bus window next to my seat where the two bullies had me cornered. The bus was moving fast, maybe 30, 40 miles per hour down the road toward school. We were all in the fifth grade and those two had decided to come after me that day.

The bullies considered their options: keep picking on me or watch me perform a death-defying stunt?

"Go for it," Dean said.

By then, I had become obsessed with showing people something they had never seen before. Something that would make them ooh and aah. Deep down, I felt if I could deliver amazement the other kids would like me. In the little playground at the center of the trailer court, I would put on carnivals complete with games (penny pitch, softball throw) and magic shows. I even had a sideshow: when my little sister Cindy drank water then jumped up and down, the sloshing sound in her belly was *loud*—freakishly loud. None of the kids could believe it. After a few such "shows," she protested. "Mi-i-ike! I don't want to *do* this anymore!" But I could always bribe her with Charms suckers or a few quarters.

Once, when I was nine, I bet the trailer-court kids a quarter that if they buried me up to my neck in the sandy soil of the sticker patch, I would find a way to escape. I even helped them dig a hole. The joke was on me, though. Even though the dirt was loose and sandy, the weight of all that sand settled around me in a way that made escape impossible. Then, in an epic case of bad timing, Mel, the trailer-court manager, came roaring up on his front loader. He was already lowering the wide-mouthed bucket when he noticed my head sticking out of the ground right where he was going to land it. At the last second, Mel halted the bucket's descent and climbed down.

"What in the hell are you kids up to now?" he yelled.

This idea of jumping off the bus, though, was my riskiest stunt yet. It was the middle of winter. Snowbanks lined the road and filled the ditches where the plows had come through. I was wearing one of those big blue parkas with the fur-lined hoods.

At Dean's dare, I stood on my seat to lower the top pane of the bus window. The opening was smaller than I had thought, which worried me a little because I didn't want to get caught dangling half-in and half-out of the bus. But I couldn't back out now. The bullies were crowded in close by then, and every kid on the bus was watching.

So I maneuvered myself through the window feet first, eased my body all the way out, and clung to the top of the window in the freezing air while I looked over my shoulder, searching for the right place to land. Strange—it never once occurred to me that the snow might be covering some backbreaking, torso-skewering object. That I might wind up in a body cast or become a pint-sized human shish kebab.

Act first, think later—that was the way I did things.

I waited for the right moment. Then, with a mighty thrust of my legs against the yellow bus, I pushed off, twisting in midair, and slamming—*whump!*—into a fluffy bank of pure white Minnesota snow. As the bus drove away, I knelt by the side of the road, brushing off snow and waving to the kids.

The thrill didn't last long.

The bus made it only another block before the driver hit the brakes. At that point, I didn't stick around to see what was going to happen. I took off running down a side street. My plan was to work my way through the neighborhood and simply walk up to school, blending in with the other walk-to-school kids. But that part of my plan didn't work. When I got there, the principal was waiting for me at the door and he did not look pleased.

The bus driver had snitched.

I followed the principal into his office, where he picked up the receiver from his old-school, curly-cord telephone and dialed my mother. He described my stunt for her, focusing mostly on the worried bus driver and the excellent reputation of Chaska Elementary—which left out all the best parts, I thought.

"Mike is a good student," the principal said into the receiver. "But he keeps doing crazy things. We just don't know what to do with him."

CHAPTER

3

Lots and Lots of Cocaine

1993

At Schmitty's one night in 1993, with my full approval, the Regulars were literally swinging from the rafters. The bar was crowded, packed wall to wall. I'd been thinking of all the little jobs that needed doing and one of them was replacing the ceiling tiles. They were those 18-inch white acoustic tiles, held in by wooden crossbeams. I glanced up and appraised the ceiling. Between the constant fog of cigarette smoke and the post-softball tournament Super Soaker water fights, the tiles had turned a dozen shades of ugly.

About that time, a couple of the Regulars, Skeeter and Kamala, walked in. I recognized the look in their eyes: they were looking for trouble. It occurred to me that I had a chance to kill two birds with one stone. I had already scheduled the ceiling demolition, but it was going to cost me money I didn't really have. I motioned Skeeter and Kamala over to where I stood behind the bar. "Why don't you guys tear down my ceiling tiles?" I said.

"Really?" Skeeter said. Both men's eyes lit up at the thought of destroying something without getting in trouble for it. "Right now?"

I grinned. "Yes, right now."

Immediately, Skeeter and Kamala jumped up on a table and began their demolition. Suddenly, the place was transformed into a jungle gym. Skelly, Petey, Toad, Pokey, Fly Man, and the rest climbed up on the bar and tables, latched onto the rafters, and began kicking in the ceiling. Tiles rained down on the floor, some whole and some in pieces, until the whole place looked like a slag heap.

During all this, some lady marched over to my bartender Jerry and huffed, "Would the owner approve of this?"

"Why don't you ask him?" Jerry said, nodding my way. "He's standing right there."

The lady turned to me with a pained expression. "Why would you ever let them do this?" she asked.

I just smiled and said, "Oh, let them have their fun."

She looked at me like I was nuts and huffed her way right out the door.

The truth is, it *was* nuts. But there was a method to my madness. I knew that woman would go and tell all her friends about the craziness at Schmitty's. You can't buy advertising like that. That's how, in the three years since I bought the place, Schmitty's had become the highest-netting bar in the area. I got people talking.

To make that happen, I first had to win over the tightly knit group of blue-collar guys who had grown up together in Victoria. When I first took over Schmitty's, I met a guy named Jeff Diethelm. Everybody called him Jiggers. Diethelm, who was a member of Victoria's founding family, told me, "We run this town. If we don't like you, we'll run you out."

They definitely tried. I was tending bar one night at LeeMichaels, the bar I still co-owned over in Chaska, when the pretty female bartender I had hired to run Schmitty's called me on the phone, practically crying. "Everyone's gone and all the barstools are on the ground in pieces!"

I held the phone between my ear and shoulder as I pulled on a Budweiser tap, finishing a customer's mug with a nice head of foam. "In pieces?" I said mildly. "What are you talking about?"

"I'm talking about the barstools, Mike! They're all taken apart!"

Here's what happened: The Regulars had grabbed screwdrivers from their trucks, quietly dismantled every single barstool in the place, and left the seats, backs, and legs lying neatly on the floor. Then they filed out. The bartender, it turned out, was so inattentive, so out-to-lunch, that she didn't even notice until they were done and gone.

The Regulars were making a statement: *We don't care how pretty you are—you're a terrible bartender.* The Regulars might've considered it a bonus if the new owner they were testing out had gotten roaring mad when he saw the damage. But when I got there and realized what had happened, I thought their stunt was genius.

"That was one of the coolest things I've ever seen!" I told them. And I meant it. They didn't just yell at the barkeep because they couldn't get drinks. Instead, they decided to do something "crazy" to get her attention. And mine.

The bartender decided she'd had enough and quit, but the incident made me more comfortable at Schmitty's. It gave the Regulars and me something to talk about, and I began spending more time there tending customers. We had bonded over their stunt.

They pulled another one soon after, when *America's Most Wanted* picked Schmitty's as a filming location. The producers decided the bar resembled one related to a crime that had taken place in Wisconsin. To serve my customers and the film crew, I set up tables outside where I kept serving drinks. But when the director ordered pizza for his crew, the Regulars intercepted, scarfed it down, and sent the delivery boy off to present the director with the bill.

I thought that was hilarious, too. (Of course, I also bought another round of pizzas for the film crew.)

With that and other antics to follow, I became the conductor of a band of fun-loving tricksters who liked to show off and who loved a good story. Finally, I felt like I belonged. It was something I hadn't felt in a long time.

With Schmitty's growing fast, I set about building a community. I created men's and women's softball leagues, took care of the fields myself, ran the lights, and even umpired games. Schmitty's sponsored a couple of the teams, and when the softball games were over, most of the players and spectators would head over to the bar. I also set up pool and dart leagues to give people another reason to make Schmitty's their regular hangout. This drove more beverage sales, of course, as well as food sales from the new kitchen I built.

I paid for the kitchen with checks written on my nearly empty bank account, then covered the checks with money from the till. I wasn't always ahead of that game, however, and racked up massive overdraft charges that year. On the other hand, I accepted as many bad checks as I wrote. Victoria was a working-class town, and I knew most of my customers were living paycheck to paycheck just like I was. So, I didn't mind when one of my Regulars wrote me a check and asked me to hold it until payday. I didn't want my employees to have to make those judgment calls, though, so whenever I went out of town, I'd post a sign on the bar:

NO BAD CHECKS 'TIL MIKE GETS BACK.

I was having the time of my life. I had my own business and I loved working, so it didn't matter if I worked 12, 15, 20 hours a day. It was easy for me to do that because of my good friend, cocaine.

I snorted lots and lots of cocaine. It seemed like everybody I knew was doing coke, although that included surprisingly few of the Regulars. In fact, many of the Regulars didn't even know I was a cocaine addict. Those who did, didn't care.

For some reason, I felt I needed cocaine to do my job. If I was alone with a customer, I felt extremely shy and awkward. I'd serve them, then pretend to be busy and hope they would leave soon or that a Regular would come in. I would slip into the kitchen or disappear down into the basement to do a quick line. When I came back upstairs, I'd feel different—full of energy, talkative, and comfortable talking to anyone.

I know that sounds crazy—a bartender who can't talk to strangers. But it's true. Cocaine was a crutch. It would turn out to be one of many.

CHAPTER

4

Peppermint Schnapps
1972–1979

W hen recalling their spiritual influences, I don't think many people put Elvis on their list. But the summer I turned 11, I added him to mine. That was the year my family visited a KOA campground an hour's drive northwest of Chaska. It might have been a family Bible camp of some sort, but what I remember about it was a song I heard there and never forgot: "I've Got Confidence," by Elvis Presley.

> *When trouble is in my way*
> *I can't tell my night from day*
> *I'm tossed from side to side*
> *Like a ship on a raging tide*

I don't worry and I don't fret
God has never failed me yet...

The lyrics seized me. I was mesmerized.

Because I got confidence
God is gonna see me through
No matter what the case may be
I know He's gonna fix it for me
I got confidence

Elvis sang on and on, about Job who was so sick "the flesh fell from his bones," about how God rescued Job, and about how Elvis himself could smile in spite of all his trials because he had confidence.

I grew up going to church with Mom and her new husband, Fred. In 1970, my mom married Fred Taylor, who worked at Cooper's Super Valu grocery in Chaska. Fred already had three kids—Shelly, Lori, and Todd—who lived with his ex but who visited with us from time to time. When Fred married my mom, he added on to our trailer and became a part of our family's life in the mobile home park. Their daughter, my half-sister Amy, was soon born. The six of us would live in the tiny trailer until 1973, when my half-brother, John, was on the way and we moved to a 5-acre hobby farm in nearby Carver.

In church, I was taught that I was going to live forever. I was certain that would be the most boring thing in the world. What could possibly keep me interested that long? I always had to be entertained. Every single minute of my life had to be an adventure. What adventures could I have in this blank place called "forever?" What would I do all day long? Sit on a cloud playing a harp?

To me, forever meant infinity. I would lie awake in bed at night thinking about it. Infinity was a gigantic notion and beginning at about age 9, I tried to wrestle it into something that made sense to me. In my mind's eye, I would project myself out, past blue sky into the dark band of space around the earth, then past the stars and into deep space. Where did outer space end? I wondered. Was there a wall that defined its edges? If so, what was beyond that? If I could actually make the journey would I ever find its end? If a person could really go there, is that where God would be?

And if God was out there, who created God?

In Sunday school, the teacher would tell us that we needed to "accept Jesus into our hearts." That way, when we died we would go to heaven and not that other place. Funny thing was, I knew instinctively that I was too young to be concerned with any kind of eternal accountability. I did believe in God, but even at 9 years old, I would do life-expectancy math in my head and think, "I don't have to worry about this for another 70 years!"

I was always good at math. For some reason numbers came easily to me, and numbers were something you could count on. They didn't change on a whim, and they didn't trick you. Percentages, ratios, odds. I especially loved game theory—the idea that success in making choices depends on understanding the choices of others. I didn't know it was called that at the time, but game theory would later play a huge role in my life.

By the time I was in high school, I was assigned to an advanced math class, one of the first calculus classes ever offered at Chaska High School. I nearly always brought home A's, but my restlessness and inattention in class were legendary and my academic reputation suffered. One calculus teacher actually asked me at the beginning of the semester, "How did *you* sneak your way in here?"

No one in the 1970s was talking about ADHD or kinetic learning. I just knew I always needed to be *doing* something, and that something was not listening to a teacher go *blah, blah, blah* at the front of the room, or sitting in my room after school doing homework, which seemed to me the peak of pointlessness. I could memorize the material and ace an exam, no problem. But homework and projects—and worst of all *group* projects—required two things that were to me like kryptonite: 1) Sitting still. 2) Talking to other people.

I had always been incredibly shy. Early in high school, though, I discovered a secret weapon: alcohol. Drinking loosened me up. The first time I drank, it was peppermint schnapps. I had somehow gotten a bottle from my friend Brad, whose dad owned a Chaska bar called Butch's Tavern. I stashed the bottle in an old outbuilding on our hobby farm. Fred wasn't using the little shack for anything, so I sometimes kept my St. Bernard, Bucky, out there and I kept a pigeon coop next to that, so I had legitimate reasons to go out there.

I was about 15 years old, and I knew all kinds of people who were already drinking by then. Like other kids, I'd taken the occasional swig of my parents' beer. It tasted terrible and I thought, why would anybody drink that? Peppermint schnapps tasted way better. After that, it was sloe gin. Those were the two things everybody got sick on at least once: peppermint schnapps and sloe gin.

That was also about the time I started gambling. I had grown up playing penny-ante stuff like shaking dice or "31," a card game I played with my parents where you put in a nickel every time you lost and the winner took the pot at the end. My friends and I would also play marathon games of Monopoly. Seriously, sometimes for 20 hours straight. I always found it more interesting when there was some kind of wager, even if it was just 5 bucks. This is how I put down gambling roots early on.

By my sophomore year in high school, I bet on anything I could, but I especially loved betting on Minnesota's teams: the Vikings and the Twins. At the time, gambling was just plain fun for me. What I didn't know was that every bet I placed was activating the chemical reward system in my brain. For me, sports betting—and later, playing craps and especially sitting at a blackjack table—was like an IV drip of pure satisfaction. In fact, that dopamine drip is a real thing, and so powerful that people will literally destroy their lives to get it.

For me, the best thing—the *best* thing—was the high I got when I won at the last possible minute. When I was all in, my last chips were down, and I hit it big. No high could top that.

Winning made me feel good about myself. Whenever I won a bet, I felt smart, that I'd used my knowledge and skill to turn chance in my favor. Still the shortest boy in my class, I didn't fit in with the jocks. But because of my love of math, gambling made me feel I fit in somewhere at least. In the end, I hung out with a subgroup of a subgroup—a handful of guys who fit in everywhere and nowhere.

That alone should tell you something about the quality of my high school love life. Someone once asked me how I felt when I tried to talk to girls. I said, "I don't know because I didn't talk to girls." I'm serious. I just didn't talk to them. I did have a crush on a couple of different girls, but I never even came close to telling them. Are you kidding me? I could never even get out of the starting gate. That would've meant risking rejection.

Instead, I would lose myself in music—like the Eagles' *Greatest Hits* album *("Ooooh, sweet darlin', you get the best of my love...")*. I'd listen and picture myself fulfilling my most cherished dream: finding a forever girl, getting married, and raising a family together in a house with a white picket fence. I didn't fantasize about what I was going to *be* when I grew up. No. It was all about finding the love of a woman and building a family together. I even daydreamed about grandkids.

Of course, there was one problem with my big plan: How was I going to find a woman if I couldn't even find the nerve to talk to one? The answer came at a drive-in.

When I was 15, I got a job at the Flying Cloud drive-in theater, selling tickets, working concessions, cleaning up. That's where I met Donna. A cute and tiny blonde, Donna attended a different high school, and I was happy when the manager assigned her to work with me in the ticket booth. Since I got to know her gradually, when I finally got up the courage to ask her out, it seemed like the most natural thing in the world.

I didn't feel "in love" or "swept away," the way I'd heard you'd feel if you were going to spend the rest of your life with someone. But that didn't stop me from plugging Donna into my long-held dream of marriage and family. The relationship sped along for a while, with Donna and I clashing often.

Before long, I was working two jobs, splitting my non-school time between the drive-in and Cooper's, the grocery store where my stepdad Fred worked. I saved up my paychecks and quickly bought a Ford Mustang, which I just as quickly totaled. Which is why I was driving Fred's pickup truck the first time death considered me, then passed me by.

I had gotten off work at the drive-in around midnight. After hanging out with a friend for a couple of hours, I headed home, exhausted. I was so sleepy that I rolled down the window and leaned my head out to stay awake. The last thing I remember before the crash is that I was a quarter mile from home driving 55 miles per hour. The next thing I remember is seeing myself standing in some farmer's yard yelling, "Somebody call Fred Taylor!"

Except that *I* wasn't yelling. I was *watching myself* standing in the yard, yelling for my stepdad. That's what I saw. That's not what really happened.

What happened was, the farmer was home in bed when he heard a deafening crash outside. Then he heard someone yelling for Fred Taylor. The farmer ran out to his yard. He did not see anyone standing in it, yelling. Instead, he saw a pickup truck wrapped around the huge ancient oak tree that stood in his front lawn and a body lying about 20 yards away, like it must have been thrown from the truck. The farmer sprinted back inside and called for help.

The next thing I remember is being in an ambulance. I heard an EMT say, "We have no pulse. We have possible internal injuries and multiple compound fractures." My mom was in the ambulance. I wanted to tell her I was okay, but I couldn't speak.

At the hospital, doctors ordered multiple x-rays, but none of the images showed a single broken bone. The next day, I walked out the front door on my own two feet. The doctors couldn't explain it.

Neither could anyone explain how I wound up in the farmer's yard. My collision with that giant oak had driven the engine block into my stepdad's front seat, the steering column almost through the rear window directly behind my head and the driver's side door was jammed shut.

How did I get out of the truck? I don't know.

A series of near misses followed that accident, so many that I began to feel invincible. I fell into a lake and was trapped under a sheet of ice. I was nearly electrocuted by a bolt of power so massive that it shut down half the town. I bought a motorcycle and wrecked it twice—the second time on the way to a skydiving lesson, during which I smashed into the ground at 60 miles per hour because my parachute didn't fully open.

Yes, I actually crashed my motorcycle and survived a skydiving accident on the same day. And walked away. Year after year, things like this kept happening to me. Over and over I asked myself, what are the odds?

CHAPTER

5

Cigarette Smoke and Aqua Net
1980 – 1985

After high school, I got more serious about gambling. I had bought a trailer in the same trailer park where I had grown up. One of the first things I did was put in a felt-covered poker and craps table. Dealing the cards, I felt I was following in my grandfather's footsteps. According to the family lore, my Grandpa Chuck—my mother's father—dealt so many hands of cards his fingerprints were worn away. He had worked at the Gold Bar, a sawdust-floored saloon in Deadwood, South Dakota. His wife, my Grandma Millie, told me Grandpa had known Bugsy Siegel in the early 1940s. Siegel, who had switched from bootlegging to gambling when Prohibition ended, dreamed of turning a dusty little desert town called Las Vegas into a glittering adult amusement park.

Grandpa Chuck thought that was a silly idea. "Gambling will take care of itself," he told Bugsy. "You don't need all these neon lights and stuff."

Both sets of my grandparents lived on farms in Armstrong, a tiny town on the Iowa side of the Minnesota-Iowa state line. Just a handful of stores and a grain elevator where farmers gathered to deliver their harvest, the town was like a safe harbor in a storm during the first unsteady years after my mother left my father. On summer nights at Grandpa Chuck and Grandma Millie's, I'd sleep with the window open, a breeze rustling the curtains. Off in the distance, I could hear the low, soothing rhythm of passing trains. The word that comes to me now is "peaceful."

Grandpa Chuck used to drive me all over Emmet County in his Cadillac. I loved it when he told me old stories about his time at the gaming tables. It had been decades since he dealt cards in Deadwood, but I could tell he still loved gambling and hated cheaters.

So maybe it was in my blood. By my senior year in high school, I was seriously into sports betting, especially the NFL, and I wagered on games whenever I could. After high school, I attended the University of Minnesota for about five minutes. In 1979, when Islamic revolutionaries seized the American embassy in Tehran, I decided the world might end at any minute. Reasoning that it would be better to spend the apocalypse having fun than studying, I quit college and moved in with my friend Jim Hansel near Cooper's. Jim's grandparents, who owned our rental, eventually lost patience with all the parties I was having there. In June 1980, they kicked me out. With no place to live, I bought a van and talked my friend Rick into driving out to California with me.

"We'll go see the Pacific Ocean," I promised.

Rick and I took a passenger with us, my Uncle Butch. My uncle, who was my mom's brother, needed a ride to Lawrence, Kansas. Uncle Butch was an alcoholic, one of those good-hearted drunks who, when he comes to visit, overstays his welcome but is so kind and funny that you kind of miss him when he's gone. He was also one heck of a gin rummy player, and we played in the back of my van while Rick drove. As we headed south and west, Uncle Butch clipped me for a lot of cash.

"When you get to Vegas, it ain't gonna matter," he told me. "Money don't mean nothing."

I wasn't sure I believed him. After Rick and I dropped my uncle in Kansas, we drove to New Mexico. Just outside Albuquerque, the van was running on fumes. In the middle of the night, we sputtered hopefully into a gas station only to find out it was closed. With no other businesses in sight, we considered our options. The place seemed deserted, but there was a car parked in the lot. Rick and I siphoned some gas from the car, wrote the driver a note, and pinned it, along with a $20 bill, under the windshield wiper. Just as we were walking back to our car, a cop pulled up, jumped out of his cruiser and stalked over. He was about to accuse us of stealing gas, when we showed him the $20 and the note. Suddenly, his attitude reversed. He seemed surprised that the young men he thought were skulking around in the dark were actually in a jam and trying to be as honest as they could. Instead of running us in as petty thieves or vagrants, the cop invited us to spend the night in the parking lot and get on the road in the morning, when the gas stations would open again.

The next day, when Rick and I drove over the mountains from the east, I saw Las Vegas for the first time, sparkling below like an open treasure chest. If Bugsy Siegel could see it now, I thought. I parked the van at Castaways, an older, Polynesian-themed casino that stood where the Mirage is today. When we walked through the doors and I saw the lights flashing, levers cranking, and coins clinking, I felt like I had just entered a giant money factory. From that first breath of stale cigarette smoke and Aqua Net, I was in love.

Still, it didn't take me long to lose every dime I had. Rick still had some cash in reserve, but back in the van, he was upset. He wanted to know, how were we going to see the Pacific Ocean now? Disappointed and exhausted, he headed for the rear of the van to get some sleep. I, meanwhile, sat in the passenger seat depressed and wondering how I was going to get out of this situation.

Just then I noticed five silver dollars lying on the dashboard. Rick must have brought them back with him from the casino. He was already snoring. I grabbed the coins and headed back inside. Looking around at the gaming options, I remembered something Grandpa Chuck had told me: "Craps has the best odds in any casino."

I headed for the craps table, even though I had no idea how to play. No one asked me about my age, but the stickman running the table looked annoyed when I asked him where to place my chip, especially since I had only one $5 red one.

"Just put it on any number," he said irritably. I put my chip on the number six. Then I picked up the dice, shook them, and promptly rolled a six.

"Just leave it all there," the stickman said, still annoyed. I did and rolled another six.

This is the easiest thing in the world! I thought. Over the next hour, it seemed my dice were stuck on six. I couldn't believe it! I thought my streak would never end, but when it finally did, I counted my winnings. I was up over $2,600. I would find out later that when you start with just $5, the odds against that kind of win are astronomical. My mind racing, I scooped up my winnings and cashed out, making sure the cashier included five silver dollars.

When I got back to the van, I placed the five silvers back on the dash. Then I woke up Rick. "Come on, let's get out of here," I said.

"I thought you didn't have any money," he said.

"I do now. Look at this," I said, and showed him my winnings with a grin. I pulled out an old Kodak camera to take a picture of all those $100 bills, then we headed to California.

That was the first time I'd been all the way down and then won big. What I didn't know was that for addicts, much of gambling isn't about winning at all. It's about betting. And my first series of bets at a craps table would cement my gambling addiction for the next 34 years.

When I was young and single and taking a carefree road trip to Vegas, this was no big deal. The stakes were small, usually no more than money for food and gas. But I kept betting more and more money. In time, the stakes for me rose so high that they became, quite literally, a matter of life and death.

My personal mini-casino in the trailer park had been illegal, of course, and before long the cops found out about it. Whenever the neighbors called in a noise complaint, I would tell the police, "I'll come out to you, but you can't come in here." Thankfully, they had more important things to worry about than my minor gambling with my friends, and never bothered to get a warrant.

As it played out, I got in much bigger trouble with another kind of betting. Since my sophomore year of high school, my friends and I had been making bets on sporting events—mostly football games—with bookies. We used parlay cards, betting on multiple games and point-spreads at once. If you won your combination bets, you could win a high payoff with a relatively small wager. I followed both college and professional football avidly and could talk teams and players, injuries and strategies as if I knew everything about the game. But on average, just like other bettors, I lost more often than I won—which is, of course, how bookies stay in business. For a while, what saved me was that my bookies let me wager only money I actually had in hand. After high school, that changed.

Through a friend, I found bookies who would let me bet with money I *didn't* have. Now, instead of making $20 or $50 bets, I could wager hundreds or even thousands of dollars at a time, regardless of what was in my bank account. The problem was, these weren't friendly, small-town bookies making a few bucks off kids. These guys were serious. Maybe not mafia, but definitely organized crime. Of course, they didn't walk up in leather coats with shoulder holsters bulging underneath and name tags that said, "Rocco." In fact, these bookies seemed like nice guys.

Between college and pro games, I had an entire weekend of action. If I lost on Saturday college games, I'd make up ground betting all day Sunday on the NFL. If I was still behind, there was always *Monday Night Football*. Even if an entire weekend was a bust and I had to pay up on Tuesday, I could always talk my way into getting more time if I needed it. I'd start all over again and somehow, some way, cover my bets.

All that worked pretty well until the fall of 1981, when I woke up one Tuesday morning $12,000 in the hole. I was sick to my stomach. I was only 20 years old. Twelve grand was an enormous sum of money, farther down than I'd ever been. It seemed insurmountable. How was I ever going to pay it back?

There was a particular location where I appeared each week to either collect my winnings or pay up. This time though, I just didn't show up. I was too afraid to find out what "the book" would do if I came empty-handed.

That Tuesday, I was scheduled for a shift at the grocery store. As soon as I got there, I grabbed my manager Lenny and dragged him into a corner where no one could hear us.

"You have to do me a favor," I said. "If you see anybody that looks like a mafia type, let me know." We agreed that if he saw anybody like that, he would page me to say I had a call on line three. The store had only two lines.

I'd been at work for less than an hour when Lenny's voice came over the intercom. "Mike, telephone, line three."

I ran out the rear door and back to the trailer court, where I hid out in a friend's trailer a couple of doors down from my own. When no one showed up by midnight to kill me, I finally went home and wedged a chair against my bedroom door, barricading myself inside.

I slept in fits, jumping awake at every creak or gust of wind. Just as the sky was beginning to lighten, I heard a car crunching the gravel outside my trailer. The engine shut off. Car doors opened and closed. I heard hushed male voices.

Terror leapt into my throat. I was trapped. I slipped into my bedroom closet, closed the door to a crack, and peered out, my heart thudding like a drum. I could see dark figures moving outside the trailer. Then the front doorknob rattled. I held my breath, waiting for someone to put his shoulder against the flimsy door and shove it open.

Instead, only silence.

Then, my heart nearly stopped as a face appeared in the bedroom window directly across from me. If he saw the chair wedged against the bedroom door, he'd know I was in here.

I heard some more low talking near the front door, then car doors again. An engine started. Tires crunching gravel, rolling away.

Fearing a trick, I didn't move from that closet or make a sound for two hours. Each minute seemed like my last on this earth. Finally, I crawled out and peeked through a window. Nobody out back. I low-crawled to the front door and opened it a crack. Nobody out front either, but my visitors had left something on the porch. It was a bag from Hardee's, the fast food joint. Cautiously, I stepped out and took a look. There was some writing on the bag:

MIKE

CAME TO GET OUR MONEY—*Book was with me—Physical Force May Be Needed*

CALL ME!

Ever since my "line three" escape, the whole experience had begun to feel like a movie. In some movies, heroes escape from bookies. In others, they get their legs broken—or worse. Which was it going to be? *Think.*

The next morning, I waited until my bank was open, then drove there and asked to see the loan officer. Mark was 30-something, and we were both long-time locals so we knew of each other already. I was totally honest with him.

"Mark, I've lost money to some bad guys with some betting, and I need cash right away. I've gotta have $12,000. You can give it to me as a mortgage on my trailer."

Within 15 minutes, Mark approved the loan and I had turned the check into cash. Immediately I found a phone and called my bookie's number. I said, "I've got the money, but I'll only hand it over in a public place. Meet me in the middle of Southdale Mall at 11 a.m."

An hour before noon, I was in the mall atrium, my nerves buzzing. Would the bookies forgive my paying late? Would it be enough just to hand over an envelope full of cash? After a brief wait, a short, stocky guy I had never seen before came walking casually up to me. I held out the envelope. Without a word, he took it and walked away.

You'd think I would have learned my lesson, but two years later, in November 1983, I found myself in even bigger trouble. After an entire NFL weekend, I was $25,000 in the red. It was more money than I made in a year. I had a new bookie, and if the Hardee's Boys hadn't been real mafia, these guys were even closer to it. Now catastrophically in debt to the mob, I bounced between friends' houses, drinking heavily to tamp down my terror. One Thursday, I decided it would be okay to stop by Mom and Fred's house, which I considered my home base. Mom and Fred still lived on the hobby farm with my younger siblings Amy and John, who were now 13 and 10.

I hadn't been there five minutes when the phone rang. Out of habit, I picked it up. Through the receiver came the most heart-wrenching words I had ever heard: "We know you don't care about yourself," said the thug on the other end of the line, "but you're living with a pretty nice family."

My blood went cold and I dropped the phone. Terror seized me as I pictured mafia leg-breakers rolling up to the farm and coming after my family.

What had I done?

Tears gushed down my face. I let out a yell that came all the way from my guts, and collapsed to the floor. I felt trapped in a nightmare from which I couldn't wake up. I had been sitting there for a long time when suddenly, a single, awful thought broke through the noise in my head:

They could be on their way right now.

That got me moving. I jumped up and ran out to my car, scrambling in through the passenger side because the driver's side door was jammed. My first stop was a liquor store where I bought a case of beer. I spent the rest of the afternoon emptying the cans down my throat, trying to numb my panic. At some point, I decided to head south on Highway 169.

I was so drunk that I had to close one eye to drive in a semi-straight line. As my car floated between the painted white lines, I thought vaguely about stopping in Iowa to borrow money from my uncle, then escaping to Vegas and never coming back. If the mob couldn't find me, maybe they would leave my family alone. But even in my drunken stupor, I realized that *they* don't play by those rules.

As I pulled into St. Peter, Minnesota, my mind kept flashing on ways to get out of this. Finally, an idea hit me: What if I just break into a place and wait there to get arrested? At least they will think I tried to get the money, and I would be safe in jail.

It was a horrible plan, fueled by fear and the warped logic of a drunk. But with a case of beer in my system and serious bad guys threatening my family, it made a twisted kind of sense. Even then though, I knew this would be the most shameful thing I had ever done.

As this took shape in my head, I spotted a gas station that was closed. I pulled into the far side of the parking lot and staggered toward the door. My plan was to smash the window and set off the alarm but to my surprise, the door was open and the place was empty. I stopped for a moment to look around, then walked over to the cash register and opened it. There were a few checks inside and nothing else. I scooped them out then stood there and waited, assuming that my messing with the register had triggered a silent alarm. I was sick inside knowing I was going to go to jail for a long, long time. But I was willing to do whatever it took to save my family.

While I was waiting, I glanced at a curved mirror placed high up in one corner of the store, and my heart almost stopped. In the mirror, I saw someone crouching in fear at the very back of the store. Someone who had stayed late, or maybe a janitor who had forgotten to lock the door.

I panicked. I had thought I was alone. Now what was I going to say to this person? "Hey, I'm not really stealing these checks. What I'm really doing is running from the mob and I'm just waiting here to get arrested."

Instantly, shame ran through me like a river. I had been a crime victim before, and now I was making another person feel the way I had. Suddenly, letting that person know they had nothing to be afraid of became the most important thing to me. I ran out of the store as fast as I could. When I reached my car, I realized I had forgotten to return the checks to the register. I threw them up in the air, jumped in my car, and hit the gas.

I circled the block then careened back onto the highway, where I almost broadsided a police car. Coming out of my swerve, I sped off down the road. The officers inside the squad car knew nothing about what had just happened at the gas station, but of course they took off after me, sirens blaring, lights blazing.

The high-speed chase through the little town of St. Peter lasted five minutes at most. I drove over a curb and popped all four tires on my car. I had a lead on the police at that point, so I was going to try to continue my flight on foot, but because of the jammed driver's door, I couldn't get out of the car in time to make my escape.

The police jumped out, weapons drawn, and ordered me to put my hands up. Amid strobing lights of red and blue, my career as a fake thief ended as quickly as it had begun.

I woke up in a jail cell. While that had been part of my plan, the reality of it was more horrible than I could ever have imagined—sickening, cold, and utterly hopeless. Almost immediately, my dad appeared at the door of my cell. I hadn't seen him in a while and shame engulfed me. As a torrent of self-justifying lies started pouring from my mouth, my dad just reached out and embraced me, then held me as I cried.

The story of the gas station theft and high-speed chase made the news all over southern Minnesota, and in no time everybody knew about it. I still burned with shame. It was one thing to be known as a gambler and mischief-maker, but entirely different to be thought of as a criminal. I wanted so badly to tell my dad what really happened, but I knew I couldn't for the sake of my family. I had to keep my mouth shut and just let everybody think the worst.

It broke my heart when that turned out to include my Grandma Millie. Having spent so much time on her farm as a little boy, she and I were very close. The day after the gas station incident, she ran into my aunt and uncle at the Fairmont mall, bragging to them that I had just gotten my real estate license and was doing really well. I had studied for a week, taken the test, and passed. I wanted to become a full-time agent but it didn't work out very well because on my first showing, my fear of talking to people took over. My grandma didn't know I had already quit. My aunt and uncle had to stop her and break the terrible news about what I had done. When I heard about that, it crushed me.

It took a couple of weeks before I got up enough courage to face people. The first place I went was to Cy's Bar in Chaska where I had been hanging out for months. The owner, Lou, walked up to me and said matter-of-factly, "Mike, you need to leave town. You are never, ever going to live this down."

Lou's words stung deeply, and I turned around and slunk out the door. The accumulated disgrace from the gas station incident, the humiliation I brought on my dad and Grandma Millie, and the destruction of my reputation ushered in four decades of living with shame.

Prosecutors charged me with DUI and fleeing the police. And because the checks I'd scooped from the gas station register and tossed into the air totaled more than $500, they tacked on felony theft. Meanwhile, I still needed to pay off the mob. Once again, I visited Mark, my loan officer at the bank. Unlike our first meeting, when he'd handed over $12,000 without hesitation so I could pay off my gambling debts, this time he turned me down for a $500 loan just to get me to the next payday.

"But I have perfect credit," I protested.

The good-hearted banker got red in the face, and his lips quivered. "Mike," he said, "part of our decision on giving a loan is based on moral character."

I walked out of that bank with tears streaming, not because I didn't get the money, but because I felt that I had forfeited something I could never get back—my reputation.

My case came to trial in March 1984 in Nicollet County District Court. I wasn't all that worried about what the judge might do to me. Instead, I was eaten up with nerves over whether I could get through this thing without making my position with the book worse.

In a way, though, my plan had worked. Since my arrest, they had kept their distance. But I knew they were only biding their time. In court, as I told my story to the judge, I left out the specifics—no bookies, no "mafia," no death threats. I was sitting at the defendant's table when a woman leaned over the bar and passed me a note:

You're doing a good job.

I didn't have to look around to see who was sending the message, or know that it really meant:

Don't give anybody our names.

The reminder was unnecessary. As it turned out, I didn't have to describe the reason for my crime in court in order to avoid harsh sentencing from the judge. In the run-up to the trial, I had spent time with a social worker who genuinely seemed to care about me and talked to me about God. I trusted him and, without naming names, told him exactly why I had done what I'd done.

I don't know if the social worker believed me or if he talked to the judge. But in a plea deal my lawyer worked out, I admitted to misdemeanor theft and DUI and was sentenced to five years of probation and five work-release weekends in Scott County Jail. But not being able to explain why I did something that went so completely against my moral compass was the worst punishment I could have ever received. Lou's words rang in my head for years. I wanted to drive through town, look each person in the eye, and say, "You are wrong. I am a good person."

The truth behind this whole story remained hidden for seven years. Then, in 1990, something miraculous happened. It came out in the paper that the bookie who threatened my family had been sentenced to 30 years in prison for leading an organized counterfeiting ring. Finally, I could tell everyone what happened back then, starting with Grandma Millie.

"Oh Mike, I knew there was something behind that," she said sweetly. "I knew that wasn't who you really were."

I felt relief in that moment, but my guilt over what she must have felt that day in the mall has never left me. After clearing things up with my grandma, I made similar rounds with family and friends. To my surprise, they all said either that they didn't remember the incident or that it didn't really matter. I couldn't believe it. I had lived in shame all that time, wondering what people thought of me, only to learn that the truth was that I couldn't forgive myself.

That, it turned out, would take a very, very long time.

CHAPTER

6

Dream Girl

1984–1985

I n 1984, while serving out those work-release weekends, I lived on my friend
Dick VanSloun's couch in a house he shared with three other friends—Dean,
Bob, and Tony. All of them were into cocaine. Despite my drinking and
gambling, I had never tried drugs and had no desire to do so. I'd been raised
that drinking was socially acceptable, but drugs were not. Besides, any time I'd
been around pot smokers, their conversations seemed ridiculous to me, as if their
brains were smothered in wool blankets. So I lived at Dick's while serving my
time, but wasn't tempted by his lifestyle.

At first.

In the town of Chaska, meanwhile, I was living under a black cloud.
Everywhere I went, I felt the almost physical sensation of small-town judgment.

In an effort to redeem myself, I once tried going to church with my mother, but the judgment there seemed even worse. As Mom introduced me around, her church friends mouthed a kind of "bless your heart" phony sympathy, but I thought I could read unspoken words behind their eyes: *Oh. This is the guy who broke into that gas station.*

Some of this was probably my imagination, magnified by my own self-loathing. Some of it was probably real. In any case, I left church that day and did not go back. The irony was that even though I had violated my own moral code, I was angry with people for judging me. And the longer this cycle went on, the further my shame spiraled.

One morning, I woke up at Dick's as he was passing through the living room on his way out to work.

"I don't feel like doing a dang thing," I told him.

Dick pointed at a mirror on the coffee table and a small pile of cocaine left over from the night before. "Try some of that," he said nonchalantly and walked out the door.

What the hell, I thought. Things can't get any worse. There was a little rock of coke on the mirror. I put that in my mouth between my cheek and gum. The effect was powerful and immediate: a rush of euphoria surged through my body. My notions of any stigma surrounding drugs vanished instantly. There was a short straw on the mirror. I used it to inhale everything that was left. Later, I asked Dick where we could get some more. That day, cocaine became my new best friend. Not only did it mask my pain; it made me feel I could conquer the world.

With this newfound drive, I went back to the drive-in and asked the manager to hire me as a janitor. Then my sister Cindy's apartment flooded, so I dove into the carpet cleaning business. I saved my Flying Cloud paychecks to buy my own machine, which was as old and crappy as the Chevy Suburban I bought to cart it around. The Suburban was so ratty that I used to hide it around the corner so my clients couldn't see it.

I was astonished when Dale Diedrick, who owned Butch's Tavern in Chaska, hired me to clean his huge restaurant and bar. Dale was a pillar of the community, and it meant so much to me that he trusted me at a time when I needed trust the most.

In early 1985, I got a part-time job tending bar at a Chaska bar called the Statesman. That summer, a woman walked into the bar and changed my life. It was August, and I was polishing glasses in the safety of my usual fortress, the area behind the Statesman bar that protected me from strangers. But from the instant this woman sat down, I didn't feel she was a stranger at all.

"Are Joe and Zany Wong around?" she asked, referring to the couple who owned the Statesman. This blond and beautiful vision set her purse on the empty barstool beside her and looked around. It was a weekday afternoon, and the bar was completely empty. She ordered a drink, then explained that she used to work at the Statesman and had stopped by to say hi to her former bosses.

I was 24 years old by then and had been in exactly one relationship. That was with Donna, the girl from the drive-in. But after six years, she left me for one of my best friends. Since then, many months had dragged by with no romantic prospects in sight. I remained as tongue-tied around women as I had been in high school.

Now, this woman sat across from me and asked me my name.

"Mike," I said.

"I'm Karen."

Reluctantly, I told her that the Wongs were out, thinking that might cause her to finish her drink quickly and leave. To my amazement, Karen stayed. She was so joyful and down to earth, and she had an amazing laugh. We talked easily about the Wongs, about the Statesman, about her being from nearby Excelsior, and anything else that came to mind. I had never talked so easily with someone I'd just met, especially a woman. We talked for over an hour but to me, the time sped by too quickly.

A few customers drifted in and out. I don't even remember waiting on them. Finally, Karen said she had to go. "Is it okay if I leave my number for Zany and Joe?"

Of course, I said yes. She jotted her phone number on a cocktail napkin, smiled her easy smile, and got up to leave.

As I watched her walk out the door it hit me: I was going to marry her. Later, as I was contemplating all the ways I could make that happen, my friend Garth Graves came in.

"Do you know a Karen who used to work here?" I asked him.

"Yeah, Karen Dickey," he said.

"I'm going to marry her," I said. I was 100 percent confident of this declaration.

"I don't think so. She's not married, but she does have a kid."

I smiled at Garth. "Okay. I'm going to marry her." My confidence did not waver.

He made some more negative noises. I don't remember exactly what he said, but it amounted to "fat chance."

Later, Garth's mom, Annie, came in. When I announced my newfound wedding plans, she sided with her son. "You have absolutely zero chance," she said. According to Annie, Karen had a 2-year-old daughter and carried a torch for the girl's father. Karen wanted to marry the guy, but he didn't share her enthusiasm. Trying to protect me, Annie told me to steer clear of Karen Dickey.

But nothing and no one was going to deter me. When I decide something, I go all in. So a few days later, I got up the nerve to call and ask her out. To my surprise, she said yes. I didn't want to show up in my rusted-out Suburban, so I traded my carpet-cleaning machine for a friend's truck. We met at one of those fancy places with a grand piano, white tablecloths, and too many forks. Karen ordered a bottle of red wine, which I never drank. When the server brought the wine to our table, he poured me a sample and stood there staring at me.

"Um, you can fill it up," I said. When I discovered the wine was warm, I fished a few ice cubes from my water glass and plopped them in the glass. Classy, I know.

With no bar to protect me and worse, no cocaine, I was extremely nervous, mostly because I didn't want to blow it with Karen. I wanted her to like me. I wanted to say all the right things, but what was I going to tell her? The truth?

The truth was bleak. I was an alcoholic and a gambling addict. I had no money and no job except bartending a couple nights a week. I'd racked up more driving citations than I could count, including multiple DUIs. I'd dropped out of college after one semester and already spent time in jail. Oh yeah, and I owed my bookies tens of thousands of dollars.

With nothing good to say about myself, I started talking about anything I could think of—making small talk, basically, which I can't stand and at which I am terrible. I later learned that Karen told her sister, "I like Mike, but I don't think he gets out much."

We went on two more dates, but when I asked for a fourth she said no. But by then it was too late. During those three dates, I experienced something I'd never felt before: powerful, all-consuming, can't-think-of-anything-else love. I'd been both captured and swept away.

I knew without a doubt that Karen Dickey was The One.

If I had dated more in high school, I might have learned how to play it cool. Had I been in love before, I might have learned to control myself a little bit. But I had done neither and so I pursued Karen with the zeal of a multilevel marketer. I began showing up at the Mai Tai, where she worked as a cocktail waitress. I would call my sister Robin and say, "I need to borrow your kid." I meant Robin's daughter Sarah, my 18-month-old niece. I would pretend to babysit Sarah, conspicuously parading her around in front of Karen to show what a good guy I was. I even bought a pair of live lovebirds, left the cage on Karen's doorstep, rang the doorbell and left.

This was the idea of some lady at the Statesman. "You have to be romantic!" she'd said. I think she was from France or something. Karen turned out to be allergic to birds.

There never seemed to be enough time to show Karen who I really was. Still, there were days when I felt I was making progress. After months of growing hope and joy, I got up the courage to call her up and ask her out again on a real date.

She completely shut me down.

It wasn't, "Sorry, I'm busy that night," or "Maybe some other time."

It was just a flat-out, "No."

I felt like I'd fallen over the edge of a cliff. I had tried to cross the bridge between friendship and romance, and Karen had blown the bridge into a million pieces. There was no going back. From that phone call on, I absolutely *dove* into cocaine and alcohol, and spent my days and nights at Cy's bar trying to drink Karen away.

Although I didn't realize it at the time, Karen's rejection poured quicksand into the hole of unworthiness I had been trying to climb out of all my life. This unworthiness had really come home to me the year before at my five-year high school reunion. As I listened to my classmates' life updates, my heart felt more and more hollow. It seemed that almost everyone had graduated from college or was established in a trade. Most had gotten married and started families.

I didn't have anything like that to talk about, so I took over the reunion with stories from my life:

How I got 17 traffic tickets in two days while trying to outrun the cops.

How I had dodged death by "mafia," and in car and motorcycle crashes.

About the time I bet Dick VanSloun 60 bucks that I could roll through a giant bonfire, borrowed some guy's leather jacket and dove into the fire, only to get stuck because Dick had purposely put a huge log in my way so he could win the bet. I showed them how I pushed myself out of the fire, but not before sustaining second-degree burns, which I hid by jumping into my car and speeding off, only to roll my car at Kelzer's corner.

And there was more.

I told my classmates about the time I talked Kenny D., my friend and fellow Flying Cloud theater employee, into climbing five stories to the top of the movie screen and mooning hundreds of theater-goers in the parking lot below. That particular stunt could have killed me. Fearlessly, Kenny scrambled up the ladder ahead of me as I crept up one rung at a time, unsure of why I had suggested this prank, given that I was terrified of heights. Higher and higher we climbed, light flickering against us as a Cheech and Chong movie unspooled from the projection booth at the other end of the parking lot.

I hadn't originally planned to moon the crowd. That only happened when we reached the top and no one in the lot below seemed to notice, even when I tried using my leg to make a shadow puppet on the screen. That was when I suggested we drop our pants.

Kenny didn't even hesitate. He pulled down his shorts and lowered himself from the ledge at the top of the screen, his buck-naked butt cheeks shining in the light from the projection room. Within seconds, I joined him, adding a second moon to the spectacle.

Below, horns started honking, first one then several then dozens. Headlights flashed on, trying to spotlight us from below. We'd done it! We'd gotten the attention we were looking for. I laughed out loud.

Kenny and I didn't hold out long, and he hoisted himself back up, no problem. For me, though, it wasn't that easy. I managed to get one arm back up on the ledge before my strength failed. As I tried to get leverage with my feet, they just kept slipping on the screen. Dangling 50 feet above the ground with no net, I went into complete panic. Sweat broke out on my forehead. My heart thundered as if a racehorse were running through my chest.

Then my shorts fell off. I mean completely off. So, there I was dangling from the ledge, naked from the waist down, giving a new definition to the term "film buff." It seemed like forever before Kenny rushed back to grab my arms and haul me up over the ledge. For a moment I just knelt there, with horns still honking and Cheech and Chong still spouting their stoner dialogue, happy to be alive.

"We called it 'The Night of the Full Moons!'" I told the crowd of reunion classmates who were gathered around hanging on my every word.

At the time, I didn't see the pitiful mix of pride and stupidity that linked these incidents, and how that characterized my need to regale my classmates with them now. I didn't see the cry for attention. Instead I thought my stories were impressive and hilarious, and that my former classmates were confirming it by laughing along. In the moment, I felt like a big-shot, an entertainer.

But later that night lying in bed, it hit me: my classmates had left me far behind in life, and I was hiding my insecurities by showing off. The realization pierced me with a deep sadness.

The year ended and as 1985 ticked by, I slid deeper into depression. The days blurred together as I bounced from bar to bar, between cocaine and alcohol. On the morning of Christmas Eve 1985, I woke up and found myself on the couch at my friend Tom's house. Two sensations pressed in on me: the pleasant scents of pine needles and good things baking in the kitchen, and the unpleasant sound of Tom's mother talking about me upstairs.

"I don't want him in our house!" she was saying as Tom defended me. She was almost yelling, which is probably what woke me up. She didn't say it outright, but I knew she was still hung up on the gas station incident.

I felt sick inside. *Maybe she is right*, I thought. *I am never going to be able to live that down. I am never going to get past my bad reputation. No one is ever going to be able to see the real me.*

CHAPTER

7

Turning Myself to Face Me

Instead of making a change, I chose to run. My destination: the only city in America specifically designed to help you hide from yourself: Vegas.

As I'd done before at low points, I pictured myself winning a fortune in Las Vegas and then coming home to Chaska to show off my money and prove to people that I was somebody who mattered. Since I was almost broke at the time, I borrowed a couple hundred dollars from a friend. Then I went back to the apartment that I now shared with my friend Wayne Salden, and my sister Cindy, who was dating Wayne. I grabbed a big jar filled with change that belonged to Wayne, along with three of his blank checks. I was only "borrowing" this money, I reasoned, since I always paid back my debts and then some.

I packed my car with all my valuable assets: a fishing pole, two reels, a pocket-knife, a pair of binoculars, a necklace, an Amoco credit card, and a cubic zirconia ring. That is a sad commentary on my life at that time. I was 24 years old and that was the extent of my worldly possessions. Well, that and an eight-ball of cocaine.

Driving to Vegas, all I could think about was Karen. Halfway there I couldn't take it anymore. I *had* to talk to her. Against all reason, I still felt a glimmer of hope. I'd already been up for several days straight, fueled by cocaine. I stopped at a gas station on a Colorado mountaintop and plugged some quarters into a pay phone.

As the phone rang in my ear, I gathered my courage to tell Karen that I loved her. But another voice answered the phone. "Hello?…Hello?…Hello?"

It was Karen's mother, Joyce. She must have been babysitting Karen's daughter, Heather. It made me wonder where Karen was. Out on a date? Everything in me was sure she was with Heather's dad. Tears welled in my eyes, and I hung up without saying a word.

Twelve hours later, I pulled into the parking lot of Circus Circus in Vegas and headed inside. I was coming down from the last of my cocaine, but just being in a casino again gave me an adrenaline rush. A few years earlier, I had turned that $5 into $2,600 playing craps. I hoped the dice would smile on me one more time.

They didn't.

Or at least I assume they didn't. I have only one clear memory of what happened the night I got to Vegas: taking Wayne's jar with $180 in change to a casino cage and trading it in for chips. I don't remember gambling away those chips, only waking up in a strange bed. Before I even opened my eyes, the misery of my situation came flooding back to me, and I found myself praying that when I did open them, I would be somewhere other than Vegas. Instead, I cracked my bleary eyelids to see a giant clown staring in at me through a dirty window.

Somehow, I'd gotten a room at the Travel Lodge across the street from Circus Circus, and the giant clown was Lucky. In real life, Lucky is 123 feet tall and friendly-looking, with a wide ruffled collar, white face, and puffs of hair like orange cotton candy poking out from under a classic cone-shaped hat. Now though, he seemed to leer in at me like Pennywise, the evil clown from the Stephen King story *It*.

I closed my eyes and prayed again, "God, please let this be a dream."

But it was no dream. A horrible feeling washed over me. I had never been that depressed or alone. I was 1,600 miles away from home with no money and no way to get back. I lay in that motel bed for hours, too depressed to move until the motel manager came jiggling my doorknob and telling me I had to leave.

At first, I just drove around town. I felt consumed by loneliness, hopeless, driven by compulsions I couldn't name, and enslaved to substances I couldn't kick. I desperately wanted to escape from the person I was afraid I had become.

But how? As daytime, hungover Vegas slid by my car windows, I tried to work out my next move. Ideas popped into my head. Maybe I could stay in Vegas and become a dealer. Just start over.

Eventually I had to stop for gas. As I was filling up my car, it dawned on me that I had one more way to get money: I could let people use my Amoco card for gas in exchange for cash, but at a discount—for example, they'd give me $10 cash for $15 in gas. I was able to make a couple hundred dollars this way before the card was finally maxed out.

A normal person would have used the money to get home. But I went to Bob Stupak's Vegas World and gambled it all away. I didn't know how I was going to get home, and I didn't care. I got in the driver's seat and pointed the car north.

Heading up Interstate 15, I heard a couple of Elvis gospel songs on the radio, including "I've Got Confidence," that song from my childhood camp. I hadn't heard it for more than 15 years. What were the odds that I'd hear it now at one of the lowest points of my life? I prayed, "God, can you please get me home?"

It took me 40 hours to get there, as I bartered my way across the country exchanging my few meager possessions for gas. Out of cocaine, cash, and alcohol, I was forced to live with myself completely sober for the first time since I was a teenager. As the little car clattered and wheezed and the miles dragged by, I came face-to-face with what gambling had done to me. I had shamed myself, ruined my reputation, even put my family at risk. And no matter how I tried to justify it, in invading that gas station and grabbing those checks I had committed an actual crime.

On the long stretches of highway, I swung between optimism and despair. I realized I had left Chaska without a word to anyone, and I felt bad about that. My friends and family had probably been worried sick. On the other hand, when I returned unharmed, I was sure they'd be glad to see me. I pinned my hopes on that because I had never felt so utterly alone.

Crossing the Colorado state line, I decided it was time to change my life. When I got back to Minnesota, I vowed I would write Wayne and Cindy a letter explaining everything. Then I would enter treatment for gambling addiction. As I made this decision, I felt a weight fall from my shoulders. Not only would I turn my life around, but my friends and family would accept me again, trust me again.

In Grand Junction, Colorado, my car fell apart. I used one of Wayne's checks to pay for the repairs. In Denver, a gas station clerk cut my over-the-limit Amoco card in half. In Sterling, Colorado, I used another check to pay for three plates of diner food. In Grand Island, Nebraska, a cagey gas station attendant let me write a check for $10 cash, but only if I threw my fishing rod into the bargain. I spent $2 at McDonald's and $8 on gas.

When I finally rolled into Chaska, I took a deep breath. I was home. I headed to my apartment excited to see Wayne and Cindy, sure they were going to be happy to see me.

"What the hell are you doing here?" Wayne snapped when I opened the apartment door. It wasn't the welcome I'd been hoping for.

I went upstairs and spent the night writing that letter telling them everything that had happened during my five-day trip to Vegas and back. It filled six pages. I was a Christian now, I claimed. Toward the end, I wrote, "I'm getting help for my compulsive gambling starting Sunday. And if I can't quit drinking and drugs on my own, I am putting myself in treatment for that, too."

The next morning, I left the letter for them and headed out to bartend at the Statesman. I figured Joey Wong would take me back. I also figured my grand explanations would smooth everything else over. But by the time I got home, Wayne and Cindy had thrown all my belongings out a second-story window, including my bed.

When I saw the pile of the few belongings that I had left lying smashed in the apartment-complex parking lot, all my good intentions evaporated instantly. The way I saw it, my best friend *and my own sister* had ignored my sincere vows to change. Screw it, I thought, and immediately drove off to find some cocaine, leaving all my stuff behind.

A few nights later, I left work drunk and rolled my car on Highway 41 in the middle of a snowstorm. (Ironically, it was in the exact spot where I jumped out of the bus window in the fifth grade.) I cracked some ribs and was in excruciating pain, but those were the least of my troubles. My real problem was that the responding police officer had ordered a blood alcohol test and I was charged—again—with driving under the influence. I knew I was looking at serious jail time.

Within a week, I had another late-night run-in with the cops. Homeless, in deep legal trouble, and out of options, I finally called my friend Brad and asked him to drive me to rehab.

CHAPTER

8

There's Still a Chance

The Willmar Regional Treatment Center occupied a facility dating back to 1912, offered treatment for drug and alcohol abuse, and also served the insane and mentally ill. At check-in, counselors told me the typical length of their chemical dependency program was three to six months, and that no one had ever graduated in less than 30 days. Since I had not been ordered by a court to participate in the program, I hoped my stay would be on the shorter side.

Walking around the treatment center grounds, it didn't occur to me that I was now not only jobless and homeless, but that my endless string of bad decisions had led me to a modern-day asylum. Nor did it occur to me that I was actually in the right place. Instead, I had an agenda, and it was not to get sober. All I wanted from Willmar was a piece of paper that would convince a judge not to throw me in jail.

Even if I had been sincere about recovery, though, I didn't like the way the program dealt with addicts. In the group and individual sessions, the counselors all said the same things:

"Your friends and family are very upset with you."

And, "Think about how much your addictions have hurt them all."

And, "Do you know how much money you waste on drugs every year?"

"I know," I'd say. "I'm so sorry."

But inside I thought, *Do you really think telling me that is going to get me off drugs?* The fact that I had hurt others and driven myself into poverty made me want to do *more* drugs, not quit. But telling the truth wasn't going to get me that piece of paper, so I hung my head apologetically and promised I was going to change.

That disconnect foreshadowed what was to come with the other rehab programs I entered over the next two decades. They all focused on the pain I'd inflicted on myself and others. But I wasn't thinking about other people. Instead, I rationalized my behavior and blamed others for my problems: Donna betrayed me. Karen doesn't want me. People like Tom's mother think I'm a loser. *I'm the one with the pain here!*

Sometimes, dimly, I realized how much of my pain was self-inflicted. But the counselors' "guilt therapy" approach didn't lessen my desire for alcohol, gambling, or drugs. In fact, those were the only things that would make me feel better, and I didn't know anything else that could.

After I checked myself into treatment, no one reached out to me. *No one*, not a single friend or family member. Until…

I received an envelope hand-addressed to me. I didn't recognize the handwriting, but when I tore it open I found a greeting card with a white rabbit on the front. Inside it read, "Some bunny is thinking of you." It was signed "Karen."

My heart soared. *There's still a chance!*

I knew I shouldn't read too much into the card, but if nothing else it meant Karen had heard about my checking myself into rehab and that she still cared about me. This gave me extra motivation to complete the program quickly.

Late one night, I couldn't sleep so I went down to the television room where another guy was glued to the TV. He said he was from California.

It was just the two of us in this great big room. "What did you do in California?" I asked, just so things wouldn't be so awkward.

"I had a food truck. I would pull up to the beach and sell food and drinks to people hanging out or to people working at local businesses."

Later, lying in bed, I began to think that a food truck enterprise might work for me, too. My mind went into overdrive, and by the time the sun came up I had a whole business plan figured out.

My new obsession motivated me even more to get through treatment quickly, so I started playing the recovery game, telling the therapists what they wanted to hear. I knew what to say and what not to say in order to get out early. I did everything right—well, except that I ran small-stakes gambling games on my ward to keep myself entertained.

Each day, I perfected my ability to talk the talk, using my growing fluency to manipulate the counselors. At night, I gambled. After 26 days in the program, I called my friend Lee Tischleder, a bartender at Cy's. "Pick me up in two days," I told him, "and come up with $8,000. I've got a plan that's going to make us both millionaires."

After leaving Willmar, I used the card Karen had sent as a reason to reconnect. She still just wanted to be friends, but my hope was renewed. And her overture gave me the opportunity to spend time with her, especially after I asked her to help me with my millionaire venture.

Lee picked me up from Willmar on the morning I had asked him to, and I immediately pitched him on my business idea. By afternoon, we were in Minneapolis using the eight grand he'd raised to buy a used food truck—and boom! In the spring of 1986, Sunshine Concessions was born. To build our clientele, I pitched the idea of lunchtime food truck service to scores of business owners in the Chaska Industrial Park. I can't tell you how many no's I got, but I wouldn't give up. I kept going back and asking to talk to someone one rung higher on the ladder. Finally, I got a meeting with the president of a huge company called United Mailing.

"How about for one week, every one of your employees can come out to my truck and get a free sandwich?" I offered.

"You'd do that?" he asked. But he still had other objections: his vending machine accounts, the length of his employees' breaks, the quality of our food. For half an hour, I answered every objection until finally, reluctantly, he agreed.

My partner, Lee, was against this idea, saying that we didn't have the money. But I argued risk versus reward: Even though we were giving away free sandwiches, United Mailing employees would also buy chips, soda, and other items, I said. "If it works, we'll have our dream. If it doesn't, we'll try something else."

In the end, I was right. Everything went off without a hitch and United Mailing's president was impressed. The company became a regular client. And having that one big client brought others. The United Mailing victory was a high I would never forget. In fact, I poured all my addictive tendencies into Sunshine Concessions. I was finding out what I was made of. I was focused and single-minded and as it turned out, very persuasive.

Karen was with me the day United Mailing said yes. Since I'd lost my driver's license, I had asked her to drive me around to call on business owners. For three months in the summer of 1986, we spent hours and hours together driving between Chaska and Chanhassen industrial parks. Excitedly, I shared my vision for the company. It was the first time I could be myself around Karen. It was the first time I felt she was seeing the real me. We became confidants. And every day, I could feel us getting closer. Our growing relationship filled me with hope.

Then one day in August, I called Karen at home. I could tell instantly that something was different. And I knew what it was: her daughter Heather's dad was back. I told myself I wasn't going to go through this again. After two days, I made a decision. I called Karen up.

"I want to go out on a real date," I told her. "If you don't want to go, I understand, and I won't bother you again."

This time Karen tried to soften the blow. She really liked me, she said, but Heather's dad—

"I understand," I said, cutting her off. As much as it hurt, I really did understand, but I didn't want to hear it. I said goodbye and hung up the phone.

Not long after that, I went to a party at a young woman's home with my friend Garth. He was the same guy I'd told I was going to marry Karen. Sadly, I had to admit he'd been right about my chances with her.

The morning after the party, I had just awakened on the party host's couch when she walked over and sat down next to me, stark naked. Surprised, I jumped up and away from her.

"What are you *doing?*" I said. I couldn't have been less interested. I was still hung up on Karen.

At that exact moment, the phone at the party house rang. Someone answered and held out the receiver toward me. "It's for you, Mike."

It was the bartender at the Statesman. Karen had been in the night before, looking for me, he said. My heart sank and raced at the same time. Why had I come to this stupid party? If I had been at the Statesman, maybe…?

I hung up and dialed Karen's number. When I heard her voice, my heart beat faster, but I tried to keep my cool. "I heard you were looking for me," I said.

"Yes, I stopped into the Statesman to see you."

Hearing something new in her voice, I abandoned coolness and jumped in. "Would you like to go with me to the Minnesota State Fair?"

"Yes," she said. She didn't even hesitate.

A few days later, Karen drove out to the hobby farm and picked me up for our date. Grandma Millie, who was visiting, took one look at Karen and said, "Ooooh, you two are going to make such beautiful great-grandchildren for me!"

I was a little embarrassed, but also secretly pleased. Maybe Grandma Millie knew as well as I did that Karen and I were meant to be together. Karen just smiled, and I knew right then—100 percent—that something had changed.

We dated only a few months before I asked Karen to marry me. In May 1987, we had a huge wedding. My mother was thrilled that I was finally settling down, but a little concerned with the amount of champagne I bought for the reception. I remember her walking through the reception hall confiscating the champagne bottles from the tables. I watched, laughing, as my friend Jill tiptoed along behind her. Every time Mom picked up a bottle, Jill replaced it with a new one.

Karen and I honeymooned in the Bahamas. Shortly after we returned, I took the legal steps to adopt her daughter, Heather, and within a year we had Elizabeth, our first child together. I was ecstatic. Next came Charlie, then Darren, who nearly didn't make it into the world.

Karen had already delivered three kids with no particular trouble. I never took that for granted—each birth was a miracle to me. Still, I was unprepared for what happened in June 1990. Karen's due date had almost arrived, so we hired a babysitter, hoping to catch one more movie before a newborn kept us close to home for a while. We were driving to the theater when Karen put her hand on her belly, looked over at me, and announced her first contraction.

"Here we go!" I said with a wide grin, and turned the car around to head toward the hospital. After checking us in, the staff mostly left us alone since Karen was barely dilated. Her contractions came far apart, and soon she fell asleep. I slumped in a bedside chair and turned on a rerun of *All in the Family*. When a commercial came on, I looked over at the monitor and saw that the baby's heartbeat had dropped to nine beats per minute.

Nine beats? Terrified, I woke Karen and showed her the monitor.

"Is this normal?" I asked.

Her eyes went wide. "No!"

I jumped up and ran into the hall yelling for a doctor. The nurse, who had been in the room just minutes before, assured me everything was fine—until I dragged her back to the room to look at the monitor. Now it was her turn to yell for the doctor, who came running. Nurses flocked around Karen, stripped off all the wires and tubes, and prepared to zip her out of the room.

She only had time to point at me and say, "Can he come, too?"

"Yes," the doctor said. "Let's go."

I raced down the hall behind the gurney. We all crammed into an elevator. On our way down, Karen went into a seizure. At the surgical floor, the medical team shot out of the elevator with Karen and into an operating room, where I could only watch through the glass as the doctors began an emergency C-section.

The next few minutes played out like a strange dream. Karen came to and looked at me just as the doctor sliced into her. As I saw him lift out what looked like a bloody, purple blob, a guy in street clothes ran past me, almost knocking me over as he rushed into the operating room.

The surgical team basically tossed him the baby. I stared in disbelief as he started performing compressions on my newborn son, then doing some kind of mouth-to-mouth resuscitation and other procedures I had never seen before. I turned from the glass and collapsed in tears.

Eventually I collected myself enough to call my mother. "Everybody is dying!" I sobbed. "Karen...the baby...they're dying!"

I don't know how much time passed after that before I got up the courage to look through the operating room window again. When I did, I saw Karen lying still, her eyes closed. For some reason at that moment, a peace came over me.

When the doctor came out, I could tell by his face that it was going to be good news. The umbilical cord had wrapped around the baby's neck, he explained, threatening his life. But the crisis was over. My wife and son were going to be okay.

Then the doctor's voice trailed off, and he looked bewildered. "You need to know, it's truly a miracle that your son is alive. That guy who came into the operating room in his street clothes is one of the few doctors I know of that could have saved your baby. But that's not the only thing. He lives 20 minutes away. I don't know how he managed to get here in five minutes."

Shortly after that, I went upstairs, where the staff handed me Darren. He was perfect.

The day I drove home with Karen and our new baby boy, my mind kept circling back to the doctor's question: How did that man get to the hospital in five minutes when he lived 20 minutes away?

CHAPTER

9

The Kids are Alright
1990–1998

Those first 10 years of marriage were one of the happiest periods of my life. I had Karen, a big family with four kids, and nieces and nephews besides. Lee and I bought the Statesman, but the Chaska city council absolutely did not want to give me a liquor license because its members considered me a drunk and a criminal. I had thought the gas station incident was dead and buried, but now it resurfaced, splashed across the newspaper in even more detail. The council aligned against me. Community leaders were split. After a two-month battle, I got up in front of the council and gave a passionate 15-minute speech.

I didn't want to speak in front of all those people, but I had to.

All I needed was a chance, I said.

Finally, the council relented. Applying a whole list of restrictions that I myself had suggested, they finally granted us the liquor license. This victory meant more to me than the business itself. I felt my reputation was on the road to recovery. Immediately, I went to see Lou at Cy's.

"Well, Lou," I said, "looks like I didn't have to leave town after all."

Lee and I renamed the Statesman, calling it LeeMichaels. In 1990, I bought Schmitty's, winning the money for the purchase on a football bet. At last, I had found my place in the world. I felt I had been handed my dreams on a silver platter.

By 1996, Schmitty's was running like a top. Every day, it seemed we were busy from morning to night. I had trained some bartenders to run the place the way I liked—nothing getting out of hand but lots of fun, too.

For example, we had an enormous rear-projection TV in Schmitty's that worked well but had just developed a solid black line through the center of the screen. One night, my dad looked at me and said, "A good bar owner would fix that TV."

After my parents divorced, my dad had married a woman named Jan. They had three children together: Corey, Marcy, and Katey. Now recently divorced from Jan, Dad had moved to an apartment near Schmitty's and frequented my bar often.

Immediately, I grabbed a hammer, smashed the TV screen, pulled out its guts, crawled inside it, and sang karaoke to a packed bar. I knew I had to replace it anyway but took advantage of the opportunity to create a memorable moment. Antics like that made Schmitty's the talk of southern Minnesota. And with cash stacking up nicely in the till, I began to think I was in a position to expand.

When my friend Wayne Hilk came to visit from his home in Kansas City, I got my opportunity. Wayne hadn't wanted to invest in Schmitty's, but when he saw our success, he suggested that we look for another bar to invest in together. With a third partner, Wayne Salden, with whom I had made amends because he had now become my brother-in-law, I bought *two* bars, one called Someplace Else and another called Suds. We agreed that the primary role of the "Waynes" would be as investors while I would manage the bars.

We marketed the three properties together using the slogan, "If you don't like Schmitty's and you don't like Suds, go Someplace Else." I thought the slogan was clever. Unfortunately, my patrons took it too literally and began spreading their business around. I found that although I now had three bars, I had far less than three times the income.

For some reason, money had always flowed through my hands like water. I'll admit I was flat irresponsible, especially for a man with a wife, four kids, a mortgage, and three businesses to run. But back then, I never worried about it. It was as though I thought I could always escape financial consequences just as I'd escaped all the rest.

All through the 1990s, our finances would rise and fall, flush and bust, but somehow Karen and I always got through. And no matter what condition our finances were in, we always took the kids on long family trips. In the spring of 1997, I thought it would be a great idea to fly into Las Vegas, gamble a little, then drive the rest of the way to California. We'd take the kids to Knott's Berry Farm, Disneyland, and Sea World.

In Vegas, we rented a van and drove to Laughlin, Nevada, a town on the Colorado River across from Bullhead City, Arizona. We checked into the Flamingo. Across the parking lot I could see the Riverside, Laughlin's very first casino.

Back in 1966, a man named Don Laughlin bought six acres of riverfront property in the middle of nowhere. He converted an old place called the Riverside Bait Shop into the Riverside Casino, and that August opened with two live gambling tables, a dozen slot machines, and an all-you-can-eat chicken dinner for 98 cents. Now the Riverside had grown from eight motel rooms (four of which Laughlin's family occupied) to a major resort. I had no idea that Don Laughlin would one day become my friend, or that his casino would one day play an important role in my life.

At the Flamingo, all six of us crammed into one tiny room, and I headed down to the gaming floor to play craps. I *loved* craps. Because of my time as a professional card counter—again, more on that later—blackjack felt like work. But craps, a very complex game with lots of wagering, was more fun than any game on any gaming floor in any casino.

On this occasion, I had so much fun that in a matter of hours, I lost $4,000— every cent of the money we'd brought for our vacation.

When that last chip disappeared, I thought of Karen and the kids up in the room and just beginning our vacation. That kicked me into salvage mode. How was I going to fix this? Luckily, my high rolling had caught the pit boss's eye, and he came over to chat. I can't remember the exact conversation, but I probably told him something like, "I'm here on vacation with my family, and I have to get back to the room. We're gonna head back to Vegas."

What I did *not* tell him was that I was broke. Absolutely not. I would never tell a pit boss I was out of cash. I wanted him to believe I was just taking a break and would be back. What a casino wants is your money. *All* of your money. The question in his mind was, *How can I get this guy to stay in Laughlin and keep laying out those big chips?*

There's a one-word answer to that: comps. The pit boss offered us a huge suite, compliments of the house. I raced upstairs to tell Karen and the kids the good news, and we dragged our half-packed suitcases up to one of the biggest suites I've ever stayed in.

After one night in the suite, we took off to California. For the rest of our vacation, we scraped by on the proceeds from four ATM cards, heading to the machines at 12:01 a.m., pulling out our daily limit to get through until midnight the next day. The night before we were to head home, we rolled into a little Best Western. The six of us had one room with one bed and no money.

The truth is, when Karen and I were living life this way, we thought it was completely normal. To us, it looked like being loving parents. After all, didn't we take our kids on these memory-making trips—to the Wisconsin Dells, to amusement parks, to the Black Hills in South Dakota? Wasn't Karen a great mom who cooked fantastic Midwestern meals full of kid favorites? And wasn't our house the one where all the neighborhood kids wanted to hang out? Didn't I coach Little League and set up tents in the backyard for all the nieces and nephews?

Since I hid my vices and addictions from the kids, I reasoned that they weren't affected. So what if I used coke and drank and gambled? So what if I occasionally spent a little time in jail? Those things didn't make me a bad person. In my mind these escapades made great stories.

By then, I was an almost-daily cocaine user. Between feeding that habit and losing on sports betting, I was usually on the verge of going broke. The year 1998 was, however, an exception.

For decades, the Minnesota Vikings had been the team of smashed hopes. Four Super Bowls, four losses. In 1998, though, there was something different in the air. All signs said this was going to be our year. We burned through the preseason undefeated. The regular season got off to a 7–0 start. Quarterback Randall Cunningham racked up a passer rating of 100 or higher. And we were scoring an average of 35 points per game, an NFL record at the time.

As the team's momentum built, Sundays at Schmitty's became a raucous party of Viking pride. The place was packed. Every time we scored, I threw a huge stack of napkins into the ceiling fan and yelled, "Drinks are on the house!" Week 5 was especially sweet. On October 5, we played our biggest rival, the Green Bay Packers, on *Monday Night Football* and beat them—*at Lambeau.*

The Regulars lost their minds.

Through all this, I had friends around me who were getting into financial trouble with sports betting and I would tell them they needed to quit, even as I bet the farm on every game. Yes, despite multiple brushes with dangerous bookies, I was still betting heavily on sports.

One of my friends was in even worse shape though, having systematically gambled away just about everything he owned. I teamed up with his girlfriend to do an intervention. Looking back, it was strange that my friends accepted this from me. Not one of them ever called me a hypocrite. I think they knew I was speaking from the heart and that, deep down, I wanted to quit too. I actually did "quit" one addiction or another for a month or so at a time, just to prove to myself that I had it all under control.

While this friend didn't call me a hypocrite, he did absolutely flip out.

"Don't you two get it?" he yelled at his girlfriend and me, his face twisted in anger. "I'm *never* quitting! *Ever!*" And he didn't, continuing to bet on professional football and losing what little he had left.

Just before that Vikings–Packers game, Skelly and I went on our annual hunting trip, one I still never miss even now. As we waited for the other guys to show up, we sat in my pickup overlooking the lake. Halloween was coming up and I supposed we should do something at Schmitty's, even though it was my least favorite holiday because of all the masks people wore.

"You don't know who is who," I said, looking out at the water. I usually avoided the bar on Halloween.

Skelly said he actually liked dressing in costume and suggested we could do something fun at the bar that would get everyone talking. And so, sitting there at the lake, we began to brainstorm the Next Big Thing we could pull off.

The Blues Brothers was one of our favorite movies. Sometimes Skelly and I traded Aykroyd/Belushi quotes while doing lines of coke off *The Blues Brothers* CD case. Sitting there in my pickup, we decided to ring in Halloween at Schmitty's by dressing up like Joliet Jake and Elwood Blues, and recreating the most famous scene from the film, the famous "Rawhide" scene. If you haven't seen it, you can look it up on YouTube: Aykroyd, Belushi and their blues band book a gig in a backwoods honky-tonk called Bob's Country Bunker. When they arrive, the waitress cheerfully informs them that customers in that bar like two kinds of music: "Country and western."

It was definitely going to be a tough crowd. The band steps onstage, separated from the crowd by a wall of chicken wire. When they launch into the Steve Winwood/Spencer Davis Group classic, "Gimme Some Lovin'," this crowd is so tough they start booing and hurling empty beer bottles at the stage. The bottles smash against the chicken wire, and broken glass flies everywhere.

"That ain't no Hank William's song!" the bar manager yells. Then he turns out the stage lights.

The band knows only one country song, the theme from the Clint Eastwood western television series, *Rawhide*. To save their gig, the Blues Brothers start singing it. The crowd keeps on lobbing beer bottles, now in appreciation.

Could we pull off a re-creation? Skelly and I asked ourselves. We looked at each other and grinned. Yes! This was going to be epic.

This wasn't just an event; it was a construction project. First, we had to create our own country bunker. Skelly got totally into it. He got us the costumes, spent a month learning lyrics, and built the big chicken-wire cage that we would need for the skit. Together we installed it on the west wall, then walked to the opposite end of the room to conduct a safety test. Grabbing a full Budweiser from behind the bar, I wound up like a major league pitcher and hurled the bottle 30 feet across the room. The bottle hit the chicken wire all right—then bounced and came winging all the way back. We ducked as it flew past us and hit the mirror behind the bar. Luckily most of the speed had bled off, so the mirror didn't break.

I looked at Skelly and laughed. "Okay, that's not gonna work." I didn't want my customers knocked out by flying bottles.

By then, it was already 6 p.m. Working fast, our friend Tony, a carpenter, reinforced the cage with more two-by-fours, and we did another test. Now, it was hard to hit the cage without hitting a two-by-four. All the test bottles smashed against the wood, beer splashed through the chicken wire, and the broken glass crumbled to the floor. Perfect.

The night came and Schmitty's was packed. Skelly and I appeared in full Blues Brothers costume—dark suits, white shirts, ties, Ray-Bans, fedoras. I had even shaved my mustache. We got in the cage, a karaoke guy hit *play* on the machine we had rented, and the show began.

As Belushi, my lines were easy. ("Hit 'em up, move 'em out.") But it was Skelly who really nailed it. As we sang the *Rawhide* theme, I looked over at him in disbelief. He *was* Aykroyd. All his practice paid off.

The crowd loved it. They hooted and hollered and sang along, going through *cases* of beer just so they could throw bottles at the cage like the rednecks in the movie. Beer (and some glass) showered into the cage, soaking Skelly and me.

We did two encores—I set off firecrackers in my pocket at the 10 p.m. show—and each time, the crowd kept getting bigger because people had called their friends and told them they had to get down to the bar and see this. I was elated. I felt like I was making a great memory for people, and eight years later that proved to be correct.

At a home show in Milwaukee, a lady walked up to me and asked if I had ever owned a bar in Minnesota.

"Yes, why?" I said.

Her face lit up. "Just a second! I'll be right back!"

Moments later, she hurried up, this time with her husband. She pointed at me triumphantly and said, "That's the guy that owned that bar!"

The woman then explained that she and her husband lived in Wisconsin. On Halloween 1998, they were driving through Minnesota on their way to South Dakota when they stopped at a bar to take a short break.

"We were so surprised when we walked into a scene straight out of *The Blues Brothers*," she said. They ended up staying the whole night because they were having so much fun. "My husband hasn't stopped talking about it since!"

By the fall of 1998, my days were filled with hunting, showing off at the bar, and doing cocaine. For once, I had no money issues. I felt like I was on top of the world. Besides all that, it was an interesting year in Minnesota for other reasons. A former pro wrestler named Jesse Ventura had decided to run for governor. Bombastic and unconventional, Ventura was running as a Reform Party candidate—whatever that meant—and he captured the interest of blue-collar people across the state. People voted who had never voted before, including most of the guys in my hunting group. We were way up in northern Minnesota on Election Day, and walked into a bar just as a newscaster was announcing that the "beer vote" had come in, and it looked like Ventura was going to win.

I thought it was cool that an underdog candidate could come out on top, but that was the extent of my interest. I was completely apolitical. I finished my beer and headed out to enjoy the rest of my trip. This trip and many like it were only part of the self-absorbed behavior that kept me away from home. There was also gambling and coke and a lot of drinking. To this point in my marriage, Karen had struggled with insecurity that sometimes manifested as jealousy.

When I returned from the November 1998 hunting trip, she and I got into an argument. She suggested that maybe I went off on these trips so often because there were other women involved. I scoffed. "Of *course* there are no women hunting with us! What's wrong with you?"

Looking back, I mourn the fact that I used my strongest virtue—being truly faithful to my wife—to justify the rest of my selfish behavior. We had the identical argument again and again as Karen's insecurities and my "justified" behavior collided almost daily. I still considered my family the most important thing in my life, but 1998 was a definite turning point in our marriage. The turbulence remained hidden, though, churning beneath the surface. To everyone else, we still looked like a family that had it all.

CHAPTER

10

Toad's Road

The month after Skelly and I did our Blues Brothers skit at Schmitty's, I got an alarming phone call. It was my friend Dean, the one who dared me to jump out the bus window, and who was Dick VanSloun's roommate during my brief stint sleeping on his couch. I had last run into him in the early 1990s, when Karen and I took the kids to Florida. Dean had married a beautiful woman, they'd had a son, and he was working on the space shuttle as a mechanic for NASA. I was happy for him, proud of the way his life had turned out.

But in November 1998, he called me at Schmitty's with a disturbing question. "Mike," Dean said, "do you think it's wrong to kill yourself?" I could tell by the way he slurred his words that he was very drunk.

His question didn't surprise me. Earlier that year, he had called me asking a bunch of questions about God. Did I think God was real? Did I think there was a heaven? Yes was my answer to both questions. Since then, Dean's world had turned upside down. He'd lost his job at NASA and his wife had left him. He said a doctor had also told him he might have a brain tumor.

"The pain is so bad, Mike," he said. "I don't know what I'm going to do." I sensed his desperation, and clearly he'd been giving some thought to ending it all. I was in shock. He was the one guy out of our group that I thought had it all together. And I knew he'd already faced excruciating pain in his life.

Once in the early '80s, five of us, including Dean, Chris, and myself, went to downtown Minneapolis and ended up at a bar called Moby Dick's. It was a dangerous place back then, and we had no business being there. We were playing pool, and Chris' mouth got us in trouble with some other guys in the bar. The bouncer stomped over and said to me, "You need to get your friend out of here—*now.*" While trying to get Chris toward the door, he made things even worse, shouting out the worst racial slur I'd ever heard.

I hustled him out of there and the five of us headed to a Burger King down the street. After we ate, I was the last one to leave the restaurant. Out in the street, I saw that a group of 20 or 25 black guys had ambushed Chris and Dean. Furious at Chris for the slur he'd used at Moby Dick's, they had him by both arms and were beating him with fists. Dean was trying to defend Chris when one of the guys kicked him hard in the groin. Dean crumpled to the ground.

I ran into the street. "Stop!" I yelled. "You're all *dead!* My dad's the biggest drug lord in the Twin Cities! You have no idea what you just did. I want names, and I want them *now!*"

Everything stopped. Dean lay on the ground in the fetal position. The guys who had just beaten him stood over him, frozen. Then one guy who seemed to be the leader walked up to me and actually smiled.

"You make me laugh," he said. He was perfectly calm in that deadly way of a man who's making a threat and intends to deliver on it. "You take your raggedy-ass suburbanite friends back wherever you came from, and don't ever come back. I'm going to let you live."

I smiled back. "Thank you."

As we were about to leave, I addressed the leader and his friends. "Hey, you guys, I was kidding. My dad's not a drug lord, and you're all going to be okay. No one's gonna kill you."

They all busted out laughing. Dean was in pretty bad shape, though. In the end he actually lost a testicle from his injuries. Obviously, this guy understood what it meant to be in pain. So when Dean told me on the phone that the pain in his head was so bad he didn't know if he could live with it, I was genuinely concerned.

"Dean, I've watched you endure more pain than anybody I've ever seen," I said. "I don't know what to tell you now, exactly, but I think I read somewhere in the Bible that it's wrong to kill yourself." The truth was, I didn't really know. I was just trying to keep my friend from ending his own life.

Dean was quiet for a second. Then he said, "Well. I don't want a funeral. I'm serious. I do not want a funeral."

We didn't stay on the phone much longer. I hung up and called Dean's brother, Mark. He confirmed that Dean was in a really bad place, and that he was very worried. A sadness came over me as I realized that someone I cared about deeply had fallen on seriously hard times, taken down by illness, alcohol, and depression.

As usual, I saw no parallels or warning signs in my own life. In fact, most nights after Schmitty's closed, I kept my personal party going. My friend Paul, nicknamed Toad, would hold a kind of after-party at his house. Toad was a hardworking single guy who put in 40 hours a week at a machine shop. He owned his own home right across the street from the Dairy Queen and kept it in immaculate condition. He could've afforded something bigger, since he'd inherited something like $300,000 from his parents. But Toad banked that money and never touched it. He wanted to use it for something that would make his parents proud.

Most nights, at least a dozen of us would end up at Toad's, drinking beer, doing cocaine, and talking about what all had gone on at Schmitty's. Going to these parties had become almost routine for me. I would work at Schmitty's, go to Toad's, and some days—thanks to the cocaine—I would stay there until it was time to go back to the bar.

Don't get me wrong: I absolutely loved being a husband and a dad. But I rationalized all the time I spent away from home. I was building my customer base, I reasoned. I was the life of the party, showing people things they'd never seen before—in this case, a good-time guy who had such a great marriage that he could remain awake for days on end, hang out with friends night after night, then return at will to his loving wife at home. What a joke.

One night, a burly guy none of us had met before came over to Toad's, looked around, and slapped money on the table. "One hundred dollars for the last man standing," he said.

Toad didn't even hesitate. He pulled out $100 of his own money and slapped it down. "A hundred bucks on him," he said, pointing to me. "He's already been up for three days."

The guy looked at me and then at Toad. "Why would you do that?"

"Because sooner or later you're going to have to go to work," Toad told him. The stranger looked back at me, and I just shrugged. He grabbed his $100 and left.

The Regulars had always looked forward to Toad's after-parties. But slowly, something began to change. One night in early 1999, my friend Kevin Chase dropped in. Kevin had been a Schmitty's Regular for years, but I hadn't seen him in about six months because he had been living up north.

It was 2 a.m. and now the only people left at the house were me, Toad, Kevin, and our friend Dan. The four of us were sitting around the kitchen island when I laid out four lines of cocaine. Instead of snorting the lines, Dan and Toad scraped theirs into a spoon and headed to separate bedrooms.

Kevin looked at me and frowned. "What the hell...?" he said.

It wasn't the first time these guys had done this. "Kevin, you won't believe it," I told him. "They're taking the coke in the back and turning it into crack cocaine." They'd been doing this for a few weeks by the time Kevin showed up.

"They go in the back and smoke it," I said. "It's weird. They stay back there for a really long time. I've seen them peeking out the windows every few minutes, all paranoid."

I had also noticed that anyone who had started smoking crack hardly came into Schmitty's anymore. And when I saw them at Toad's, all they wanted to do was grab their coke and disappear into the bedrooms. "We don't even talk anymore," I told Kevin. "It's ruining us."

Kevin and I looked at each other. "I don't want to get like that," I said. "Let's promise each other we will never, ever smoke crack."

CHAPTER

11

Coke Times Ten

W ith *The Blues Brothers* blowout and the Vikings' dream season, in late 1998, I was riding high. But January brought what turned out to be an earthquake year. I know the exact day things headed south: Friday, January 15, 1999.

We were headed into a huge weekend. The Vikings had gone 15–1, the first team ever to win 15 regular season games. The NFC championship was set for that Sunday, the Vikings versus the Atlanta Falcons, and we were 11-point favorites. The whole town, and really the whole state, was high on victory. We all had our sights set on the Super Bowl, our first in 22 years. This time, we were going to win.

This being Schmitty's, we weren't confining the party to game day only. I had planned promotions to draw people in all weekend and expected the place to be an absolute zoo. As she sometimes did, Karen had agreed to come in and help out behind the bar beginning on Friday. I was rushing around the house that morning, getting ready to head over to the bar when Karen looked at me and said, "I'm not coming in."

I stopped dead in my tracks and whirled around. "What?"

I had already tried to hire extra bartenders for the weekend but with the big game on tap, couldn't find any. There was no way I could handle this crowd myself. I tried to talk her into coming in. We usually had each other's backs, but this time Karen made a stand.

She had been up all night partying, and she wasn't coming in. Period.

We'd been arguing more lately, our patience worn down by hectic schedules, being apart all the time, and especially by drinking and drugs. This argument, however, escalated into a full-blown fight. My rage kicked in, a kind that crept up on me more and more. I was furious. She was furious. We both said and did things we had never said or done before. Karen stormed into the bedroom and locked the door, I stormed after her and kicked the door in.

Then I stopped. I would never lay a hand on Karen, but I felt betrayed. As far as I was concerned, she was messing with our livelihood, this being maybe the biggest money-making weekend of the year. I felt abandoned, my pride wounded, and I wanted her to know that if I wanted to come into my bedroom, I damn well would. Later, I felt terrible about breaking the door and tried repairing it myself. That, too, was a disaster.

I went in to Schmitty's and ran things myself that Friday, fueled by thick lines of cocaine. I was angry all day, so much so that I was glad my wife and I weren't speaking. I didn't want to talk to her and she didn't want to talk to me. Things were bad, but the next day, they became horrific.

Early Saturday evening, Dean called me. He was so distraught I couldn't even understand what he was saying. Not an hour later, Dean's brother, Mark, called me.

"Dean's dead," Mark said. "He shot himself."

That night, I sat outside Schmitty's for an hour and sobbed. I was in shock. My mind reeled and for a long time afterwards, I asked myself what else I could have done. Sunday, the day after Dean's suicide, those of us who had been close to him walked around in a state of disbelief. But our friend had been living out of state for 20 years, so most people in town were more concerned about the Vikings playoff game. As people crowded into Schmitty's, I had to set my feelings aside. The team lost, blowing a seven-point lead in the final four minutes, then losing by a field goal in overtime. The Regulars were crushed. They filed out one by one to drown their sorrows elsewhere.

After everyone left, I sat alone in the bar, shell-shocked. Karen and I were still fighting, so I never went home that night. Just stayed in the bar, doing coke all night long. The next morning, I decided to keep Schmitty's closed. It was like I was sealed in a bubble of sorrow, with no communication in and none going out. Finally, my friend Tony got worried and called Skelly. "Mike's never shut the bar down. I think you need to go check on him."

Skelly did, and on Tuesday morning I opened my eyes and saw him passed out beside me on the floor of the bar. Looking around, I realized the janitor had come in and swept up around Skelly and me as though we were chalk outlines in the middle of a crime scene.

That was the terrible beginning of a terrible year that would change the course of my life. Not long afterward, I was down in the basement at Schmitty's. I was out of coke, and a friend of mine said, "Here. Take this."

I looked down and saw a crack rock in his hand. Vaguely, I remembered the pact I'd made with Kevin Chase. We weren't going to do crack. We weren't going to become creepy and paranoid like those guys at Toad's house. On the other hand, I was out of coke, and it had been an almost universally crappy year.

I looked down at the rock. "What's it like?" I asked my friend.

"It's a lot like coke," he said.

Well, it *was* coke, sort of. I knew crack was made from coke—with baking soda, water and heat. I did not realize that it is an almost completely different drug. With that first rock in my hand, I decided it wouldn't hurt to fill in the gap in my supply just this once. So, I smoked it and…nothing. It was no big deal.

But the *second* time…

The second time, the high was magnified beyond anything I'd ever felt. When I inhaled, there was a *whoosh*, and I was instantly "there." It was coke-times-ten, at least. I smoked another rock and another. Over the next few hours, I also noticed that crack didn't seem to carry the negative side effects of coke. With coke, I was tired but couldn't sleep. I wasn't hungry but wanted to eat. With crack, I could sleep *and* eat.

All that was the devil's lie, of course. This would soon flip. Not only would I not want to eat, I would not want to sleep. All I wanted was more crack.

I tried it a few more times in the weeks ahead, picking up some here and there from friends, including the paranoid ones who'd stopped coming to the bar. One day, I talked one of my dealers, Ray, into driving all the way out to Schmitty's from Minneapolis. He pulled up outside the bar, and I walked out to meet him. He rolled down his window and handed me a baggy of coke.

Then I asked him a question that had really been worrying me. "Hey, Ray," I said. "Do you know anyone that's done crack then went back to just doing soft cocaine?"

Ray stared at me hard, and his face became a question mark. "What?"

I repeated my question and his eyes narrowed. "You didn't do it, did you?"

"Yeah, I did."

Ray's face collapsed. "I *told* you—never, ever smoke crack!" he said. "You're done now. You're *through*. You just ruined your life."

1966 The Lindell family (my father Jim, Cindy, me, Robin, and my mother Barb) on our neighborhood street in Fairmont, Minnesota.

1964 I was 3 years old here when I led neighborhood kids in a parade.

1969 My card skills began at a very young age. Here I am shuffling cards at our kitchen table.

1973 Pictured left to right: me, Barb, John, Robin, Amy, Fred, and Cindy.

1975 Christmas Day, pictured left to right: John, Cindy, me, Amy, and Robin.

1975 Camping at a Minnesota KOA, pictured left to right: Lori, Robin, me, John, Cindy, and Fred.

1977 Closing time at the Flying Cloud Drive-In Theatre in Eden Prairie, Minnesota, I didn't mind mopping the floor. In fact, I found it relaxing.

1977–1982 Exterior view of Cooper's Super Valu where I worked as a cashier and a stock boy in the produce department.

1978 My stepdad Fred's truck after my accident.

1979 The Honda motorcycle that I crashed on my way to go skydiving.

1980 Just before my friend and I departed for Las Vegas, my Grandma Millie snapped this photo of my Uncle Butch and me. My friend and I were going to drop him in Kansas on our way to Vegas.

1980 Wayne Salden and I hanging out at Butch's Tavern in Chaska, Minnesota.

1983 Me pictured with Lee Tischleder, we opened Sunshine Concessions lunch wagon and then went on to open LeeMichaels together.

1984 Front row, pictured left to right: Cindy, Robin holding Katey; Back row: me, Marcy, Jim (my dad), and Corey.

1981 Hardee's bag with bookie's threat: MIKE CAME TO GET OUR MONEY—Book was with me—Physical Force May Be Needed CALL ME!

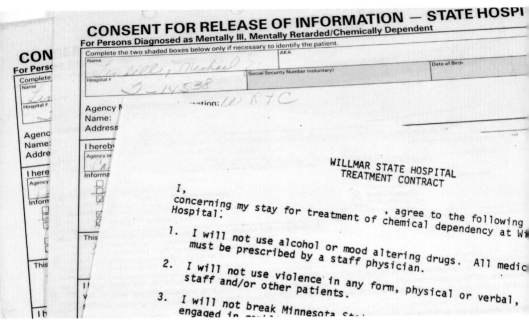

CONSENT FOR RELEASE OF INFORMATION — STATE HOSPI

For Persons Diagnosed as Mentally Ill, Mentally Retarded/Chemically Dependent

Complete the two shaded boxes below only if necessary to identify the patient.

Name
AKA

Hospital #

Social Security Number (voluntary)
Date of Birth

Agency
Name:
Address

I hereby
Agency or

Informa

This

WILLMAR STATE HOSPITAL
TREATMENT CONTRACT

I,
concerning my stay for treatment of , agree to the following
Hospital: chemical dependency at Wi

1. I will not use alcohol or mood altering drugs. All medic
must be prescribed by a staff physician.

2. I will not use violence in any form, physical or verbal,
staff and/or other patients.

3. I will not break Minnesota Sta
engaged in

1986 Treatment Contract and
Consent for Release of Information
documents from Willmar State
Hospital, the facility I checked
myself into.

1986–1989 One of the first
businesses I started was Sunshine
Concessions, a food truck carrying sandwiches, snacks, and soda.
I would park this truck outside of
local businesses and sell goods to
employees during their breaks.

1987 Grandma Millie, pictured here with Karen and me on our wedding day.

1985 With my daughter Heather, age 2.

1993 Lindell family portrait, pictured left to right: Charlie, me, Karen, Darren, Heather, and Lizzy.

After a delay, Statesman owner gets liquor license

By LaVonne Barac

This week, the Chaska City Council granted a liquor license to Karen Lindell for Lee's of Hazeltine, the former Statesman Restaurant. Approval came after a stipulation was added that is designed to prevent the applicant's husband and another man from serving liquor after 6 p.m. The stipulation is also supposed to be in employment contracts between Karen Lindell and the two men.

The initial hangup occurred because the original license applicant, Lee Tischleder, for whom the business is named, has a 1985 liquor license violation conviction and state statute bars people with convictions (within the last five years) from holding licenses.

Before the application came before the city council on Dec. 19, however, the three principals directly involved in the business -- Tischleder, Lindell and Lindell's husband, Mike -- had come up with a restructuring that gave Ms. Lindell legal ownership of the business.

After the restructuring of legal documents and agreements, Tischleder and Mike Lindell became employees of the business, which in council discussion prompted Alderman Robert Lindall to ask: "We're supposed to believe they'll have no involvement in the operation?"

Karen Lindell was represented by her attorney, Jim Croft, at the meeting. Croft told the council, "We hope our focus would not be on the employees...The whole thing I worry about is the issue of guilt by association."

Lindall, noting the statute allows the city some discretion, told the council, "This doesn't say if the principal operator is clean, you have to grant (the license)."

With that, the council tabled the action until this week, when it was approved.

This week, the Lindells and Croft were back again. In approving the liquor license of Karen Lindell, the staff had suggested a condition prohibits her husband and Tischleder from dispensing liquor at the establishment unless she is on the premises. In discussion, council members Robert Lindall and Dan Ress both supported a compromise offered by Mike Lindell and it was adopted.

According to information discussed at the mid-December council meeting and included in the police department's background check, Lee Tischleder owns a mobile concession route. Mike Lindell, a bartender at the Statesman, has also been employed by Tischleder.

In November 1985 Tischleder was observed as the bartender at Cy's Bar. It was 2 a.m. and he had seven or eight people still in the bar. He was cited for allowed patrons in the bar after hours, entered a guilty plea to the charge, and was fined $33. Other than alcohol related motor vehicle violations, Tischleder has no criminal history, according to the police report.

Mike Lindell has a liquor violation charge pending against him. According to the police report, he was issued a citation for selling liquor to minors at the Statesman. According to the report, while the citation was dismissed, a formal complaint is being issued. Also in 1986, a charge of illegal consumption after hours was issued at 4:49 a.m., The charge was subsequently dropped as the result of a plea negotiation. In addition, Mike Lindell's history has a range of violations, including several of driving while under the influence, some of which were aggravated offenses according to the police department.

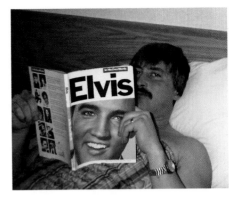

1992 Me pictured here reading up on Elvis. I've always been a big fan.

1989 LeeMichaels finally gets liquor license (right); newspaper article (above) published in the *Chaska Herald*.

1989 LeeMichaels Restaurant and Lounge; I owned this establishment from 1989 to 1990.

1990–2003 Outside view of Schmitty's Tavern, Victoria, Minnesota.

1993 Talking with some of my Regulars while tending bar at Schmitty's Tavern.

1994 Schmitty's co-ed softball team.

1994 Pictured left to right: Darren, Charlie, Heather, and Lizzy.

1996 My dad, Jim, and me at Christmas.

1998 Performing at Schmitty's on Halloween, I dressed as Jake and Paul (Skelly) dressed as Elwood from the characters in the 1980s' hit *The Blues Brothers*.

1997 Entertaining a crowd at Schmitty's.

2001 Setting off firecrackers inside Schmitty's. (Notice the napkin "snow" on the floor.)

2001 Me with lit firecrackers in an ashtray under my hat.

2002 Family vacation to Florida, pictured from left to right: Charlie, Karen, Heather, Darren, me, and Lizzy.

BOOK

2

CRACK
Minnesota…and Casinos Everywhere
2002–2007

CHAPTER

12

Storm Warning

From inside Schmitty's, I could hear the sounds of a growing storm. Thunder rumbled in the distance, like drumrolls on sheet metal. Rain poured through the parking lot and bent the trees at Stieger Lake. It was about 2 a.m., and I was closing up, tidying behind the bar. Counting the money in the till, I found there wasn't as much as I would've liked.

Again.

It was the summer of 2002, and a bar down the block called Floyd's had been siphoning away my business for a couple of years. The new owners bought the place at about the same time I started using crack. They did a good job creating a fun atmosphere where customers felt at home, just like I had. They also started bringing in live bands, something we didn't have room for at Schmitty's.

I responded with one of my trademark grand gestures, organizing all-out-party field trips I called "Schmitty's Goes to Vegas." After I gambled away our vacation money in 1997 and the Flamingo Casino pit boss comped Karen and me the luxury suite, I had learned a lot about "comps." Like most regular gamblers, I had a "player's card" for each casino where I spent significant amounts of time. I discovered that when I used these cards, the house tracked my metrics. What games did I play? How long did I play? And most importantly, how much was I betting per roll or per hand?

If the metrics rose high enough, there were perks: meals, rooms, show tickets—all for free. Casinos will give gamblers pretty much anything to keep them gambling. To maximize my comps, I promoted the idea that I was a big-time player, which meant trying to look and act like I had money when I didn't. It wasn't long before the Riviera, the Stardust, and the Westward Ho—my favorite casinos on the Strip—had each issued me a *gold* player's card. That entitled me to things like suites, unlimited food, even limousines. After a while, I learned I could extend my comps to others. So, I organized a pair of four-day trips for the Regulars and friends.

The Schmitty's crew was as obnoxious outside the bar as in, which meant the flights to and from were just as entertaining as being at Schmitty's. But for me these trips were also a lot of work. I wanted to make sure each and every person was taken care of and having a great time. Plus, I had to play four hours a day at each of my three gold-card casinos to keep the comps flowing.

On one of these trips in 2000, a friend ran out of cash and took out a $100 marker at the Stardust. A marker is like an IOU, a way of borrowing money from the house to place a bet. But as with bad checks, an unpaid marker is a felony in Nevada, so it's critical to pay it back. Since I was a gold-card holder, the Stardust let me sign for the friend's marker. I quickly scribbled my signature on this minor IOU and forgot all about it.

Each trip was a huge success, but even taking my Regulars to Vegas didn't stop some from defecting to Floyd's. That really hurt me. I felt I'd poured a lot of love into Schmitty's and into my customers, and their defection felt like a betrayal.

The real story—that I was also defecting—was harder for me to accept. In the '90s, when I was building the business, I worked double-digit hours seven days a week, tending bar and running the softball and pool leagues. After my family, Schmitty's was the most important thing in my life, and I poured all my energy into it. Now though, crack sucked away my passion little by little. I was becoming a clock-puncher at my own business. I rationalized my increasing absences. After full weekends of entertaining my customers, I reasoned that I didn't really need to be at Schmitty's on Monday nights. Then, before long, it was also Tuesday nights. And so it went. Crack was incompatible with running the bar. I used to run down to the basement, do a quick line of coke, and reappear behind the bar as the life of the party. Cocaine had become just another recreational drug. But crack required secrecy, and keeping that secret was a lot of work. The drug carried a stigma, and I certainly didn't want anyone to know I was smoking crack.

When I finished counting the till money, I tucked it in a zip-up bank bag and walked out into the storm, locking the doors behind me. Rain poured in sheets from the dark morning sky, and I pulled my jacket up over my head as I hurried to my truck. Feeling low about the night's skimpy earnings, I cranked the engine and turned on the wipers. They beat back and forth, smearing the view, but the handwriting on the wall was becoming clear. Crack was now more important to me than my livelihood.

Crack takes you down fast. I was watching it happen all around me. One day, the wife of my friend John called. John had been staying away from the house for long periods, she said. Also, their bank accounts were disappearing. John's wife, along with his mother, suspected he had a gambling problem and asked me to come over and help them do an intervention. This remained an ironic feature of my life, that friends and family would call me to talk other addicts off the ledge even though they knew I was an addict myself. This happened many times, and I still don't quite understand it.

It was two in the afternoon when I arrived at John's house, and a dozen of his family members were already there.

"This last time, he was gone for three days," John's wife said the minute I walked in. "He's cheating on me. I know it!"

His mother chimed in. "He said he was at Mystic Lake Casino."

Many times, I'd cleaned out the till at Schmitty's and headed to Mystic Lake with friends. Taking friends with me was kind of like an insurance policy in case I lost right away. I could always get them to give me a short-term loan against the Schmitty's till. I later learned that when Skelly came with me, he'd hide behind the slot machines so I couldn't find him when I needed more cash. He didn't have a problem loaning me money; he just didn't want to see me go deeper in the hole.

Now, I looked sadly at John's wife and mom. "You're both wrong," I said. "John isn't cheating on you, and he's not gambling. He's on crack."

Surprise washed over both their faces. "Really?" his wife said. She sounded somewhat in disbelief, but also strangely relieved.

"You don't get it," I said. "Crack is the most powerful drug I have ever done in my life."

After the fourth or fifth time I used it, crack turned on me, causing terrible paranoia. I would be filled with fear and not know why. I found myself lifting the corners of window curtains, peeking out, searching for something that wasn't there. The paranoia thing is common among crack users. You can be sitting with your best friend since high school, wondering if he's an undercover cop. At first, the paranoia hits you two out of 10 times you smoke crack, then three or four out of 10. Pretty soon, it's every time.

I would find myself shut in a house with strangers, isolating myself just like the paranoid guys at Toad's house. Once I got to that point, I would smoke a rock, then take everything, including the hot pipe, and hide it—in a hole in the wall, a secret pocket cut into the couch, under a sink behind the pipes—anywhere I thought no one else would look. Then 10 minutes or so later, I'd pull it out and smoke another rock. Then hide it again and start all over.

Everything about crack required secrecy and cunning. I was always making small, makeshift pipes. I'd buy a tire pressure tester and take the insides out or maybe use a wrench socket or a glass pipe. To complete the pipe, I'd buy a Chore Boy scrubber, tear a piece off, and scrunch it up inside the pipe so that it functioned like a screen in a tobacco pipe. Whenever I arrived at a store checkout counter with a spoon, baking soda, and a Chore Boy, I was sure the clerk knew exactly why I wanted that stuff and was just waiting for me to hit the parking lot before calling the cops. The paranoia that came with crack was exhausting.

Yet even with all the fear and secrecy, even as I knew my behavior was getting stranger and stranger, the high I got from crack was so euphoric that I was willing to endure it all rather than stop.

At the exact moment I revealed to John's family that his real problem was crack, John came walking down the stairs. "What's going on?" he said, looking around at the familiar faces crowded into his living room.

One by one, his family spoke. "This is an intervention," they said. They were worried about him and had already reserved him a spot at a Granite Falls, Minnesota, treatment facility that would help him with his gambling addiction.

Gambling addiction? I thought.

"I told you guys he needs to go in for crack addiction, too!" I blurted. John glared at me like I'd stabbed him in the back. I understood his sense of betrayal. After all, I didn't want my friends and family to know *I* was hooked on crack. But if John's family was already at the intervention stage, I felt they needed to know the truth. Even if I couldn't be saved, maybe it wasn't too late for John.

I returned my friend's gaze. "John, we've talked about this," I said.

"We both know this is the most powerful drug either of us has ever done. We have no control over it."

There was nothing he could say at that point. Reluctantly, but to please his family, John left that day for Granite Falls.

As it turned out, John could not be saved. After a 28-day addiction program, he returned home and came out as a full-blown crack addict, now with nothing left to hide. I had tried to help, but failed.

I also failed to control my own crack use, and by now Karen was into crack, too. Even though I was functioning better than some of my friends, I noticed I was starting to pick up more of their strange behaviors. While smoking crack alone or with friends, I'd run out of the drug and start crawling around the floors, searching for any little scrap that might be a piece of an unsmoked rock. It's called "farming" and every crack addict has done it.

And remember my friend Toad? For all the time I had known him, Toad put in the hours at that machine shop, never cut corners, and hung onto his inheritance. Then he tried crack. Remember that neat, clean house across from the Dairy Queen? It was now a full-blown crack house. Toad had papered over the windows with cardboard, cutting in peepholes and slits to accommodate the crackhead paranoia. The yard, which he had always kept neatly clipped, became overgrown with weeds. After a while, he stopped paying his electricity bill, and the power company shut off his lights. Toad just snuck a long extension cord onto his neighbors' property and stole power from them.

Crack had its claws in my friend so deep that he was smoking it around the clock. Since the high lasts only five or 10 minutes, Toad started using a timer to keep from running through his supply too quickly. His increasingly bizarre behavior cost him his job. Now, at lightning speed, he was burning through the money his dad had left him.

I had always loved debating with Toad over everything from new inventions to the existence of God. Now I was watching him free fall toward disaster. One day when I was at his house, I confronted him about it.

"Look at this place!" I said, gesturing around at the mess. "Where does it end, Toad? You've spent almost all your dad's money. Where does it end?"

Toad's eyes narrowed to slits like the ones he'd cut in his window cardboard. "When it's *gone*," he whispered.

In the voice that came out of his mouth, I did not recognize my friend. The difference in Toad, the diligent nice guy who wanted to please his parents, and the man I saw before me, brought me a deep sadness. This Toad sounded desperate, determined, defiant and lost, all at the same time. I'll never forget it.

When I pulled into my driveway on the night of the huge summer storm, I saw lights on in the kitchen. By then, lightning was forking down around the neighborhood. The thunder that followed sounded like explosions at a demolition site. Inside, I found Darren sitting at the kitchen table, watching the storm through the open sliding glass doors.

"Hey, are you the only one up?" I asked.

"Yes. The thunder woke me up."

"Haven't seen a lightning storm like this before," I said, glancing outside. It was like watching a light show at eye level—that's how close the lightning was.

I walked over to the fridge. "Are you hungry? I could cook us up some deer steaks."

He smiled and nodded. I put the steaks on the stove and sat down next to him. I was in a reflective mood and for a few minutes, I watched lightning flicker on Darren's face as it danced around the trees outside.

I was in love with my kids. You know how it is: Raising them seems to take forever, but that precious time also flies by in the blink of an eye. Darren, who'd barely made it into the world, was already 12. Charlie was 13 by then. I remember when he was about 18 months old, we had to take him to the emergency room for dehydration, and we couldn't figure out why…until we noticed Lizzy over in the corner drinking Charlie's baby bottle. It turned out she'd been stealing his bottles from his crib, drinking them dry, and putting them back empty. She was 2-and-a-half then. Now she was 14, heading into high school. Heather, a spirited preschooler when Karen and I got married, was now driving. Where had the time gone?

For 15 years, Karen and I had been so close. Now, we were both into crack, and it was beginning to chip away at the integrity of our family. The pace of family life and running Schmitty's had always kept us busy, but the secrecy that developed around our crack use caused us to spend even more time away from our kids. Keeping our addiction away from the house and the kids meant we'd go hang out with our crack-smoking friends. Also, I often went off to smoke crack on my own—at Toad's house, for example. This, combined with the awful crack paranoia, caused Karen even greater anxiety. She'd always worried I was cheating on her, and now my longer absences magnified her fear.

Darren and I sat watching the storm until the deer steaks were done. I pulled them off the stove and we dug in, listening to the rolling thunder and the patter of rain. Still in a nostalgic mood, I started telling him stories about my life. I can't remember how the subject came up—maybe it was that I knew Schmitty's was headed south and I'd begun to think about career options—but I began telling Darren about my days as a professional card counter.

If you're not familiar with card counting, I'll tell you how it works. A card counter is an "advantage player" who tries to overcome the house's built-in advantage in the game of blackjack by keeping mental track of the cards as they are played. By doing so, he is also tracking cards that *haven't* been played. As a result, he is able to predict with a fair degree of accuracy which cards will be played next. I learned the trade back in the '80s from a card counting master named Vas Spanos. In Spanos' system, players memorize "matrixes"—tables that quantify the advantage to the house versus the player by assigning each combination of cards a positive or negative value—and use them to "count."

Now, if you've ever lost money on casino blackjack, you know the odds always favor the house. However, using probability as his or her secret weapon, a good card counter actually has a steady advantage over the house of about 1.5 percent.

"That's why it isn't gambling," I explained to Darren. "But it also isn't really a lot of fun."

Counting involves keeping careful track of cards played to build your advantage. But as a dealer turns up cards from a deck or a shoe, the advantage seesaws back and forth between players and the house. To come out on top, you have to sit at the tables for hours and hours, running through the matrixes in your head, grinding it out.

"It's a job, an occupation," I told Darren, clearing the mess from our little 3 a.m. snack. "But if you stick with it, you can make a good living."

"Why did you stop?" Darren said.

I paused and looked at him. "Well, when I was in his course, Vas Spanos said I was one of the best he'd ever seen. But he also said I'd never be a successful card counter because I was a gambler at heart."

Vas was correct. I always became impatient with the plodding pace and pressed my bets too far. Except for the one time I did it right.

By the summer of 1983, I had already tried Vas' system, then given up counting. Now I was working on my uncle's pig farm in Iowa. Uncle Al raised feeder pigs, the kind people buy to fill their freezers with pork. I was putting in 80 to 100 hours a week at $5 an hour, slopping, cleaning stalls, delivering tiny little piglets, clipping tails, clipping teeth (yes, teeth), and nursing sick and injured pigs back to health. But that was the loneliest year of my life.

I was living with my grandma, two hours from home, from my folks, my friends, and my girlfriend, Donna. Eventually, I hit on an idea: The feeder pig market was going gangbusters and Uncle Al was making a mint. Why didn't I raise and sell my own pigs? Mom and Fred had their hobby farm back in Carver. I could set up my business there.

As the saying goes, it seemed like a good idea at the time. I managed to get a small bank loan, built a pen on Mom and Fred's hobby farm, and bought 60 frisky, 40-pound piglets. And then, almost immediately, the bottom fell out of the pig market. I had paid $65 for each pig and was forced to sell every one of them at a catastrophic discount. Now, I not only owed the bank about $4,000 for the pigs, but I also owed the feed company a couple of thousand, and a bookie $10,000 for some baseball games that hadn't fallen my way.

I wracked my brain: How could I pay back the money? Solution: I would go to Las Vegas and count cards. I was going to do it right this time, I promised myself. I would be frugal and hyper-focused. I would follow Vas' rules. And I wouldn't have a single drink.

Borrowing some gas money from my grandma, I jumped into my beat-up old van and headed west. On the way, I came up with a plan. I had already mapped out all the casinos. I knew I would have to bounce around between them, never staying too long at any one so that I didn't attract attention. My goal was to make $300 a night, which I would send back to my mom daily.

When I rolled into Las Vegas a couple of days later, it was so hot I swear you could have boiled water on the dashboard. At least 120 degrees. I took that into account as I put my plan in motion, trying to win my money as early in the evening as possible so I could sleep in my van during the coolest hours. Eventually I figured out how to sneak into the Stardust pool, and I would spend my days sleeping on a lounge chair, catching little bits of Casey Kasem's *American Top 40* between stretches of shut-eye. For 40 days, I was a machine, sleeping at the pool by day and counting at night. Every morning, I sent $300 home.

I knew a lot about cards by then. I had even read a book on how to catch a cheat. One night, I was sitting at a casino table when I got a surprise: None of the players were cheating. The *dealer* was cheating. I spotted him second-dealing me—dealing me the second card in the deck instead of the one off the top.

Excited to have caught him, I called over the two pit bosses. "This guy is cheating me and I can prove it," I said. "The next card is going to be the jack of diamonds."

I looked right at the dealer and said, "You're in trouble, buddy!"

Sure enough, he flipped over the jack of diamonds. I didn't have time to say anything else before the pit bosses circled the table, picked me up, and dragged me to the front of the house, where they threw me through a pair of swinging doors out into the street. It was just like you see in the old Westerns.

I lay on the sidewalk as they stared down at me. "Come back here and we'll kill you," one of them said. Suddenly I realized I had forgotten a critical fact: The dealer works for the casino.

But the most defining moment of the trip happened at the Flamingo. I was up $500 before a pit boss came over and asked me to leave the table. He knew I was counting. Since I had already overshot my daily earnings goal of $300, I decided to play some slots. It would be the only time during this 40-day trip that I would gamble. Progressive slots machines were relatively new at the time. The big draw was that the jackpot just kept building until someone won it. That night, the jackpots at the Flamingo's three progressive slots were up to $1.5 million.

Winning that kind of money was just a fantasy, of course. Still, I thought, *wow*. That's all I'd need. I sat there and plugged all three machines for a while. I was winning some and losing some when this young guy and his family walked up behind me. It was the kid's 21st birthday. "Do you mind if we play one of the machines?" he asked.

The kid and his family only wanted one pull, just to say he had done it. "Sure, go ahead," I said. After all, it was his birthday.

I stepped aside. The kid plugged in three silver dollars and pulled the lever. Then I heard some of the worst sounds I've ever heard in my life. The machine started to jingle and ring and flash bright lights. The kid and his family leapt into the air, then started laughing and hugging each other. The kid had won the jackpot.

For a couple of moments, I stood there in shock. I had been one pull away—*that* pull away—from $1.5 million. That was change-your-life money, especially back then. Suddenly, I needed to get out of there fast. The family was still celebrating, and I just couldn't watch anymore.

I spent the rest of the night going from casino to casino, replaying the events of the night over and over in my head. The worst thing was that the news was everywhere, all over the Strip:

"TOMMY BANANAS WINS $1.5 MILLION ON
HIS 21ST BIRTHDAY AT THE FLAMINGO!"

No matter where I went, I couldn't get away from it. At that time in my life, that near-win was the most devastating feeling I had ever experienced.

Somehow, I managed to spend the rest of that trip sticking to the plan, and as soon as I had enough money to pay back my bookie, the bank, the feed company, and my grandma, I was out of there. I had done it. I had accomplished what I came for. But it had taken me 40 days to dig myself out of debt, and I had spoken to virtually no one besides dealers and pit bosses the entire time. It had been lonely, drudging work. I missed my family and friends even more than I had working for Uncle Al.

As I drove away from Vegas, I knew I would never count cards again. Darren listened to my story and was quiet for a moment. Then he said, "But you're saying that when you follow the rules, you win?"

"You'll lose some hands," I said, "but at the end of the night, if you follow the system, you pretty much always come out ahead."

"Then why did you quit?" Darren asked.

"Like I said, it was really, really lonely. Plus, Vas was right. I always gave into gambling. Those 40 days were the only time I ever did it right."

"Well, why wouldn't you card count again," Darren said, "and do it right again?"

His question hit me like a lightning strike.

CHAPTER

13

Casino Bound

Sometime later, Darren and I headed off to bed. As I lay there, my head spun with excitement. With Schmitty's in decline, I needed a new way to make money. I was a small-town guy with a high school education and no skills to speak of, but I didn't like the idea of working for someone else. What if I took Vas' refresher course and tried counting cards again? As a professional counter, I could combine cards, which I loved, with mathematics and probability, which I also loved.

I knew I couldn't call Vas in the middle of the night, and morning seemed an eternity away. Unable to sleep, I let my mind drift back to my first course in card counting. Vas Spanos was a stout, swarthy Greek who had first become fascinated with the game of blackjack years before, when he was a student in Greece. He had gone on to earn a Ph.D. in mathematics at the University of Minnesota and stayed in the area to teach his system of card counting.

I tracked down Vas in Minneapolis and signed up for his class, which he held in a huge, old brick house south of Lake Street. Vas had the whole bottom level set up like a casino gaming floor with real blackjack tables. The course lasted six months and, if I recall correctly, cost $900. Each class was small so that he could work closely with his students. I took the class with two guys I didn't know, Russ and Pete. We memorized the matrixes, which track the occurrence and relative advantage to the house or player of 10s, face cards, and aces, versus the numbers two through six. (Sevens, eights, and nines don't count.) This required putting in hours and hours at home. On class days, we played at Vas' tables, for which he hired real dealers. Using the matrix numbers, we learned to predict the next card that would be played.

Meanwhile, Vas would pace behind us, hands clasped behind his back, barking rapid-fire commands in his thick Greek accent:

"Hit! Hit! Hit!"

"You must be fast and always thinking!"

Or, when someone made a mistake, "Poor! Poor! Poor!"

I soaked it up like a sponge. I understood the sequences and matrixes, and there was a logic to it all that appealed to me. In addition to matrixes and style of play, Vas taught us to look for casinos that offered what he called the right "conditions." In a nutshell, you want to go head-to-head with a dealer rather than count at a table with other players. That way you can play as many hands as possible. Also, you want the dealer to go deep into the deck (or deep into the "shoe" if he or she is dealing from multiple decks shuffled together). This allows you to establish a good "running count" and identify when the advantage has swung your way. (Playing with one deck, you have to start the count over every time the dealer shuffles.) Finally, for good conditions, you want betting limits high enough that you can make a decent profit on each hand. If you don't have that, you could win for a week and still not earn enough money to make it worth your time.

As part of the course, Russ, Pete and I made a couple of practice runs to Las Vegas. And as Vas had predicted, I found that I liked to cut corners. Instead of grinding out a long series of small, steady wins, I liked to press my bets when I had the advantage—in other words, a deck rich in face cards and aces. In Vas' system, you could increase your bets within limits when you had the advantage, but I would go well beyond the limit. Observing that tendency, Vas understood I was a gambler at heart, and wouldn't succeed as a counter. Still, my conversation with Darren had electrified me. I forgot all about the drudgery and loneliness of counting, and focused instead on the glamorous idea of making a living at cards.

Back in the '80s, I'd developed an act. See, on the one hand, card counting isn't illegal as long as you're not using some kind of technology, like a signaling buzzer, for example. On the other hand, casinos hate card counters and will kick them out if they're caught, just like those pit bosses had once tossed me out on my can. Why? Because of that 1.5 percent advantage over the house. Casinos hate anything that costs them money.

That's why, whenever I went counting, I gulped down an endless stream of free cocktails to fool the pit bosses and the "bubble people." That's what I called the professional counters and card cheats casinos hired to watch the gaming tables. This surveillance took place via live camera feeds installed in inverted plastic domes that hang down from the ceiling—"bubbles."

As I played, I kept the cocktails coming. Already a regular drinker, I had a high tolerance for alcohol, but the casino people didn't know that. I also kept up a running conversation with the dealer and any players who happened to be at my table. The casino watchers usually, though not always, thought I was too drunk and chatty to be counting cards.

The morning after Darren and I talked, I called Vas. He said it would be at least two weeks before I would be able to get into his refresher course. I decided I couldn't wait that long. Immediately, I made the rounds between the bank and the bar till, draining both like an idiot. Then I jumped in my truck and took off for Kansas City, carrying at least two eight-balls of cocaine. I had a white camper shell on my truck, so I figured I could sleep in the truck bed to save money on hotels.

Six hours later, I arrived at a major riverboat casino, which was really a building "moored" to a pier, and headed to the blackjack tables. It had been decades since I'd counted, but I figured I remembered enough about Vas' matrixes to give it a try on my own. Trouble was, I couldn't find good conditions. All the tables had betting limits so tight that I would not be able to make money there, no matter how long I sat to play. Finally, I headed to the craps table, drawn there as surely as metal to a magnet.

You have to understand that my gambling addiction was like an autopilot with bad programming. I made bad decisions like these without even realizing it. In this case, I stepped up to a craps table, rolled the dice once, then stayed there all weekend. Though my luck turned solidly against me, I refused to leave. I called this "playing through," and it usually required a lot of cocaine. Whether I was losing in a casino or had a problem to solve elsewhere, I would often play through, staying up for days, refusing to surrender until my luck changed or I'd solved my problem.

It didn't always work, and it didn't that night in Kansas City. Within hours, I lost all the money I'd brought except for six crumpled one-dollar bills, some of which I'd used to snort cocaine on the way down from Minnesota. The only reason I still had those was because they were stuffed in a random pocket. Finally at 3 a.m., I stomped out of the casino, broke and furious. On the way to my truck, I berated myself. I had just told Darren I would "do it right" this time, but I apparently had no self-control whatsoever. I had just blown every bit of extra money Karen and I had in the world. I was still a gambler, just like Vas said.

When I got out to my truck, I rolled up one of those dollar bills and inhaled a huge line of cocaine to numb my rage. It didn't help much. Still beating myself up for being so stupid, I steered out of the parking lot. I figured if I got started right away, I'd make it home by mid-morning, in time to spend most of the weekend with Karen and the kids.

Not knowing the area well, I steered down one dark street after another, looking for Interstate 35. My friend Wayne Hilk had told me there were some seriously dangerous areas in Kansas City and warned me not to get lost. Now my truck rumbled over a street so torn up it looked like a war zone, in a neighborhood that didn't look much better. I drove slowly, looking left and right for a turn that would lead to the highway. Then I hit a massive pothole, and my front end took a wild bounce. A second passed before I heard a crash behind me. I braked to a stop, looked in the rear-view mirror, and saw that my camper shell had flown off the truck bed and was lying in the street.

Because of the broken streetlights, the night was pitch black. Reluctantly, I got out of the truck and looked around. I couldn't see much, just a battered neighborhood that looked abandoned. I walked back and inspected the camper shell. A couple of the clamps that held it in place seemed to have taken a beating. Would they still work? Even if they did, how was I going to get the shell back on my truck? I knew I couldn't do it alone, and I definitely couldn't stay here all night. Should I just leave it?

Just then, two guys came walking out of the dark toward me. As they got closer, I could see that one of them was holding a gun. I know I should have been afraid but in that moment all I could feel was anger. It was shaping up to be a lousy weekend and at this point, I'd had enough.

"Put your f***ing gun away!" I roared as they got close. "I've got all of six bucks on me, and you can each have three! But first you're gonna help me put this camper shell back on my truck!"

Fits of rage like this one had continued to plague me since the gas station incident, and I still didn't know why.

This time, I was still so angry with myself over my rash spur-of-the-moment trip to Kansas City that a guy with a pistol seemed like the least of my problems.

These would-be robbers were young. I didn't wait for them, but grabbed the camper shell and started dragging it toward the truck. They looked at each other then without saying a word, walked over to the camper shell and helped me lift it back onto the truck bed. As soon as they finished, they started walking away.

"Get back here!" I yelled after them. "I told you I had $6 on me. I'm good for my word!" Then, strangely, I felt guilty for yelling at these guys, even though they were about to rob me, so I added, "And I've got cocaine if you want to do a line."

They looked back at me like I was crazy then disappeared into the night.

I just shook my head. *Why does all this crazy stuff happen to me?* I thought, yet again. *Why do I keep getting into these bizarre scrapes, then getting out again?*

I attached the camper shell as well as I could with the mangled clamps, then drove carefully down the pocked street so that I wouldn't lose it again. After about half a mile, I saw a police car. The officer flipped on his emergency lights, and I pulled over.

"Do you know where you're at?" the officer asked through my window.

"No, not really," I said. "I'm trying to find I-35. I guess I'm lost."

The cop gave a little laugh. "Yeah, you're lost all right. You're in one of the worst areas in Kansas City. That neighborhood you just came out of? We don't even go in there."

"Really?" I said, smiling. "I just had two really nice guys help me out back there."

My anger over my impatience and my losses in Kansas City solidified my determination to repeat Vas' course and "do it right." After my refresher, I began a series of weekend counting excursions, not making enough money to get rich, but enough to justify the trips. I saw these absences both as adventures and as necessary to keep my family afloat. In between, I tried very hard to keep my promises to Karen and the kids. But those boundaries soon began to crumble away. We would make plans, "Hey, we're going to do X today," then I'd make up an excuse to cancel. Not because I wasn't physically capable or didn't have time, but because I wanted to do crack instead.

Charlie and Darren were young, 11 or 12, and I had always loved to take them hunting and fishing. Duck and goose hunting, in particular, were my passion, something I had done since I was 9 years old. Now though, when we'd go, I didn't dress the boys properly, or I ran out of time to get the right licenses, or generally just wasn't as responsible a parent because I was too busy with my addiction. Then, on a local fishing trip, I really crossed the line.

This particular day, we were meeting a friend named Troy at a lake a couple of miles from my house. The kids were excited, as usual. When they were both little, I had taught them to bait their hooks and cast their lines. There was nothing like watching the thrill on their faces when they reeled in a big one.

We made the short drive, parked on the side of the road, walked out through a field, down an embankment and through some woods to a big lake. Troy showed up a few minutes later with a guy I didn't know. His name was Alex. Not too long after we set up to fish, Alex whispered, "Do you guys want to go smoke some crack?"

I said no right away. I looked at Charlie and Darren, happily casting away from the lakeshore. I had no intention of leaving my boys.

Then I caught movement from the corner of my eye. Alex and Troy were already headed for the woods. A switch flipped inside me, and suddenly the lure of that crack high started pulling me after them like a 10-pound line. Within minutes, I was crouched in the woods with Troy and a perfect stranger sucking on a crack pipe while my boys fished alone.

Even as the *whoosh* came, even as I hit that high, I felt an all-consuming shame. I gazed at Charlie and Darren from my hiding place in the trees, separated from my sons by a wall of secrecy. This time could have been so special, I thought, and it was being stolen right in front of my eyes. I was at the same time both the victim and the thief.

CHAPTER

14

Tunica

Card counting started to keep me away from home and from Schmitty's for longer periods. I was trying to earn a living to support my family, but my increasing absences also placed a greater burden on Karen, who stayed home and wrangled teenagers.

After I went bust and lost my truck topper in Kansas City, I found myself in a similar neighborhood in Memphis, Tennessee. Too low on cash to fund another card-counting trip, I had asked one of my crack buddies, Gary, to go to a casino with me for a week. Our arrangement was that he would provide the cash and I would do the counting. Between gaming tables at Tunica Resorts, a cluster of casinos in northwestern Mississippi just over the state line from Memphis, we would get high.

Gary and I arrived in Memphis around 11 p.m. We needed to accomplish two things: Get directions to Tunica and get crack before we got there. Gary and I checked off the second item on our list, buying some crack in a neighborhood of sagging two-decker houses. It was a very bad area. The streets rippled with dark moving shadows that had eyes that lit up when our headlights moved past.

We smoked the crack, but it turned out to be as bad as the neighborhood. Now it was 3 a.m., and we needed more. The neighborhood was a mile-long street shaped like the letter U. At the top of the street, clear of what seemed to be the most dangerous area, there was a liquor store. Across from the store was a median strip, and when Gary drove by, I spotted a young black man sitting on a mound of dirt. He looked to be in his mid-20s.

"Stop here," I told Gary. "Let's ask him."

Gary pulled over so that the young man was on the passenger side of the car. "Do you know where I can get some crack?" I asked him.

"Yeah," he said. He jumped in the car and pointed back toward the neighborhood we'd just left. "But I'm not going in there alone."

"What's your name?" I asked him as we rolled back toward the shadows.

"Tony."

Tony, a good-looking kid, was casually dressed. He didn't look like someone down on his luck—in other words, someone who would be sitting on a median strip at 3 a.m. "What were you doing back there, sitting in the middle of the road?" I asked him.

Tony started telling us his story. He was from Kentucky and had come to Memphis to visit his uncle, who owned stores in a chicken restaurant franchise. It was supposed to be just for one weekend, but Tony had spent all his money on crack and couldn't get home. He'd been stuck in Memphis for two weeks. There was a warrant for his arrest back home and he needed to get it cleared, but he didn't have any money. Then he said something that broke my heart.

"I have a fiancée back home. She goes to church and doesn't drink or do drugs or anything." Tony had blown it with her before over crack, and she had given him a second chance. He added, almost crying, "I told her I'd never do this again."

As Tony talked, Gary steered the car through the dark. We could see people sitting on the balconies and lower porches of the two-deckers even though it was the middle of the night. I felt for Tony. I knew what it was like to disappoint the people I loved. I asked him where he was staying, and he said he didn't have any place to go. I told him we were professional gamblers on our way to Tunica.

"Why don't you come stay with us?" I said.

Gratefully, Tony agreed. In front of one of the houses, he told Gary to stop. He disappeared inside, then returned. I couldn't tell whether he'd gotten us some crack, but he did come back with a very scary passenger, a white guy with hard eyes, who stared at me and said, "I want everything you've got."

The guy didn't seem to have a gun, but he twitched and rambled and mumbled, reminding me of one of the harder cases at Willmar. I tried to coax him into getting out of the car. Deflecting his odd and slightly menacing remarks, I explained that we were in town to gamble in Tunica. I didn't mention that between Gary and me, we had about $10,000.

"Can we drop you somewhere?" I said.

"No," he said. "I'm not going anywhere."

What was I going to do? Call the cops and say, "Hey, I was buying crack and now I've got some nut-job in my car. Can you help?"

Once again, my addictions had placed me in a situation where I was at the mercy of bad people. It was a lesson I seemed to have to learn over and over.

Eventually, I convinced the nut-job that we didn't have anything that would interest him. After a few blocks, he told us to pull over and let him out. Relieved, we drove south across the state line. Twenty miles later, we rolled into Tunica, Mississippi, a town that Reverend Jesse Jackson in 1985 called "America's Ethiopia." Until the 1990s, Tunica felt like the old rural South, surrounded by rice, cotton, and soybean. It was so poverty-stricken that people in one neighborhood, called "Sugar Ditch Alley," lived among open sewers. Now though, Tunica had become the fifth-largest gaming city in America, and the neon lights of nine casinos glowed against the night sky.

Gary found our casino hotel. When we checked in, we got caught up in smoking crack and never made it to the casino floor. Night became day and day became night again. Between hits on the pipe, Tony and I talked about crack and the hold it had on us. About how it tears apart relationships and sucks away everything you love. Tony told me about his family, especially his fiancée. He felt terrible that he let her down. Tears filled his eyes, and I could see in him that battle between addiction and conscience that affects so many of us.

Your actions betray your heart. You want to quit and try to quit but a great, unseen well of pain, as well as physical chemical dependency, drags you back down. Pretty soon, you've tried and failed to get clean so many times that nobody, including you, believes you anymore.

I told him about my life, about all the strange coincidences and near-misses. "I look at my life and think, what are the odds of all these things happening to one person?" I said. So many crazy things happened to me that I'd been telling people I was going to write a book. More and more, I told Tony, I wondered if God was trying to get my attention.

We stayed at the casino hotel for four days. Three times, we all piled into the car and drove back to Memphis to find more drugs. The third time, trouble found us.

Gary was driving and I was in the passenger seat. Tony sat in back, holding $300 I had given him to get more crack. At about 11 a.m. on a Sunday morning, we were about a block into the same run-down, U-shaped neighborhood when Gary said, "There's a cop behind us."

I glanced back and saw that he was right. We hadn't seen a hint of law enforcement in this neighborhood at night, but now a black-and-white was following us.

We passed a couple more two-decker homes before Tony tapped on Gary's shoulder. "Hey, pull up here. Honk the horn and let me out." Gary pulled to the curb and the cop slowed to a crawl. Gary tapped the horn twice. My nerves tingled and I took a deep breath. I expected to hear the *whoop-whoop!* of the patrol car pulling us over, and maybe a cop's voice through a loudspeaker, "Step out of the car!"

Tony got out of the back seat and walked up to a house—a different house than the one he'd led us to before. The cops accelerated and drove on past.

I finally exhaled. Gary and I sat in the car and watched the patrol car roll down the street and disappear around the U-turn. Tony returned and jumped in the back seat, slamming the door.

"What was that all about?" Gary said.

Tony grinned. "I wanted them to think we were just picking somebody up."

We waited. Then, through the spaces between houses, we could see the black-and-white head back out of the neighborhood along the road on the other side. When the cops were gone, Gary steered on to our actual destination and pulled over again.

"Drop me off here," Tony said. "I'll go get the stuff. You guys get out of this neighborhood. Wait for me at that little store."

Back at the liquor store across the street from where we'd first met Tony, the sun beat down on cracked asphalt and broken-down signage. The shop was closed, and the surrounding block was deserted. The whole place looked even scarier during the day.

Gary gave me a skeptical look. "You know Tony's got $300 of your money, right?"

I had complete faith in Tony. "He'll be back," I said.

My words were still hanging in the air when the patrol car reappeared, red and blue lights flashing. It pulled into the parking lot and skidded to a stop behind us. Two cops jumped out, one black, one white. The black cop was at least 6-foot-4. He walked to my side of the car, bent at the waist and looked in.

"Step out of the vehicle," he said.

The white cop had gone over to Gary's side. The second I got out of the car, the cop saw a wad of money sticking out of my shirt pocket, and a pen sticking out of the other. I think the pen must have looked like a crack pipe, because he turned me around and slammed my head against the car. Gary got the same treatment.

"What are you *doing*?" I yelled.

"Where did you get that money?" Between us, the cops found about $8,000.

"We're professional gamblers," I said. "We're on our way down to Tunica."

The black cop gave me a look that said, *"Who are you kidding?"* He asked to see my ID. Gary showed the white cop his. Neither officer was satisfied. The cash, the suspicious pen, and the fact they'd just seen us, a couple of white guys, rolling through one of the worst neighborhoods in the United States. It all added up to probable cause.

The officers stashed us in the back of their squad car and went back to search our rental. I started to sweat. I knew they wouldn't find a pipe, because I'd thrown mine out back in the neighborhood after the cops drove by. But there was other evidence: baking soda, and a spoon with crack residue and burn marks on the bottom. Beside me, Gary sat with a dazed look on his face. We both knew we were probably going to jail. Tony was long gone, though. Lucky him.

My mind raced. How bad is it going to be? Can they get us on that spoon residue? After several minutes, the black officer came back carrying the baking soda and the burned spoon. "What's this?" he said, holding out the baking soda.

With a straight face, I said, "I've got really bad feet. I use it for foot powder."

His expression said he knew better. He was about to ask about the burnt spoon when Tony came out from around the nearby building. He walked up and started talking to the police. I couldn't hear what he was saying from inside the squad car, but he was talking to them like friends, like he knew them.

He set us up! I thought. Wasn't this where we'd met him in the first place?

Gary and I waited anxiously. Finally, the cops came over and let Gary and me out of their car.

"I'm going to tell you something," the black cop said. "People die in there. You go back to wherever you came from. Go to Tunica. Whatever. But don't ever come to this part of town again. Do we have an understanding?"

"So, we can go?" I said, astonished.

He nodded.

He didn't have to tell me twice. We jumped in the car and drove away before the cops could change their minds. As soon as we were on the road, I asked Tony, "What happened back there?"

As he was walking out of the neighborhood he saw the squad car, he said. Suspicious, he sent two little kids to see if there were a couple of white dudes in the cop car. "They came back and told me, 'Yes,' so I had to make a decision. I could either let them take you in or do something to try to save you."

"What did you tell the cops?"

"I told them you were just gamblers. I told them you wanted some drugs but that they showed up before the deal went down," Tony said. "I said you were harmless and that we were going back to Tunica."

"They didn't check your ID?"

"No, they didn't."

I was still confused. Tony could've walked away with my $300. He could've been arrested himself, because of his outstanding warrant.

"Why'd you decide to talk to the cops?" I asked.

"I don't know, man. Something just told me I had to get you out."

That was one of those moments when my life could've taken a whole different path. I'd been arrested for DUI, but never drug possession. In the back of that police car, I was sure I was going down, that I was going to shame my family once again and lose my business. Then suddenly, I was free to go. But the blessing of my narrow escape did not produce wisdom.

"Did you get the crack?" I asked Tony.

He had, he said. He'd hidden it behind the store, and like fools we went back to get it. Afterwards, as we drove toward Tunica, my near-miss with the cops and all the relief I'd felt at not ruining my life vanished. All I could think about was that first hit of crack. Nothing else. The drive seemed to take forever. Once we were back in the hotel room Gary fell asleep, and Tony and I got deeper and deeper into conversation.

The next morning, Gary still had his cash, but I'd spent almost all of mine on crack. I'd come to Tunica to earn money counting cards, but I hadn't played a single hand of blackjack. I had a few hundred dollars left and considered how to spend it. I decided I would wake up Gary to get cash for card counting, and I would give Tony the rest of my money to get us more drugs and beer. I had begun to carry out this plan when I looked into Tony's eyes and saw a deep sadness.

I knew exactly what he was feeling because I'd felt it myself. Searing regret. A remorse that yawns like a hole in your soul. Wondering how you got so low and whether you'll ever be able to climb up again.

I held out my hand and offered him all my cash, maybe $300 or $400. "You know what?" I said. "You take this money and go home. Don't look back."

Tony burst into tears. On the spot, he called his fiancée, confessed what he'd been doing, and begged her for another chance. She gave it to him.

"Thank you," Tony said as he hugged me. I saw a new glint of determination in his eyes. He turned and walked out of that hotel room, and I never saw him again. Years later though, under very strange circumstances, I would learn exactly what happened to him.

CHAPTER

15

It's a Small World

In late December 2002, I was sitting on my back deck wrapped in a blanket. It was well after 2 a.m., and Karen and the kids were in bed. I'd just come home from Schmitty's, where I'd received some news that might mean the end of the bar. Staring into the dark, I thumbed the wheel of a lighter, and the tiny flame lit up my face. As I sucked in white smoke, I tried to figure out how to fix things.

Increasingly, the Regulars, a couple of my employees, and even some of my family members were abandoning Schmitty's for Floyd's. In the spring came something that really hurt: A couple of members of the softball teams I sponsored also made the switch.

Who had built up the softball leagues in Victoria? I asked myself indignantly. Me, that's who! I started them, ran them, umpired them—did everything the city required. I even took care of the fields and the lights at night. Now, some of the teams I'd built up were wearing the Floyd's logo on their jerseys and going to Floyd's for drinks after the games. I felt deeply betrayed.

One day, feeling angry and sullen, I tacked up a sign on the front door of my bar: "For all my friends, family, and bartenders who are on the Floyd's team, I would prefer if you didn't come in till the season is over."

People started calling me right away:

"You're crazy!"

"You're going to ruin your business!"

"Take it down!"

But I wasn't persuaded. "It stays up," I said to everyone who called. And it did—for one whole day.

A couple of my friends who played on the softball league called me the next day, saying they hadn't realized how hard I took their defection to Floyd's. We got through the rest of the season, but things were different.

Now on my deck, looking out into the night, I took another hit off the pipe and thought about the bad news I'd gotten. I was about to lose the only revenue stream that had been keeping Schmitty's afloat—pull tabs sold at Schmitty's by the Chaska Lions Club. Pull tabs were like little scratch-off lottery tickets, except instead of scratching one to reveal whether you had won, you pulled a little cardboard tab to reveal a row of three symbols like those on a slot machine, three cherries for example, if you had a winner. Customers could win up to $500. The odds of drawing a winning pull tab were pretty high, turning some customers into regular buyers. Some became compulsive buyers, leading to a nickname for the pull tabs: "cardboard cocaine." The tabs usually cost $1 each, and some people would sit there and buy them all night.

At Schmitty's peak we sold more than $1 million a month in pull tabs, more than any other bar in Minnesota. Obviously, I didn't get to keep all that money. The Chaska Lions Club rented space in the bar, sold the pull tabs using someone they hired, and used the profits to fund their service work. For me, it provided a modest but steady source of income.

But as the number of customers coming through my door dwindled, so did pull tab sales. By 2002, it was no longer profitable to the Lions and they wanted to pull out. For me, that would be a disaster—probably the death blow. I needed the rent and fees they paid me. Hoping to hold on to the Lions, I suggested a way to make our arrangement more profitable for them. I could sell the pull tabs from behind the bar. If they didn't have to pay their employees, they would still be making money at Schmitty's, and I'd still get the Lions' rent. Karen, along with Rick, the Lions' president, had to appear before the Victoria City Council to request approval of behind-the-bar sales. I'd just received their answer earlier that day, which is where the bad news comes in.

The city council wasn't exactly happy with me. I'd spent the last year fighting for changes in the pull tab laws. There was also the inconvenient fact that I'd just spent almost three weeks in jail.

Because of repeat DUIs, I'd lost my driver's license in 1990. Since then, I sometimes let other people drive me around, but mostly I'd been driving without a license. Finally, in May 2002, I got caught. A cop pulled me over for an unrelated minor infraction, and I was charged with a "DAC"—driving after cancellation—a serious offense.

A judge sentenced me to home monitoring with the stipulation that I couldn't use any drugs or alcohol. Also, I would be tested for alcohol with a home breathalyzer. I had to blow into this thing every night at midnight. While on home monitoring, I used crack and coke since the breathalyzer didn't test for those. But I didn't drink. That is, until my friend Wayne Hilk came to town. I decided I could have a couple of afternoon beers with Wayne without triggering the breathalyzer later that night. But I cut it too close. I blew into the machine at the appointed time and a little alarm sounded. I looked at the breathalyzer. The alarm signaled a demand that I blow into the machine again.

The next morning, my phone rang. "Mike, you failed your monitor," the home monitor officer said. "I have to arrest you. I'm going to wait until your kids get to school and then I'll be over."

I was so high and paranoid that I couldn't even fathom what he was saying. When I finally did, my heart sank. All I wanted to do was crawl out of my skin.

A judge ordered me to check in as a guest at the Hennepin County Adult Corrections Facility in Plymouth, a suburb of Minneapolis. I was to serve 19 days, again with work release. My sentence was to begin on November 12. That morning, I checked myself into jail and was shocked at how nice it was. My "cell" was like a hotel room. I even had my own television.

I can do this, I thought.

On my first day of work release, I spent most of the day at home, which I wasn't supposed to do since the whole point of work release is the work part. Then I rode with Karen and Darren to check on Schmitty's.

"Dad, will you play a video game with me?" Darren asked when we got inside. Pinball and video games were Darren's favorite things to do at the bar.

"I sure will," I said, eager to spend time with him. "I just have one thing to take care of first. Let me run downstairs. I'll be right back."

You already know what I had to take care of: I wanted to get high. Think about this: I had just landed in jail because of all my substance abuse, but the instant I was out, I found a way to get high. To a normal person, that doesn't even make sense. But the connection between addiction and the serious consequences I was enduring made zero impression on me. And when some guy in the bar that day offered to sell me a $60 concoction that would guarantee my urine was clean when I returned to jail, I jumped at the chance.

Downstairs at Schmitty's, I told myself I was only going to take one hit of crack and then go back upstairs to play that video game with Darren. I prepped a pipe, flicked on my lighter, and inhaled the smoke deep into my lungs. I waited 10 minutes.

I'll take just one more hit, I thought. Of course, that hit led to another, then a fourth and a fifth. Before I knew it, I'd spent over two hours in the basement. When I finally climbed the stairs back up to the bar, it was time for me to head back to jail, and that fact produced a searing type of shame within me. The whole ride back I sat in remorseful silence. I had chosen crack over my child. Again.

I checked in at the front desk and officers led me back to my cell. There was no drug test. I felt confident I had beaten the system, but the system had actually beaten me. Three hours later, officers pulled me from my cell to do that drug test after all. They weren't stupid. I'm sure work-release prisoners used all kinds of urine-cleansing potions, but they worked only for a limited amount of time. I'm not sure whether the potion I bought ever worked at all. In any case, when my urine came back positive for crack, I denounced the test.

"It was defective!" I howled.

Officers were having none of it. With frightening efficiency, they hustled me off to solitary confinement, where I spent what I thought were the longest six hours of my life. But it was about to get worse. An officer appeared to tell me that the judge had revoked my work release. I was being transferred from the "hotel" portion of the facility to exactly what you think of when you think of a prison.

An officer made me put all my belongings in a plastic bin, then strip searched me. (Yes, *that* kind of strip search.) As I went to put on my new uniform, a set of jail coveralls, the guard happened to be looking the other way. I palmed a deck of cards from the bin and slipped them inside my underwear. As I carried my bedding down a first-tier walkway past tiny, barred cells, veteran inmates on the second tier greeted me with cat-calls and a shower of crumpled paper and garbage. Though I had been in jail before, I'd never experienced anything like this. It was like a scene right out of a movie.

Walking toward my cell, all I could think was, how did I let this happen? Step by step, I had made choices and this was where those choices had led me. We arrived at a tiny cell that had only a sink, a toilet, and a hard bench to lie on. The bench held a thin mattress and a flat rubber pillow. It was an isolation cell, and for me this was torture. I was to be alone for nearly three weeks. Just me and my failures, 23 hours a day.

My first night was a complete nightmare. There were bars on the front of my cell, but I couldn't see the other inmates. I could hear them, though. All night, they yelled at each other or sang horrible rap songs about killing people and degrading women. It went on and on, and I didn't get a wink of sleep.

At 5 a.m., exhausted and frustrated, I sat up in my bunk and pulled out my contraband deck of cards. From that moment on, I spent every waking hour with it. I had just finished my refresher course with Vas and re-memorized all the matrixes. So, I practiced them hour after hour. During my time in that cell, I must have dealt myself several thousand hands of blackjack, quickly stashing the cards under my pillow when I heard the footsteps of the guards.

After several days, the rap songs were driving me crazy. Maybe, I thought, I can inject a little humor and get them to sing something else. I jammed my face between the bars on my cell-front and yelled to the two guys on either side, "Hey, our cells are so small we should sing that Disney song!" I started singing, and soon other prisoners joined in.

It's a small world after all,
It's a small world after all,
It's a small world after all,
It's a small, small world

Quickly, more men joined and then even more. Soon the two-story concrete cell block rang with a couple of hundred deep male voices singing the silly Disney tune. We kept getting louder and louder until it became almost deafening. At first, it was funny. Unfortunately though, I had suggested one of the most irritating songs in the English language. And the joke was on me because they wouldn't stop singing it.

It's a small world after all,
It's a small world after all,
It's a small world after all,
It's a small, small world

The chorus echoed through the cell block over and over again, all night long. When morning came, two guards appeared at my cell and hauled me off to see the jailhouse shrink. When I walked into his office, I saw my medication bottle on his desk.

The psychiatrist pointed at the bottle. "What's this for?"

"It's buspirone," I said. "My doctor's got me on it to keep me off cocaine."

"Well, it's also an anti-anxiety medication," the doctor said. He paused and regarded me thoughtfully. Then he added, "We had a report you were leading the prisoners in a Walt Disney song."

Translation: *I thought you might be a mental patient.*

"Yes, I did lead the song," I said. "But now can you please make them stop?"

I completed my sentence at Hennepin on November 30, and it was no secret to city leaders in Victoria. And when Karen went with Rick, the Lions Club president, to make their case for behind-the-bar pull tab sales, I knew the city council could say no. But I really didn't think they would. After all, the bar was in Karen's name. I couldn't see the council denying both Karen *and* Rick.

The bar was packed as I sat there anxiously waiting for Rick to give me the news. He walked in with a sullen look on his face and didn't waste words. "Mike, they denied it," he said.

But that wasn't all. Rick repeated what the mayor of Victoria had told him at the city council meeting: "If somebody else ran the place, we'd let Schmitty's have the pull tabs behind the bar. But not Mike Lindell."

When Rick told me that, tears welled in my eyes. In that moment I knew it was over, the end of an era. I was going to have to sell. And fast. Before the pull tabs were gone and the value of the bar dropped. My mind raced.

"Can the Lions stay at least until I can get the bar sold?" I asked Rick.

He put his hand on my shoulder. "I can't, Mike. The labor is killing me. I'm going to have to leave by the end of the month unless you can think of something."

Later, I got Rick on the phone. "What if I worked the pull tab booth every single shift? You wouldn't have to pay me, so you wouldn't have any labor costs."

Rick thought about it for a minute, then said, "That would really show them now, wouldn't it?" So that's what we decided to do, a temporary solution until I could sell Schmitty's.

That had only been a few hours ago. Now, on my back deck, I lit my pipe again, remembering how I'd felt after hanging up with Rick. I'd looked out at everyone in the bar, putting a smile on my face as cover. Inside though, I felt excruciating sadness.

Schmitty's was a family, and now it was over. All 13 years flashed before my eyes. Schmitty's was the place where it snowed in summer, the home of Super Soaker water fights, where bikers sang along to David Cassidy, and everyone put up with Petey worshipping Alex Trebek. It was where you might find people kicking down the ceiling one day and hurling beer bottles at the Blues Brothers the next. There was Vikings mania, firecrackers in the ashtrays, and if you couldn't afford your drinks, everyone knew you could always write Mike a bad check.

I realized I was standing in the same place I had been the first time I went to Schmitty's. "We run this town," a Victoria leader had said back then. "If we don't like you, we're going to run you out." It had seemed like a challenge at the time. Now it seemed like a prophecy.

CHAPTER

16

Those Were the Days

That December passed in a haze of dread and sadness. We had a family reunion coming up on February 1. The location was Phoenix, so it was a good thing we'd bought our plane tickets in advance. Because the bar wasn't making its normal money, we were nearly broke. In fact, it would take $5,000 just to catch up on our mortgage payments and keep our vehicles from being repossessed.

On January 31, 2003, we flew to Phoenix where my brother and sisters had already gathered. Since the reunion didn't kick off until 2 p.m. the next day, I had decided to count cards in Laughlin, Nevada, the same place Karen and I had discovered in 1997. My plan was to raise cash to cover our debts and keep us afloat. I had brought only about $300 of my own to count cards with, so I tried to talk my siblings into contributing some money for my bankroll, promising to return their money with interest the next day.

Most of my siblings equated card counting with gambling. All except for my brother Corey. In some ways, Corey was my opposite. While I listened to and acted on what I thought was intuition, Corey was so analytical that I joked he would analyze the water chemistry and temperature before dipping his foot into a swimming pool. Corey was, and is, very frugal and cautious, so when he supported the idea that card counting is a statistically legitimate way to earn money, it meant a lot to me.

In the end, my siblings loaned me about $700 to take to Laughlin. That brought my stake to $1,000. With that in hand, Karen and I rented a car in Phoenix and drove north. On the way, I explained to her that I could only afford to play with smaller chips. I had about 20 hours to count, which meant I needed to make $250 an hour to earn the $5,000 needed to avoid losing our house and our vehicles.

Steering north through the beige desert landscape along US-93, I told her, "I'm going to have to play all night. With the kind of chips I can afford, if I take a break I'll have to increase my bets to make up for the lost time." Upping my wagers would mean I wasn't card counting but gambling, and this time I couldn't afford to gamble.

We checked into the Golden Nugget Laughlin at about three in the afternoon, and Karen went up to the room. Meanwhile, I headed for the blackjack tables. I felt excited but a little nervous because when I returned to counting the year before, I hadn't done so well. Again and again, I had given in to my instinct to gamble. On the other hand, since then I'd finished both Vas' refresher course and my self-inflicted 19-day card counting intensive at the Hennepin County jail.

On the casino floor, I found a table with good conditions. I played there for a couple of hours and when I pushed away from the felt, my earnings were right on target. After that, I hopped from casino to casino, methodically building my total take, while staying on the move to avoid getting caught. But by about 1 a.m., I was exhausted. I hadn't slept since we'd flown into Phoenix the day before. I needed a nap. I went back to our room at the Golden Nugget and opened the door quietly, trying not to wake Karen.

Slipping over to my side of the bed, I was starting to undress when Karen's voice cut through the dark. "No! You can't go to bed!"

"Just wake me up in two hours," I said, wearied.

"No! You told me it would be gambling if you sleep. Go down and order some drinks and keep playing."

I knew she was right. I sighed, turned around, and headed back downstairs.

It was now after midnight on the gaming floor of the Nugget. Foot traffic had thinned out, and I found myself alone at a table with the blackjack dealer.

Three pit bosses roamed the floor. I started my act, keeping the cocktails coming.

In card counting, the act is a big part of it. Some counters escape the pit bosses' notice by pretending to be drunk. Others keep up running chatter with the dealer and the other players. I was able to do both. And sometimes I would just glance at the cards instead of studying them so that the pit bosses and Bubble People would think I wasn't even paying attention.

I used this strategy on one of my first trips to Hole in the Wall, a casino in Danbury, Wisconsin. I was winning steadily at blackjack using Vas' strategies and my glancing technique, all while keeping a conversation going with the pit boss, Mike Robinson. Vas had actually warned me about this guy and told me never to play there when he was working. Robinson used to be a card counter before he went to work for the casino. But the Hole in the Wall dealt the best odds in the country, and I thought I could manage Robinson. He and I talked for over an hour while I put on my act and won hand after hand.

Eventually he became suspicious. "You don't even look at the cards, but you're making all the right moves," he said. "I'd swear you were wired."

I tensed up. I needed to remain friendly with as many casinos as possible. If the famous Mike Robinson suspected me of counting, he'd kick me out of the Hole in the Wall for good. It was time to employ a little amazement. Immediately, I stood up and stripped down to my underwear.

"Do you see a wire?" I demanded.

Everyone stared. Robinson's face turned beet red and he didn't say a word. Four security guards surrounded me as I was putting my clothes back on and asked me to follow them. They took me to Robinson's boss who demanded to know what was going on.

"I'm not going to tell you what your pit boss did," I said, as though Robinson had done something wrong, which he hadn't. "I don't want to get him in trouble."

I was asked to leave the casino that particular night for displaying my tighty-whities. But as an offended customer "unfairly" accused of cheating, I was welcomed at the Hole in the Wall for years to come. It was actually the beginning of a long friendship with everyone in the casino, including Robinson and his manager.

Now in the Golden Nugget, I was alone at the table, tracking the cards while pretending to be drunker than I was. Slowly but steadily my chip stacks grew taller, and the two roaming pit bosses became very interested. Both came to my table to watch me play. Suddenly the count went negative. The dealer dealt me 15 and he had a six. By the normal strategy of blackjack, you would never take a hit on this hand because, odds are the dealer's down-card is a 10 of some kind and dealers are required to hit on a 16, producing a likely bust. With these cards showing, only two kinds of players would hit a 15—a fool or a card counter.

I had to hit. And that's how I got caught at the Golden Nugget.

I hit my 15 and got a five, now I was at 20. The dealer hit five more times and he had a 21. I lost the hand.

"That's it!" One of the pit bosses said. He flipped the deck over and fanned out the cards. There wasn't a single face card to be seen. "You're card counting. You're done playing blackjack."

"Counting?" I said, as though insulted. "I've had 20 drinks. I can barely see the cards!"

"That's the part we don't understand," the pit boss said. "With an act like that you should take it down to the Riverside."

Taking the pit boss's advice, I headed down to Don Laughlin's casino. The second I walked in, a strange feeling came over me, a sense that this place was somehow going to be connected to my life. I can't explain this. I can only tell you that it happened.

I counted all morning at the Riverside and then spread my play to other casinos in town. At one casino, I was caught again, but I didn't care. I was up $5,380, in addition to the $1,000 or so I had started with. Karen and I got back to Phoenix just in time for the start of the reunion. I repaid my siblings and delivered the promised interest. When we got home, I dug us out of our financial mess one more time.

Then, reluctantly, I began looking for a buyer for Schmitty's.

It took me a couple of months to find one; a little longer, I suspect, because I was trying to keep it quiet. We agreed on a sale price of $500,000, a lot less than the $1.2 million valuation I had enjoyed during the height of Schmitty's popularity. On the other hand, half a million bucks was a lot more than I would have gotten if the bar had completely lost the pull tabs before the sale. Rick had been true to his word, letting me work the Lions' booth inside the bar without pay.

The buyer's name was Craig. He agreed to buy the bar on a "contract for deed" from the corporation Karen and I had formed several years back, which we called Twin Silver. In case you're not familiar with the term, the contract for deed meant that Twin Silver would carry the loan, and Craig would make monthly payments to us for five years, with a balloon payment for the balance at the end. Craig and I agreed on our terms, but for now we would keep our deal a secret. I didn't want to lose more customers, or have any angry Regulars trash the place in a fit of loyalty before Craig and I closed on our deal. I felt like it was my fault our Schmitty's family was breaking up, and I had no idea how I was going to tell them.

Just as I had when I closed LeeMichaels in the summer of 1990, I planned to throw a weekend-long party to send Schmitty's out in style. I decided to call it

Masterpiece Weekend. Soon, rumors were flying so I spread rumors myself. I let it get out that I was losing the bar. Losing my house. I was broke. It didn't take long before everyone in town heard about Masterpiece Weekend. I knew people were going to show up to see what Schmitty's was going to do.

The first night, Friday night, I charged $5 for a ticket that would cover the whole weekend of entertainment. Many of my Regulars went up the road to Floyd's instead of paying the $5 for the ticket. I decided to give out free drinks for two hours straight to the ones who had.

That night, the booze flowed and my customers danced to a very expensive live band we made room for by shoving the pool tables aside. All weekend long I brought out case after case of small white napkins. My Regulars and I would throw them into the ceiling fan, creating Schmitty's trademark snow. On Saturday, I went to the bank and withdrew $2,000 in $1 bills. I threw the cash in the fan and the whole place turned green as the money floated in the air. Everyone stopped and stared. It was like they couldn't comprehend what was happening. After a long, suspenseful pause, the crowd broke into a mad, joyful dash to pick up as much of the cash as they could. Knowing it was going to get around town, I told everyone I had just launched $10,000 into the air.

Several of my friends came over to me with fists full of cash. "We can't take this, Mike. We heard you were about to lose the bar. You need the money."

I just smiled. "No, it's fine. You keep it and have a good time."

Though Craig and I would not close the sale until September, we agreed that he would give me some earnest money and take over operation of the bar on June 1. That meant that May 31, a Saturday, would be my last day at Schmitty's. As the time approached, I decided to throw another party.

Masterpiece Weekend was big, but so was my final day. Hundreds of people showed up. I played all our old favorites on the jukebox. It was a joyous night that became incredibly emotional when "To Love Somebody" by the Bee Gees came on. Karen and I climbed up on the bar and the Regulars cried as the song played. At the end of the night, we played one of the bar's favorites, "Those Were the Days" by Mary Hopkin. I thought the song captured the spirit of Schmitty's, and the end of an era, perfectly.

Once upon a time there was a tavern
Where we used to raise a glass or two.

Remember how we laughed away the hours
And think of all the great things we would do.

Those were the days my friend.
We thought they'd never end.

We'd played that song hundreds of times over the years, and the Regulars now climbed up on the bar, linked arms, and we all sang it together, tears streaming. When the bar closed and everyone moved outside, the emotions turned into chaos. Fights broke out and someone even lit the street on fire. It was as if the pain of breaking up the Schmitty's family had spilled out into the town. The cops showed up, but I heard one of them say, "We're not arresting anybody unless they drive drunk. It's Mike and Karen's last night."

Soon, the crowd settled down and we set off fireworks. There were tears and hugs, memories and laughter. Well after midnight, the crowd thinned. I tried to say thank you and goodbye to every single person. Finally, only Craig, Karen, and I remained.

We went back inside. I looked around Schmitty's one last time. Then I handed the keys to Craig, fighting back tears as a thousand memories flashed through my mind. Yes, I thought. Those were the days.

CHAPTER

17

Good and Evil

One Sunday morning after handing over the bar, I was lying in bed in that weird place between sleep and dreams. That place where you can either wake up all the way or doze off again and finish your dream. As my mind hovered in between, strange words filtered into my consciousness like a fountain. I opened my eyes, but the words were still coming.

My nerves tingled. I can't say why, but I could tell this stream of thought was somehow important. I began to feel an urgency to capture it. Sitting up in bed, I grabbed a pen and a notebook off the nightstand and started writing. But it wasn't like *I* was writing. It was more like I was taking dictation. My hand moved the pen and words appeared on the page. It struck me that these were words I didn't even use.

I could hear Karen out in the kitchen as ink flowed rapidly across the page. Without a conscious decision, I scribbled a title at the top of the page: "God Against Crack."

What followed was a scale of some kind, a "crack addiction scale," as strange as that sounds. It had numbers, "C1" through "C5." A crack user at C1 had just started his downhill slide. He was smoking rock, but still had a job, his possessions, and his relationships. Addicts who had reached C2 through C4 on this scale had lost some or most of those things. By the time a person reached C5 on this scale, he had lost everything.

Without stopping, I scrawled page after page, including a step-by-step plan for getting off crack. But as I sit here and write this, I'm telling you, it wasn't *me* coming up with these ideas. Was I having some kind of out-of-body experience? Were these thoughts from somewhere—or Someone—else? I didn't know.

In under an hour, I had filled six pages. Karen walked into the bedroom with a basket of clean laundry. "What are you doing?" she asked.

I waved the notebook at her like a flag. "Look at this! It has something do with wiping out crack addiction. I don't know where it's coming from!"

Karen was used to this kind of talk from me. We would be out with our friends and she would listen as I tried to persuade all of us to quit. I could never remember what I said, but it had something to do with odds and with miracles. Some of them would quit, and I wouldn't know why. Strangely, instead of being happy, I would think to myself, "Wow, I'm just losing friends."

But even though I loved the crack high and had no intention of cleaning up anytime soon, I sensed that one day I would be free from this drug and from all addictions. The strange experience of waking up to write down this weird crack essay made me sense this even more.

I looked at Karen and waited for a response, but she just flashed a smile and walked out of the bedroom. Still propped up in bed, I began reading through the pages.

"You will know when the time is right," I had written, "and you will be provided a platform."

What? Where in the heck had that come from? And why would I be referring to myself as "you?" How would *that* come from my own subconscious? And a platform? I didn't even know what a platform was.

Finally, I got out of bed, went to the kitchen, and poured some coffee. What I would come to call my "out-of-body essay" bugged me for the rest of the morning. Then around noon, I was out in the garage with my crack pipe, smoking where my kids wouldn't see me, when my cell phone rang. It was my sister Cindy.

"Did something happen to you today?" she asked.

Immediately, I suspected what she was referring to. "No, why?" I said.

"You're lying," she said without hesitation.

Cindy then told me what had happened to her at church that morning. She and Wayne had divorced. Now Cindy and her new husband, Bryan, were members of Living Word Church. Every Sunday, they drove an hour each way to attend. Why would anyone do that? I wondered. I just didn't get it.

"My pastor called me up in front of the congregation," Cindy said. "He asked me if I had an older brother named Mike."

"Cindy, everybody knows I'm your older brother," I said.

"Maybe. But he also told me that something happened to you this morning and that I needed to tell you that it's important. That's what he said, Mike. He said, 'Whatever happened to your brother, it's important. He has to follow through on it, and you need to tell him.'"

This is crazy, I thought. How would she know *any* of this?

"So, what happened to you today, Mike?" Cindy said.

I hesitated. "There was something I wrote," I finally said. "I don't know where it came from. I don't even know what it means."

"Well, you need to do exactly what it says," Cindy insisted.

"Part of it said I will know when the time is right."

"You will. And when that time comes, you have to do it. Promise me that."

I promised my sister, and we hung up. As you can imagine, I was a little freaked out. I rushed back to my bedroom, grabbed the notebook, and hid it behind a framed album cover I had hanging on the wall. I would not see those pages again for four years.

Whatever that platform thing had been, whatever that bizarre, early morning writing experience had been, it wasn't going to interfere with my plan for life after Schmitty's. I had decided to become a full-time card counter. As I'd told Darren, it was hard work, but it was a living.

My plan was to borrow $50,000 against the contract for deed. With so large a stake, I would be able to afford to play bigger chips—the black ones, $100 each. It would be tedious work with long hours. But if I could find the right conditions—going head-to-head with dealers going deep into their shoes—my steady 1.5 percent advantage over the house would earn me at least $500 an hour, or about $200,000 a year. As far as I was concerned, that was way better than any kind of job I could find with only a high school education.

I talked over the card counting plan with Karen. With the monthly payments that would be coming in from the contract for deed after we closed the sale, we both felt it would add up to a pretty nice income.

Then life threw a couple of glitches into my plan. First, Craig had begun to reconsider the financials on the Schmitty's sale. We'd been going back and forth on terms for months and when we finally sat down for the closing, he insisted on a price reduction if he was going to go through with signing. At that moment, I considered pulling out of the deal. But there was an outstanding mortgage on the bar, and I could no longer keep up with the payments. In the end, Craig and I settled on the price and our corporation, Twin Silver, ended up selling the bar for less than $500,000.

I felt deeply disappointed. The new terms did not reflect the sweat-equity I'd poured into Schmitty's for 13 years. They also left Karen and me with far less financial stability than I'd been counting on. On the other hand, Twin Silver was now a corporation with assets—a contract for deed worth a few hundred thousand dollars, with receivable income years into the future. In the final analysis, with all the emotion wrapped up in selling Schmitty's in the first place, I was relieved to have the transaction behind me.

Then life threw in the second glitch.

Before I could find someone willing to lend me the $50,000 stake against the contract for deed, I was shocked to receive official notification that Twin Silver was being named as co-defendant in a lawsuit. The previous winter, a couple of people had gotten drunk at another bar, jumped on a snowmobile, and crashed it. Both were injured. Instead of taking responsibility for driving drunk, they hired a lawyer and ginned up a lawsuit based on Minnesota's dram shop act.

Dram shop is the old term for establishments that sold gin in 18th-century England. Dram shop acts are laws that hold bars and alcohol retailers responsible for injuries and deaths that occur after someone is "overserved"—for instance, when a bar patron is clearly drunk and the bartender keeps serving him anyway. Tavern owners in Minnesota are required to insure themselves against dram shop claims. But the greedy lawyers in the case against us wanted more than insurance. They wanted the equity in Twin Silver, too.

The plaintiffs in the suit had not been served any alcohol at Schmitty's the night of the accident. But one of them had made a phone call from my bar, so their lawyer decided to name us in the suit. I guess he thought he could rake in cash for his clients from two bars instead of just one.

I was mortified. I had not been about to walk away from Schmitty's rich, but at least we would have had money to survive. This lawsuit could wipe us out.

I had only two choices: settle or fight it out in court. In trying to figure out how to respond to this new challenge, I realized that if I were going to borrow $50,000 against the contract for deed, I'd have to do it quickly. Once the contract was fed into the gears of this lawsuit, I might not be able to borrow against it at all.

I knew I couldn't go to a bank because I didn't have any credit. That meant looking for a private deal. I quickly found a potential lender, a man whose last name was Neff. But Neff came with red flags waving.

Red flag #1: I met Neff through my bookie's stepson.

Red flag #2: The bookie's stepson said flat out, "Neff will take risky investments, but don't trust him."

I ignored the red flags. I needed the loan.

We met at a hotel bar. Neff was a dumpy guy with oversized glasses who ordered scotch-and-milk. (I had owned a bar for 13 years and never heard of such a thing.) Despite the red flags and disgusting cocktail, Neff seemed nice enough. I told him I wanted $50,000 in cash to count cards and explained the complication of the frivolous lawsuit. At our second meeting, he told me his plan.

"Mike, here's what you do. You sell me the contract for deed for $60,000, then put 10 grand in the bank and take 50 grand with you to Vegas."

"Sixty thousand? Are you kidding me? That contract is worth hundreds of thousands," I said.

"Hang on a minute. Let me explain. You sell me the contract for deed for 60 thousand—and then you declare bankruptcy."

"But I'm not bankrupt."

"Not a problem. You make up some creditors that you supposedly owe money to."

I was starting to catch on. Once I declared bankruptcy, the dram shop lawyer would drop Twin Silver from the case because he'd know we had no money.

"But what about the rest of the value in the contract for deed?" I asked. If I sold Neff the contract for $60,000, that left hundreds of thousands of dollars in equity. Put simply, the way he had outlined the deal, I would be selling him a bar with a valuation in the mid-six figures for the bargain basement price of $60k. Also, the monthly payments from Craig would now go to Neff.

When I mentioned this last concern, Neff said, "I'll give you some money every month out of the payments." He went on to explain that after a year passed, he'd sell the contract for deed back to me for $80,000, and Craig would resume his monthly payments to me. "It's a win-win. You'll get out of the lawsuit and have a little steady income, and I'll make 20 grand plus a year of payments."

The deal he'd described amounted to a loan with an interest rate of something like 50 percent. And the bankruptcy element was weird, shady at best. Of course, it wouldn't be the first time I'd colored outside the lines of the law. Besides, in this case the law was twisted against me: The dram shop lawyer's scheme may have been legal, but it was definitely immoral. The lawsuit threatened my family and everything we'd worked for. If I had to skirt the law to beat him, so be it.

I did have one worry, though, and it was a big one. Neff wouldn't give me a written contract, which meant I would have no proof of our agreement. And without proof, there was nothing to prevent Neff from keeping the bar. At the end of a year, he could simply refuse to sell the contract back to me. If he did that, he would have purchased a bar worth almost half a million dollars for just $60,000.

I asked Neff about this.

"Are you kidding?" he protested. "You'd kill me if I did something like that, Mike. It's not in a contract, but my wife knows about it." Besides, he said, he hadn't stayed in business all these years by reneging on his deals.

So, desperate for cash, I filed for Chapter 7 bankruptcy with the State of Minnesota in December 2003.

In early January, on nothing but a handshake, I sold the contract for deed to Neff for $60,000.

Two days later, I headed to Vegas.

CHAPTER

18

Leaving Las Vegas

As I flew in over the mountains east of Vegas, the city glittered below, reminding me of an open treasure chest, just the way it had when my friend Rick and I arrived when I was just 18. I'd had a love-hate relationship with this city since. After hitting it big with Rick's five silver dollars, I'd crashed and burned with Wayne's $180. But then there were those six weeks I'd spent here counting cards in 1983, grinding out $300 a day in earnings to pay off a $15,000 debt. That gave me hope.

In fact, I was buzzing with optimism. This was a new era in my life. A new career doing something I was good at—playing cards. I knew that if I put in 10 hours a day under good conditions—and if the pit bosses let me play—I was going to win. It was simple math.

I was determined to be very careful with my cash. When I arrived on the

Strip, I decided to visit multiple casinos, stopping only when I found tables where I could go head-to-head with a dealer.

It felt good to take my seat at hot tables at the MGM Grand, New York-New York, and the Mirage and throw down a few thousand dollars to buy in. With piles of chips stacked in front of me, and $40,000 more in my pocket, I felt very confident. Of course, that also drew the attention of the Bubble People and the pit boss. A lone gambler betting $100 chips had to be carefully watched. The pit boss would make sure a gambler didn't get "up" too high before approaching him with some tempting comp offer that would both break his rhythm and keep him in the casino long enough to lose it all back.

That's the whole casino game. Keep the player playing.

In blackjack, the odds favor the house by approximately .05 to 2 percent. That means that for every $100 you bet, you're going to lose between 50 cents and $2. That doesn't sound like a lot, and it isn't if you play only a couple of hands. But almost no one plays a single hand of blackjack. Instead, they play more like 60 or 100 hands. That's when they have you. The certainty of the casino winning over time is so solid that there are actually formulas that predict a gambler's hourly loss rate.

Let's say you're betting $100 a hand at a table where the dealer is pumping out 60 hands per hour. Even if you're a perfect strategy player and the house edge is only .05 percent, you're still losing $30 an hour. But most people aren't perfect strategy players, and in that scenario, the casino pockets their money at a rate four times faster—about $120 an hour. And the longer you play, the more certain those odds become.

Bottom line, if a generous pit boss can keep you gambling, you will lose. Period. Why do you think they give you free drinks?

But I was not gambling. I was counting. Which is why I accepted the endless stream of free cocktails and, as always, acted much drunker than I was. In the conventional way of thinking, a card counter should be intense and focused. There was no way someone as drunk as I pretended to be would be able to track the cards.

There's a phenomenon in gambling. Some call it a trend, others call it a streak. Vas Spanos called it "stability." You can have the best odds in the world and the best conditions, but if you don't have stability, you're supposed to pull out. Card counters are technicians—cold-eyed mathematicians who don't get caught up in either the dopamine rush of winning or the adrenaline response of losing. In periods of stability—a streak where you're winning when you should be losing—good counters will press their bets. When they're losing, they'll back off or simply walk away. Vas taught me this. It's the exact opposite of typical gambling instincts. Gamblers, especially amateurs, will bet less when they're winning. You'll see them tidying their chips like a kid gloating over a stack of his favorite cookies. But when they're losing, they panic and bet more to try to win back what they've lost.

Vas also taught me never to play with "worried money." In other words, never play with money I couldn't afford to lose.

That, of course, was my first mistake. That $50,000 was all the cash Karen and I had left in the world.

Instead of walking away from tables where I was losing, I stayed put, gritting my teeth and *willing* the cards to fall in my favor. Because I was playing black chips, the money drained away in huge $5,000 and $10,000 chunks. Fairly quickly, I panicked. I transformed from card counter to gambler and began to bet more when I was losing and less when I was winning. It was as though everything I'd ever learned disappeared from my brain. I felt detached, almost like I was watching someone else play. It was surreal, as if that $50,000 were slipping through another guy's fingers.

I convinced myself to play through, just stay at the tables until the trend changed. It was a tactic I'd often used to turn my luck around. But this time, my luck didn't change. I should've walked away or gone to bed and lived to fight another day.

But I didn't. I couldn't stop.

My gambling addiction was in charge now, and I knew it. Within 24 hours of landing in Vegas, I went into a complete spiral, and I knew how the nightmare would end. I knew I was going to lose it all even as I was doing it. So, I began to drink more. I always drank as part of my act, but now I got very serious about it, pounding down whatever the cocktail waitress brought me. That way, when the music stopped, I would not have to feel the pain.

This, of course, increased my error rate. A good counter can afford about one mistake per hour. I was making at least five per hour. Still, I hung onto hope. I had dug out of losing streaks many times in my life, so when I was down to my last $10,000, I fixed my mind on those times. I waited for that wave of relief, that dopamine rush that comes with narrowly avoiding disaster.

I remember where I was when disaster came. I was sitting at a high-limit table at New York-New York. That last hand is a blur, but I remember the queasy doom that spread through my body when the dealer swept my last chips away.

Walking out of there I felt so empty and sick that I can't even describe it. My mind spun desperately, searching for something that hasn't been invented yet: a way to turn back the clock. The money I'd brought to Vegas was our future. It was our chance, and I'd blown it. I'd taken us down before and had always come back. But there was no coming back from this.

I went to bed finally, and I don't even remember where. I don't remember leaving Vegas or how I got home. Even now, as I write this, that whole section of my memory is blank. But I do remember that somewhere in there, I had a sudden, horrible flash of insight: Neff was going to betray me.

When I told Karen I'd lost the money, she didn't flip out. Her attitude was, "We'll get through it. We always do." It was true. We'd never suffered. We raised our kids. We took our trips. We didn't have fancy clothes or cars, but we bought what we wanted—like a satellite dish the size of a car before satellite dishes were popular. Looking back, I know my catastrophic loss must have scared her. She was able to remain calm about it mainly because I had not told her how bad things really were.

After I got back to Minnesota, I showed up unannounced at a cafe to see Neff. I planned to ask him to borrow money against what he would be paying me when I bought back the contract for deed. Neff insisted on talking in his car. Then he did something that put me on high alert: He patted me down to make sure I wasn't wearing a wire.

Satisfied that I wasn't, Neff got in the driver's seat and then pointed his car toward the Twin Cities. For the next hour and a half, he became the man my bookie's stepson had warned me about.

"Mike," he said, "I'm not giving you any more money right now. And legally I don't have to sell you back the contract. We have nothing in writing."

My worst fears were coming true. My apprehension when making the deal. The premonition I'd had in Vegas. Was it really a premonition, though? All the signs had already been there. I looked at Neff, driving down the freeway as he calmly told me how he had total control over me now. His Coke-bottle glasses reflected light, and I couldn't see his eyes. It was as if he didn't have any. It felt like I had made a deal with the devil.

"You're an addict," Neff said, spitting out the last word like something rotten. "You'd lose it all anyway, just like you lost the $50,000."

Despair filled my heart as I saw everything I'd worked for vanishing before my eyes. Then anger washed over me. This man was stealing from my family. I started to speak, but he cut me off.

"What are you going to do about it?" he snapped. "If you try to tell the cops, you're gonna have to tell them you declared bankruptcy when you weren't really bankrupt, and that's a crime. You'll go to jail."

My mind went into overdrive. For the thousandth time in my life, I thought, *How can I salvage this situation?* You have to understand that I'd been an addict for 30 years by then. I had lived in constant chaos for so long that it never occurred to me there was another way to live. I was like a fish who doesn't know he's wet. Epic highs and catastrophic lows didn't just *seem* normal to me—they *were* normal.

But I could still read a room. Suddenly, it hit me that Neff wasn't just a con artist. It wasn't just that. No, he hated addicts, literally hated them. Later, his wife would confirm this for me. Neff had found a hunting ground where he could stalk and trap people precisely because they were desperate. Neff had laid his trap for me, and I had blundered into it like a fool.

Quickly my instincts took over. Reading Neff, I realized that cruelty was his drug and that a wounded, panicked reaction from me would only feed him. I immediately backed off trying to get any more money against my contract for deed. Instead, I reminded him that since we made our deal, the bankruptcy trustee had begun looking into my finances. I wasn't sure, but there was a good chance they would soon be asking why I would sell a $500,000 contract for $60,000. It would sound shady to them, just as it had to me. That was something to keep in mind, I told him.

"We're both going to be in trouble if they realize that I'm not really bankrupt," I said.

On the outside, I was staying cool, but on the inside, I was sickened as the realization hit me that this man's intention all along was to take everything from me. In the end, I convinced Neff to give me a few thousand dollars to take care of my family.

One more chance. That was all I needed—the story of my life. One more chance with the mafia. One more chance with my DUIs, with money, with Karen, with my career. When was it going to end? I'd asked the same thing of my friend Toad as I watched his inheritance literally go up in smoke. I could see the addictive insanity in other people. I could even see it in myself, but I had no idea how to escape. No "bottom" had been deep enough, and no rehab had touched me. Now, here I was at the end of the line with just a few thousand dollars to my name. And as crazy as it sounds, I thought all I needed was one more chance in Vegas.

This. Was. It. This time, I'd do it right, like Darren said. This time, it was going to be different. But it wasn't, of course.

Within eight hours of landing in Vegas with Neff's money, I'd won $3,000 playing craps at the Fremont then lost it all back. I had $110 left.

It was time once again to numb the pain. I'd been doing cocaine since I got off the plane, but now my despair was so deep that I knew only crack would do. I was wandering down a street in downtown Las Vegas wishing I had a pipe when this guy walked up to me and asked me if I wanted to buy some pot.

I stopped and looked at him. He was black, very clean cut, and articulate. I sensed immediately he was a nice guy.

"No, but I've got some coke," I said. "If you have a pipe, we can smoke some crack."

The guy agreed and after a stop at an all-night grocery to pick up some baking soda, a Chore Boy scrubber, and a spoon, he and I took a cab to the Westward Ho. Because I held a gold card there, the hotel comped us a room. I did not leave that room for seven full days.

My new friend and I shared a name: Michael.

He was a smart guy who used to work in aerospace, but like Toad, he'd lost everything to crack. He took a trip to Las Vegas and tried crack for the first time. His first hit led to another and another, each of which led him to remain in Vegas one more day. And here he was, two years later. That was the power of crack. Michael simply never went back home to Kentucky, to his job, his wife, or his two kids.

"I even missed my grandmother's funeral," he told me. At that point, he broke down crying.

I absolutely understood his pain. I actually made it to my Grandma Millie's bedside right before she passed away. But I should have been there sooner, and would have been if I hadn't been waiting to come down from my crack high.

As we loaded the pipe again and again, Michael and I bonded over how much we had in common. On the second night of our bender I could see that we were going to run out of drugs. Michael made a call and within a half an hour, there was a knock at the hotel room door. A big, burly guy and a petite, tattooed woman walked in. Crack paranoia had seized me by then, and I didn't want to go out in public. It was after midnight, so a new banking day had begun. I wasn't sure how much money was in my account, but I gave Michael my ATM card, told him my pin, and asked him to go try and make the maximum withdrawal, $300.

When the door shut behind him, the woman shook her head and looked at me with a mix of pity and disdain. "You're crazy. He ain't never coming back."

"Oh, he'll be back," I said.

A very long time passed. Every now and then, the woman looked at me and shook her head. Meanwhile, her big friend was getting very impatient with me. He kept looking at the door and it hit me that he probably didn't know Michael very well. Every once in a while he would mumble something like, "He better come back."

Finally, there was a knock on the door and when I opened it, Michael walked in with my ATM card and money. The woman's skeptical expression was replaced with complete shock. The burly guy, still annoyed, made a swift transaction and left.

"What took so long?" I asked. Michael confessed that he had accessed my bank account and was at least a quarter mile away before something came over him and made him turn around. He just couldn't steal my money, he said.

For the next few days, Michael and I smoked crack and commiserated. I stayed awake for seven days, and the room at the Westward Ho became a treatment center, therapy group, and church all in one. By the seventh day, I was broke again and also just a couple of hours from running out of crack. Coming off my high and returning to reality was going to be one of the worst experiences of my life, and I knew it. I'd misplaced the $110 from the Fremont and now I rifled desperately through my suitcase until I finally found it.

Then, suddenly, I stopped. Maybe buying more drugs wasn't the best use of this money. During my week-plus without sleep, I hadn't come up with any insights about how to improve things in my own life. But after hearing Michael talk about his regrets over his life decisions, I thought maybe at least I could do something for him.

"You know what? It would mean a lot to me if you went back to your family," I told Michael, emotions rising in my throat as I said the words. "Go home. Save yourself. I'd rather buy you a train ticket with this money than buy any more crack."

He teared up.

We called to get the price of a train ticket to Kentucky. It was $104 and the departure was that afternoon. Around noon, Michael came out of the bathroom, cleaned up and ready to go to the station. At that moment, the reality of my situation hit me and I started to cry.

"Come over here," Michael said to me. He put his arm around me and surprised me when he began to say the Lord's Prayer.

Our Father, who art in heaven,
Hallowed be thy name...

I hadn't heard the prayer in a very long time, and it brought me peace.

At the train station, after Michael picked up his ticket, he turned to me and said, "Can I get some money from you for food on the train?" This request stopped me short for a second. After I'd given him money for a ticket, he wanted my last six bucks? On the other hand, what good was six dollars going to do me? And it *was* a long way to Kentucky.

I handed over the cash, and Michael started down the platform toward his train. Looking after him, I couldn't help but wonder whether he had, over the last seven days, put on some kind of Oscar-worthy act. But just as that thought formed in my head, Michael rushed back to me and wrapped me in a hug. We both burst into tears. I don't know how long we stood there tangled up and sobbing, but when we let go, a crowd had gathered to watch this white guy and black guy hugging and crying in the middle of the train station.

The crowd parted as Michael walked toward his train. He turned and yelled, "Thanks, Mike. I'll never forget you."

Now penniless, I stowed away on a tram and rode back to the Westward Ho, where I collapsed from lack of sleep. I woke up and reality began to creep in from every corner. To escape, I turned on the TV and began to watch a *Gunsmoke* marathon, drifting between sleep and hopelessness, then to escape again, I'd lose myself in another episode. This cycle went on for two days as I thought about my kids. Darren, our youngest son, was starting high school and Heather was already in college studying fine arts. I may have helped Michael, but my family had been counting on me and I had failed them.

CHAPTER
19

The Dream

I don't even remember how I made it home from Vegas, but I remember vividly what happened next. One night in the spring of 2004, I sat straight up in bed, holding on to the tail of a dream. I glanced at the clock. It was 2 a.m. Words from my dream were still running through my head. It was my own voice repeating the words, "Where's my pillow?"

The phrase was what you'd say if you laid down at night and found your pillow missing. A pillow is a very personal thing. No one says, "Where's *the* pillow?" But why was I dreaming about pillows? I wasn't sure, but as I sat there in bed with Karen snoozing quietly beside me, the images from the dream were still vivid. It was me, running around yelling, "Where's my pillow?" Really weird.

In all my years of trying to find a good pillow, I had found only one that sort of worked. It had been a gift from my father-in-law. Until it finally fell apart, I had insisted on sleeping on it everywhere I went.

"MyPillow." I thought it could make a good brand name. Then I thought, well, no. That sounds dorky. Who would put "my" in front of anything? On the other hand, there was something about it.

I got up, headed to the kitchen, grabbed a notepad, and started writing.

my pillow...

MyPillow...

MYPILLOW...

Over and over again. Something about it just felt right. Excited, I kept experimenting with different ways of writing the name until it began to take the shape of a logo. I wrote it hundreds of times, the same way you practice signing your name when you're a kid.

I was still doodling at 3 a.m., and now the kitchen was papered with sheets from the notebook, as if some mad scientist had spent hours brainstorming a new formula.

My daughter Lizzy came upstairs, poured herself a glass of water, and sipped from it as she looked around at the blizzard of pages. She asked what I was doing.

Still scribbling, I told her I was going to invent a pillow. "It's going to be called 'MyPillow' and it's going to change the world."

Lizzy gave me the kind of look only a teenager can give. "That's really random, Dad," she said, and went back downstairs.

Change the world? Where had that come from? How was a pillow going to change the world? I didn't know. But when I woke up from that pillow dream, I felt hope for the first time since losing the $50,000 in Las Vegas. I had a purpose now. I grabbed onto that purpose and held on.

That night, my brother Corey and I had plans to head to a nearby casino. I'd been able to borrow money to card count, which was how I was keeping food on the table. Corey showed up at my house, and we got in my truck to head over to the blackjack tables in Danbury, Wisconsin.

"We need to make a little detour first," I told him.

"Where to?" Corey said.

"Duluth."

I wanted to go see Heather at the University of Minnesota campus in Duluth, at the tip of Lake Superior. At 8 p.m., Corey and I showed up at her townhome unannounced. I held out one of the many scraps of paper on which I had experimented with a version of the words MyPillow. "I want you to turn this into a logo."

Heather took the paper, sat down at her desk, and pulled out a sketchpad. As Corey and I watched, she rendered different versions of the words. I urged her to connect the "y" at the end of My with the "P" in Pillow. It didn't take long before Heather had created what would become the first MyPillow logo.

"Perfect!" I said. Corey and I visited with her for a few more minutes then left.

After two weeks, I was still babbling about MyPillow. "When is he going to quit talking about this pillow thing?" the kids asked Karen, one after the other.

"It's just a phase," she said. "He'll get over it."

As you already know, I did not get over it. I knew a few things about the pillow I wanted to invent. First, it would have to be adjustable. You would be able to shape the pillow to fit your head and neck, and it would hold the shape that was perfect for you. Second, the pillow would stay cool. Third, you would be able to wash and dry it. Finally, I wanted the pillow to last a long time.

One of the first things I did was market research. I stopped in at Bed Bath & Beyond in the Southtown Shopping Center in Bloomington, where I spent hours examining every pillow on the shelves. The manager finally came over and asked me if I needed help.

"Nope, I'm good," I said. "Just doing some pillow research."

"Can I show you some of our bestsellers?" he said. "These pillows over here are really popular."

"Those pillows are all awful," I said. "I'm going to come back someday with the best pillow you've ever seen. You're going to sell them in your store one day."

The manager didn't seem to know quite what to say. He smiled politely. "Well. Okay. Just let me know if you need any help."

I left Bed Bath & Beyond with some zip-up pillow covers I could use to develop MyPillow, as well as information about potential types of pillow fill. It wouldn't be down fill (flat and shapeless) or memory foam (sleeps too hot.) But I did feel that foam was what I was looking for. The next stop was Rochford Supply, and I took Darren with me.

Rochford was the leading midwest supplier of textiles, marine fabrics, vinyl, leather, and foam. I told the owner what I was interested in. After we talked it through, I decided on a certain type of foam, bought a huge batch of foam blocks, and carted them away in my truck.

Back home, Darren and I went out to the back deck and got right to work, ripping golf-ball-sized pieces from foam blocks and stuffing them into the zippered cases. Tiny flecks of foam soon covered the deck and swirled around us, getting caught in the late spring winds. Even with the two of us working, it took a while to hand-tear enough foam to fill just one of the zippered cases.

When we finally did, I zipped it up and took it inside for a test-drive.

Lying down on the couch, I nestled my head into my prototype and almost immediately stood up again. Nope.

The next day I went back to Rochford Supply for a different type of foam. This went on the next day and the next and the next. One foam was too hard and the next was too soft. I was living the story of *Goldilocks and the Three Bears*, except that nothing I found was just right. Some foams crumbled in my hands every time I tried to tear them. Others were so tough I could barely rip them with my hands and had to resort to chopping them up with the electric knife I used to filet fish.

Some of my friends thought I was crazy. A couple of them said, "What? Are you on crack?" Then they'd say, "Oh that's right, you are!"

Soon Darren was coming with me to Rochford's at least three times a week. Then, we'd sit out in the backyard tearing up the latest foam sample until our hands ached. Those hours remain special to me, a time of bonding with my youngest son. I used our breaks to sketch out maps and diagrams of the factory I envisioned owning someday.

I showed him a blueprint-style drawing I'd done, pointing to different rooms. "Whatever pillow-fill we wind up using, we'll fill the pillow covers in this room. We'll sew them over here, and in this area we'll have quality control."

"What's quality control?" he said, dusting foam flecks from his hair.

I paused, wondering about the best way to explain quality control to a kid. Finally, I had it. "That's where you make sure your product is as good as what you would make for yourself or your best friend."

I kept that first drawing. Today you can overlay it on the site of the MyPillow factory in Shakopee. It's an almost perfect match.

After trying 94 different foam types and combinations, we were close. And then one day, we did it. I could shape the pillow and it would stay put.

It worked!

But not so fast. The shaped foam wouldn't come apart. Which means it didn't work.

What I envisioned was a fill that held its shape, but released with just a light touch. We kept working day after day, shredding and tearing until, finally, we hit on a prototype filled with a special foam of three different types and sizes. That was in my backyard in August 2004. The fill in MyPillow hasn't changed since.

Still, the pillow didn't release correctly. After some more research and with the help of foam engineers, we hit on a solution: an additive that caused the foam to stick or slide, depending on the type and amount of pressure applied. Even better, this new additive, which would become proprietary, treated the foam in such a way that the pillows could now be washed and dried. Another problem solved.

As the pillow project took shape (literally), so did my bankruptcy case. We began to receive notices that the trustees of the court were doing a deep dive into the Lindell family finances. Which were, of course, a disaster. Karen knew I'd lost all our available cash on my two trips to Las Vegas, but she didn't know that I suspected Neff was never going to sell the contract back to us. If Neff followed through on his threat, we would lose hundreds of thousands of dollars that should have been ours for the sale of Schmitty's.

In January 2004, Karen and I took a week-long trip to a beach town in Mexico, using money I borrowed from a friend. This was part of our pattern. It didn't matter whether we were flush or broke, we took our annual vacations. I'd heard it was easy to get coke in Mexico and it didn't take long for us to meet that beachfront dealer I mentioned before, the one we called the Greek. I stayed up for seven days straight, fueled by a steady supply of cocaine.

The whole time, I thought about Neff. How was I going to get the Schmitty's contract back? On the plane home, while I was staring out the window at passing clouds, I came up with a plan.

Soon after we got back from Mexico, I went to see Neff, again unannounced. As before, he checked me for a wire, and we talked while driving the perimeter of the Cities in his car. I resumed my reasonable nice-guy act. I had realized the only way to win with a guy like Neff was to keep acting as if I believed we were friends.

"Neff, the bankruptcy hearing is coming up soon," I said, repeating my earlier warning that the court was going to challenge the legitimacy of my filing. That was now coming to fruition. "I know the lawyers are onto us."

"Forget it," he said abruptly. "I know where you're going with this, and you're not getting anything. You're an addict. No one will ever believe you."

"We talked about this," I reminded him. "What's going to happen when the court finds out I sold that contract to you for pennies on the dollar? I've been looking into it. It's called a 'clawback.' They will pull that contract in as part of my actual assets. They'll also know it's a fraud. Then we're both gonna be in trouble."

Neff had warned me that I'd go to jail for bankruptcy fraud, but the possibility that he might go with me seemed to him an entirely new concept. I suspected that he'd been able to steal from addicts before, because most deals likely didn't involve lawyers and judges. Because of the bankruptcy, this one did.

Neff said nothing, just drummed his fingers on the steering wheel.

"I think I've got a solution that will work for us both," I said. "You could sell the contract to a friend of mine for 70 thousand. That's 10 grand more than you paid for it, plus you've made money on payments from Craig, so you're coming out way ahead." When the court looked at what would now be two sales, I hoped they'd conclude that the valuation on the bar wasn't as high as they'd thought. After all, it was only worth what the market would bear.

At first Neff resisted, but in the end, he surrendered. He would sell the contract to my friend Bob, who had agreed to buy the contract as a favor to me. I had arranged to pay Bob a good rate of interest, so it would be a win-win. Bob, would make good money, and I'd get some of my equity back. As importantly, I'd get rid of Neff.

On the day of the closing, Neff showed his colors one more time. He demanded an additional $10,000. If he didn't get it—and I mean *right then*—he was going to walk. I felt sick, but told Bob to quick-sign the papers anyway. I would accept another $10,000 loss. The instant the deal was done, I told Bob to put Neff on the phone. Then I unloaded.

"I sat up night after night thinking about how you were taking everything from me and worse, from my family!" I shouted into the phone. "I want you to know that I think you are the most evil person I have ever known!"

Neff laughed. "You're an addict," he said. "You'd have lost it all anyway."

I hung up on him and stared at the phone as if it contained a poisonous snake.

CHAPTER

20

Learning Curve

From the day I first dreamed up the pillow until the day the first batch was ready for sale, time sped by in a blur. When I wasn't working my way through the bankruptcy case or counting cards to pay the mortgage and feed the kids (with money borrowed against the contract for deed now owned by Bob), I was working out the details of MyPillow.

After a long string of bad luck and terrible decisions, I was energized. Darren and I had finally hit on the right fill for the pillow, but we couldn't sit on the back deck and tear foam by hand forever. We had to come up with a way to automate.

We tried several methods: graters, electric knives, wood chippers, and even a blender, but nothing worked. It was frustrating at times, but I wouldn't trade anything for the time I spent with Darren week after week, sitting outside and talking as we reached for a dream. Then a friend of mine made a suggestion that changed everything. I was discussing my automation problem while playing cards with my regular poker buddies: Wayne Hilk, Lyle Lund, Slip Mahoney, JD, and Joe Wickenhauser.

"Mike, you used to work on a farm," my friend Joe said. "You should try one of them old hammer mills."

A hammer mill is used to shred or crush materials into smaller pieces by repeated blows of little "hammers" or blades. These cutting or crushing tools can be changed out to produce final products of differing sizes. Farmers use hammer mills to crush grain into coarse flour that they can feed to livestock. Hammer mills are also used to grind shipping pallets into mulch, and to shred paper, scrap automobile parts, or crush rocks.

Joe's comment got my son Charlie involved as he and I drove around the midwest for weeks looking for a hammer mill. No luck. I was playing cribbage with Lyle one day when, out of the blue, he said, "I seen one of them hammer mills out there on the Olson place."

A plainspoken man of German roots, Lyle is an old-school Minnesota farmer right down to his handlebar moustache. I looked at him. "Are you sure?"

"I think so."

I jumped up from the table. "I gotta go see right now. I'll be back."

I sped out to the Olson farm, which was less than two miles from my house, to see if Lyle was right. In the middle of a field sat a beat-up old hammer mill, with sunrays glinting dully off the rusted metal. Charlie and I had driven across a dozen counties looking for one of these things. What are the odds that I'd find one less than two miles from my house?

I located Mr. Olson and inquired about his machine. As we headed out into his field to take a closer look, he told me hardly anyone used these old models anymore. Even he didn't, it turned out. As we got closer, I saw that grass covered half the hammer mill and was also growing up through it. It must have been sitting out there for years.

Mr. Olson sold me his machine for practically nothing. I got it home and tinkered with it for days, trying different combinations of hammers, knives, and screens until it finally shredded foam in the sizes I needed. This was not without risk. Changing out the screens that determined the ultimate foam size was a dangerous job that cost me a little in blood every now and then. I didn't mind. I had cobbled together a machine that did the job.

Speaking of jobs, I didn't have one. My friend Bob was still lending me money against the contract for deed, and I had run through it like water, using the cash to develop the pillow, keep the refrigerator full, and the lights on. I decided to take a break and do some more serious card counting as I was almost completely out of cash.

The Beau Rivage was a towering hotel casino in Biloxi, Mississippi, overlooking the Gulf of Mexico. Karen and I headed down there to turn $2,000—our remaining spare cash—into a mortgage payment and other monthly expenses. For a little over 24 hours, I sat at the blackjack tables while Karen played slot machines. Accepting what seemed like a gallon of free cocktails, I stuck to my usual act. I hoped I looked to the pit bosses like a good-timing drunk having a lucky run at the cards, but I was actually ticking off Vas' matrixes in my head. I counted meticulously until about 3 a.m., when I walked away from the table with more chips than I'd had in a very long time.

By the time I cashed them in, the cocktails were catching up with me. Very intoxicated, I stumbled to our room, where Karen was still up drinking herself.

"Hey, I've got something to show you," I said, my voice half mystery, half excitement. "I just won $14,000!"

It was the largest sum of cash we'd had in a while that didn't belong to somebody else. But that wasn't my biggest news. Vas Spanos had called me that evening. A couple of members of a high-end professional card-counting team had been watching me play that night—scouting me, actually. They planned to invite me to join.

The most famous card-counting team is portrayed in the movie *21*, which tells the story of mathematics professor Mickey Rosa and a group of Massachusetts Institute of Technology students who used their math skills to win big in Vegas.

Card-counting teams use different strategies. Sometimes a team is just two players, friends maybe, or even a male/female team pretending to be a couple. In this kind of team play, one player, usually the better counter, may use signals to indicate how the other should bet. They might roll up their sleeves or move their cocktail from their right to their left. In another version of a two-member team, one player bets big chips and appears to be paying very little attention to the game. In fact though, this player is counting very accurately and reading signals from the other, who is playing small chips at the same table while pretending to be a stranger.

The team Vas was recruiting me for was the kind I really liked playing for—a "spotter" team. In this style of play, one member warms up the table with low stakes bets while carefully tracking the cards. Because of the player's $5 and $10 bets, pit bosses and Bubble People usually do not recognize that he or she is counting. When enough cards have been played, and the odds at the table turn against the house, the spotter signals the "big player" or "jumper," who then joins the game. As the spotter leaves the table, he or she passes the count to the jumper, usually with a pre-arranged verbal signal, a kind of code. Something like a random comment to the dealer, "I can only play a little while longer. I've got a big meeting with 15 buyers tomorrow." That means the count is "plus 15." Now, with the count favoring the player, the jumper sits down, immediately starts betting the big chips, and if all goes well, cleans up.

The team that was scouting me had lost their leader, who had been caught and banned from a lot of casinos. Now they were looking for a new leader. Vas had recommended me, and the scouts liked what they saw.

"He said this team is one of the best in the world and that I could make a lot of money if I join," I told Karen. "He's going to call me tomorrow and tell me when we start. I'm going to be making over $500,000 a year!" Karen jumped up and we danced around the room celebrating. When I neared the hotel room window, I could see the hotel pool glowing blue in the early morning darkness many floors below. That gave me an idea.

I turned back to Karen. "Do you remember that scene in the movie *Vacation* where they jump in the pool?" Her face lit up with a smile.

Minutes later, we were poolside, and the place was deserted. Right before we jumped in, I pulled the $14,000 out and threw it up in the air. Later that morning, I woke up back in the room, wondering if I had dreamed all that. But when I looked around, all I could see was 140 still-limp hundred-dollar bills drying all over the room.

With my foam composition and shredding issues settled, I now needed pillow ticks, the covers that hold the fill. At first, this was a bit of a comedy show. Instead of laying out the money to hire a professional to sew them, I invested the money in an industrial sewing machine. Each tick required just a few lines of seaming, and I'd already reengineered the hammer mill. How hard could it be?

Hard, that's how. The machine seemed to have a thousand tiny parts with movements that made about as much sense to me as a cuckoo clock. Charlie and I looked through the manual, which didn't even show how to thread the bobbin. The first time I hit the foot pedal, the thing went nuts, tangling the thread into a mess the size of baseball. But it did thread the bobbin automatically. It took me a week to sew 300 ticks using a fabric I'd bought at Rochford. It was embossed with tiny stars.

By now I needed a space for the hammer mill and production, so I rented an old bus shed across the street from my house. (The landlord, Dick Lenzen, had also sold Karen and me our first house.) The kids helped me stuff the new ticks with the pillow fill. We labeled them with Heather's logo, sealed them in plastic, and stacked them in the bus shed. After months of dreaming, brainstorming, and jerry-rigging, we had our first 300 pillows ready to go. Now, I had just one thing left to figure out: how to get people to buy them.

It wasn't long before I got some terrible news. The card-counting team Vas had recruited me for had disbanded. All of its members had been caught and barred from casinos. I got the word the same week I was going to join them.

Vas tried to console me. "I have another team we can put together," he said, naming my brother, Corey, and two guys I didn't know, Jim Furlong and Nick Callahan. I didn't feel any better. I predicted I'd make peanuts compared to what I would have made on the other team.

Jim was tall and a little cranky at times. He was an excellent player, though, so good he had been making a living at it for about a year by the time we met. He did have one dangerous run-in after leaving Grand Casino in Hinckley, Minnesota, though. Jim had cleaned up that night, winning about $9,000. But a guy who'd watched him cash out followed Jim's car down a foggy backroad, ran him onto the gravel shoulder, put a shotgun in his face, and robbed him.

Nick Callahan, a shorter, stockier guy, was a great counter, too. But he was also very conservative and seemed to be in it more for the adventure than to make money. Jim would get irritated with him for not betting enough. Even when the count was in his favor, Nick would rarely press his bets beyond laying another $5 chip on the table. Jim called him "Five Dollar Nick."

My brother Corey, who had also taken Vas' class, joined us, making a team of four. Corey was slow and very precise. His plodding pace drove me nuts, but it actually helped our act. Together, we traveled to casinos in Mississippi, Nevada, Wisconsin, Washington, and Minnesota. I was basically the team leader, although decision-making, such as where we were going to play and what method we were going to use, was a shared responsibility.

Because of the cloak-and-dagger element, like pretending we didn't know each other, team play was more fun than solo counting, which as I've said is pretty much a grind. It also took the pressure off financially. Having multiple players on a team tends to overcome deviations—statistical anomalies that cause you to lose when you should be winning. Sometimes that 1.5% advantage that counters have over the house doesn't pan out. With team play, if I'm losing $50 every hand, but Jim, Nick, and Corey are winning at $50 a hand, then we're still netting $100 a hand as a team.

Another good thing about team counting was this: With the other guys counting on me, I stuck to the matrixes and kept a tighter rein on my inclination to gamble.

Between counting trips, I tried to figure out how to sell my product. Eager but naïve, I stopped first at the Bed Bath & Beyond store in Bloomington, where I had started my pillow research. With a sample pillow under one arm, I marched up to the manager.

"I have the best pillow ever made. You're going to want this in your store," I said. "How many would you like?"

The manager burst out laughing. "Sir, I don't decide what we sell. I just work here."

"Well, who chooses the products for your store? If I could just get five minutes with…"

"I'm sorry, sir," he interrupted. "We're a part of a chain and it has only one buyer for the entire country. You can't just walk in here and see him. He isn't here."

As you can imagine, every chain retail store I visited gave me a version of the same message. The rest said something like, "Why would we buy a pillow from some guy off the street?"

Sometimes, I got so passionate that a manager would say, "You need to leave. Now."

My sister's brother-in-law Brad suggested that I sell MyPillow from a kiosk. I told him I didn't even know to spell kiosk. Brad then said he knew of a guy who could get me on the QVC shopping channel. He set up a meeting with the rep who, when I arrived, sat behind a desk wearing a suit and an attitude.

The rep told me not so subtly that my product was a joke. I told him I had already given away a lot of sample pillows and everyone loved them. Then I walked out, glad the guy didn't want to sell my product because I didn't want to do business with him anyway. (When I ran into the guy years later, he was still wearing a suit but definitely had a different attitude about MyPillow.)

Never one to give up, I decided to try Brad's kiosk idea at a mall show in Eden Prairie, Minnesota. It was December 2004. I paid $1,000 to be in the show when the exhibitor fee was really only $100. The show manager later admitted he gouged me because he thought I was fly-by-night, which of course, I was. I designed a show booth, stenciling signs and using markers to color in the letters. Not only was the whole thing really hokey, but I realized immediately that I had created my own worst nightmare.

Having no bar or beer taps between me and my customers left me absolutely terrified. Every ordinary question from a potential buyer felt like a CIA interrogation. On the first day, Karen and I talked our heads off for four hours until finally, some guy came up and bought a pillow. He also asked me for a business card in case he wanted his money back. I didn't have a business card, so I scribbled my number on a scrap of paper. (Like I said, hokey.) As soon as he walked away, we both exploded with excitement. We had just sold our first MyPillow!

Still, by the time the show was over, we had sold a whopping total of 12 pillows at a loss of around $1,300, including the inflated entry fee.

Several weeks passed, and I was out of ideas. I had more than 250 pillows that cost about $8,000 to make, and I had no place to sell them. For Christmas that year, I had to borrow money from a friend to buy presents for the kids. New Year's Day came and went. Then one day in January 2005, I was wracking my brain for a solution when my cell phone rang.

"Are you the guy who invented this MyPillow?" a man said when I picked up.

"Yeah."

"Well, I bought one from you at the Eden Prairie kiosk," he said. "This is the best product I've ever purchased." I noticed that he didn't say "best pillow." He said "best product."

"Seriously," he continued, "this pillow changed my life."

It turned out that the caller was a key organizer at the Minneapolis Home & Garden Show, and he wanted MyPillow to be an exhibitor there. My heart did a flip. Tens of thousands of people attended that show! I told him I'd love to participate. We exchanged details and hung up. Then it hit me: He was the guy who'd asked for my business card in case he wanted his money back. The Eden Prairie show had been a huge failure, and *this* is the guy who gets my phone number? What are the odds?

CHAPTER

21

A New Drug

T he Minneapolis show drew hundreds of exhibitors. Most of them
operated from expensive booths, many with professional lighting and
graphics. I didn't have money for that, so I set up my space with carpet,
a table, and an inkjet-printed version of my new slogan, "The most comfortable
pillow you'll ever own." I slipped the printout into a plexiglass sign holder that
I bought at Staples. Still hokey, but at least good enough to be in the show.

Before the show opened, I spent a lot of time thinking about how to improve
the pitch that had managed to sell only 12 pillows at Eden Prairie. I decided on
a problem-solution presentation. If it were me, I thought, I'd want to see how
MyPillow was different. I decided to set up my booth as a demo.

By the time the doors opened, I had placed three large jars on the table,
each with one of the three types of foam in my fill. When people walked up,

I explained that I'd always had problems sleeping: The pillows I was using would go flat. I'd use my arm to prop them up, but my arm would fall asleep. And most mornings, I'd wake up with a neck ache or a headache.

From the nodding and murmuring, I could tell this was a problem that lots of people shared. I would then demonstrate the solution, that MyPillow could be molded to fit their preferences.

"Can you put your hand here and push down?" I would say, indicating the spot where a person would lay their head. "See? The foam stays put. You can put six pounds of pressure on it—which is less than your head weighs when it's supported—and it will hold its shape."

"Wow!" was the usual reaction.

Then I would ask them to press a little harder and watch their amazement as the foam released and returned to its three separate components.

At that point, I'd throw out the bonuses: "I make MyPillow right here in Minnesota, each pillow has a 10-year warranty, plus you can wash and dry it. Also, I'll give you a 60-day money back guarantee. If you don't like it, come back and I'll refund your money."

People came back all right. On the second day of the show, at least 15 people came back. They'd slept on the pillow the night before and came to buy more. These return customers told all the new customers at the booth how much they loved my product. One guy took his pillow home, took a nap and came back the same day to buy more. That day, one of the show organizers walked over and said he'd seen more MyPillows walking out of the show than any other product. Before the event was over, Karen and I had sold nearly everything we had— about $10,000 worth of product.

But the real thrill for me wasn't the money. It was the change in me. I had invented something that helped people. The feeling I got from knowing that was a revelation. The emotion took me all the way back to Mother's Day 1968. As gifts for our moms, everyone in my second-grade class had decorated flowerpots and filled them with soil and seeds. That Friday afternoon, we took the flowerpots home. I was standing in line for the school bus when a boy ran up to the girl in front of me and deliberately knocked her flowerpot out of her hands. As it smashed on the ground, he ran away laughing and the girl burst into tears.

I held out my flowerpot. "You can have mine," I said shyly.

"But it's for your mom," she protested.

"That's okay. I've got lots of presents for my mom."

That wasn't true. But helping my classmate that day filled my heart so full that I never forgot it. Now at the Minneapolis show, when I realized that MyPillow was helping people, I felt I had found something I'd been searching for most of my incredibly self-centered life without even knowing what it was. As a result, I could talk to people about my product without fear and without drugs or alcohol. When I was demonstrating MyPillow, the hours flew by, and I couldn't wait for the next day to start. I wasn't conscious of the connection then, but looking back, I realize that I'd found a new drug.

While the Minneapolis Home & Garden Show was a big success, it didn't make us rich. Credit card vendors were slow to pay us for purchases made through "paper processing," where you run the customer's card through one of those old manual "knuckle-busters" with a carbon-copied slip. To stay afloat, I kept up my card counting with Corey, Jim, and Nick.

Card counting and managing MyPillow kept me not only away from home, but out of town, which further fed Karen's insecurities. Even when I was in town, I often stayed away from home so that I could smoke crack. With the kids getting older and more aware, I was too paranoid to use crack at home, worried they'd walk in and catch me.

During this season, we usually had cash on hand, but we were still scraping to get by, maneuvering, robbing Peter to pay Paul. Our family business was small but growing, and that gave us hope. The Minneapolis Home & Garden Show led to more shows, but even more importantly to the Minnesota State Fair.

The State Fair drew not tens of thousands of people, but hundreds of thousands. When we were accepted as exhibitors, my kids pitched in, helping haul in the materials and set up the booth. Even Heather, home from college, sold pillows. By the second day, we had customers lined up so deep they were blocking walkways.

We hit it out of the park, selling tens of thousands of dollars in product. Suddenly, I realized we could exhibit at the Minnesota State Fair and basically not work for the rest of the year. That wasn't what I wanted to do, but I could if I had to.

During the event, an older guy walked up to our booth. He stared at my signs and read them aloud. "'Guaranteed the most comfortable pillow you'll ever own'" he said, scowling. "Hah! How can you guarantee that? I'm 82 years old. Do you have any idea how many pillows I've owned? That's a crock of—"

Well, you know.

This old guy was probably the crabbiest human being I had ever met. I rubbed the back of my neck and looked longingly at the deep line of customers behind him waiting to see my demo. There was no way I was ever going to please this guy. I was anxious to talk to customers who might actually be interested, not this crank. But instead of moving on, he shuffled over to the couch we had set up at our booth, hitched up his pants legs, and sat down.

He picked up a pillow, pushed on it a few times. "How the hell is this supposed to be comfortable?" he demanded. "It's got lumps in it!"

Now the crowd was watching *and* listening. Suddenly, making this guy happy became a customer service challenge. "Well, sir, the pillow may feel lumpy, but that's part of the design. You can shape it to fit your head. I guarantee it, and I'll give you your money back if it doesn't work for you."

"Hah!" he snapped again. "Where am I supposed to find you? Over at your factory in China?"

"No, sir. I make these pillows right here in Minnesota."

"I don't believe it. There ain't no pillow made in the United States. They're all made in China."

"Well, look at the tag." I pointed to our "Made in the USA" label.

"Well, I'll be damned," he said, staring at it.

He was quiet for a moment, but I could see he wasn't convinced.

"Sir, where do you live?" I asked.

"I live in Plymouth, Minnesota. Lived there all my life."

"Okay. How about if I *give* you a pillow? You give me your phone number, and I'll call you in about a week. If you don't like the pillow, I'll drive over and pick it up. If you do like it, you can pay me then."

The man raised his eyebrows. "You'd do that?"

By now, the waiting crowd was really into it, urging us on. "Yes! Do it! Let's get this line moving!"

The old man squinted up at me, still skeptical. "You don't want to see my license first or something?"

I held up my hand. "Nope. I just want you to write down your phone number and your name."

"Well. All right."

I searched around and found a napkin and a pen. The man jotted down his name, which was Joel, and his number. When he walked off with a pillow tucked under his arm, the crowd cheered.

A couple of weeks later, I dialed Joel's number. "Hi Joel, this is Mi—"

"Is this that damn pillow guy?" Joel interrupted. "Are you gonna come over here or what? You said you'd be over."

"Yeah, I could probably come by today. I'm heading in that direction."

"Well, bring three or four more of them damn things with you," he said, and hung up.

I smiled. Challenge won. When I pulled up in Joel's driveway later that day, I could see him sitting in a recliner staring out his front window. No book. No magazine. Just staring. I banged on the door but heard nothing. I knocked two or three more times before I heard him yell, "What the hell do you want?"

"It's Mike from MyPillow!" I called out. "I've got your pillows."

"Well, get in here and hurry up! I'm busy."

I carried in an armload of pillows and set them down on his living room floor. Joel pulled out his checkbook and asked, "How much do I owe you?"

I hesitated. "Well, I'll give you a deal since you're buying a four-pack..."

Joel scowled. "I don't need no damn deal. Just tell me what I owe you. And hurry up about it! Can't you see I'm busy? I've got better things to do than deal with you."

I told him the price, and then inspiration hit. Ever since the return customers at the Minneapolis Home & Garden show, I had been asking people for testimonials.

"Hey, Joel?" I said. "Could you maybe write me something you liked about the pillows? I'm just starting out and I'm trying to collect testimonials to help me advertise."

Joel heaved a huge sigh, as if this were the biggest inconvenience in the world. "All right, I'll write you something." I handed him a scrap of paper. He scribbled something down, slapped the paper on top of his check, and shoved both in my hand. "Now get the hell out of here."

Back in my truck, I read what Joel had written: "I'm 82 years old and I don't like a damn thing, but these pillows are OK."

Today, we've sold tens of millions of pillows, but Joel's testimonial is still my all-time favorite.

CHAPTER

22

Saving Uncle Butch

December rolled around again and along with it came my annual Iowa deer hunting trip that I never miss, even to this day. This year, a huge snowstorm was expected. Usually Skelly, Tom, Mark, Jeff, Doug and I camped. But this year because of the stormy weather, we decided to stay in a motel in Fairmont. One night near the end of the hunt, we closed down the Fairmont VFW hall and everyone headed to the hotel. But I was high on cocaine and there was no way I could sleep. Instead of going to the hotel, I decided to go see if my Uncle Butch was still up.

This was the uncle who'd hitched a ride with my friend Rick and me and beat me at gin rummy all the way from Minnesota to Kansas. More than 20 years had passed and Uncle Butch's alcoholism had worsened over time. He was still a good-hearted drunk, but he had also become what is known as a maintenance drinker. A maintenance drinker is someone who has consumed so much alcohol for so long that his or her body now requires a certain level of alcohol in order to function.

That was Uncle Butch. He started off drinking around the clock because he liked to. Then he drank around the clock because he had to.

My uncle's real name was Charles Booth Jr., and he was the son of my grandfather, the Deadwood card dealer, as well as his namesake. The two had a terrible relationship, one that had ended when my grandfather died in 1967. I wasn't sure if that was part of the pain that drove him to drink, but he had become the most serious alcoholic I had ever known, and I'd known plenty.

Divorced, with a grown son and daughter, Uncle Butch had always been a jack-of-all-trades, drifting between jobs, bunking in with different relatives. Now, he was doing odd jobs and living rent-free in an apartment over a grocery store called Gunther's Foods, thanks to the kindness of one of the store's owners.

When I left the VFW, the snow was falling in fat flakes that swirled in the glow of the streetlights. I climbed the steps to my uncle's apartment and tapped on the door. He was happy to see me, and we sat down in a tiny run-down living room to talk. Looking around, I saw a clutter of empty liquor bottles and also, in a dark corner, a man I'd never seen before. Sipping something brown from a half-empty highball glass, he was about 20 years younger than my uncle and had stringy hair that touched his shoulders. He glanced at me, then returned to nursing his drink. Uncle Butch did not introduce us.

I was worried about my uncle. This was a man who hadn't had an alcohol-free day in at least 40 years. Where his relatives had once welcomed him, they now more or less tolerated him. He'd gotten to where he would drink himself to sleep in broad daylight in someone's living room, or break something valuable and not remember it. When my sister Cindy got married, she and her first husband kept a commemorative bottle of champagne from their wedding day. They held onto that bottle for years, until the day Uncle Butch found it, popped the cork, and drank it.

Incidents like that strained Butch's relationships, but I knew he didn't have a malicious bone in his body. I sat down with my uncle, who reminded people a little of George W. Bush. We chatted about this and that for a few minutes. Out of the blue, I started talking to him about his drinking.

To this day, I have absolutely no recollection of what I said, but I suspect it went something like this: "You know what, Uncle Butch? We all care for you so much. Life can be so good, but you're missing it because you spend all your time with these bottles." I gestured around at the mess. "It's such hard work to be an alcoholic, isn't it?" I then named one of his recent misadventures, something I knew he'd done in a blackout state. "That's not you, Uncle Butch. I know that's not you. You're a good person."

I realized it was a speech I could have, and should've, been giving to myself. As I've said, being an addict was incredibly hard work, too. Through all this, Uncle Butch looked at me sadly. But every now and then, I thought I saw a glimmer of hope in his eyes. Just a spark. I told him that my friends and I would be finished with our hunt the following day. "How about if I come over and get you when we're through? I'll drive you up to the Cities and get you some help."

To my amazement, Uncle Butch agreed.

The next day, after we finished another successful hunt, I told my buddies we were going to pick up my uncle. We drove Uncle Butch up to the Cities and checked him into the Salvation Army. I visited him there a few months later, and for the first time in my life I saw my uncle sober. He was doing great. Working the front desk with all his natural-born charm on display, he was practically running the place. I was thrilled for him and gratified that by just giving a little of my time, I'd been able to help.

Looking back, I find it interesting that I could talk the talk so well, but never walk the walk. By 2005, my addictions were accelerating. With no boundaries and no self-control, I had become a runaway train.

My drug habit was getting more and more expensive. Also I hadn't stopped gambling, especially sports betting, my first and most dangerous addiction. One football weekend in the fall of 2005, it started out badly on Saturday and got steadily worse. By Tuesday morning, I owed my bookie Ed $20,000.

Ed was a short Asian man with deep pockets and a long fuse. He and I had become friends, so whenever I was unable to make good on a bad bet, he let me make payments. He knew I was good for it, and I never let him down. But this time I was into him for 20 grand—not the kind of debt I'd ever take care of with a payment plan. That Tuesday morning, I met with Ed and pleaded with him for more time, promising to pay him everything I owed the following Tuesday. Finally, he agreed.

I needed a big win the next weekend to cover my losses. More, it had to be a sure thing.

A friend of mine had once told me about someone you could call to find out about fixed games. With the obscene amount of money involved in sports these days, fixed games are not as common as they once were, but they're still around. My friend gave me a phone number, and I dialed what was basically a direct line to the East Coast Mobster Department of Rigged Sports. In a Jersey accent right out of the movies, the guy on the other end of the phone checked me out. Then, for a fee of $5,000, he told me about a fixed college football game coming up that weekend. The mob was paying the quarterback big money to throw the game.

With the inside information, I placed a $25,000 bet (money I didn't have), taking the team with the honest quarterback (who had no idea he'd already won) and a two-point spread. That meant that if my team won by at least three points, I'd make $25,000. Then I could pay off Ed, as well as the $5,000 I had borrowed from a friend to pay the fixer. My debt would be erased. But if I lost I would be out over $50,000. I couldn't let my mind go there.

On game day, I went pheasant hunting with some friends near Aberdeen, South Dakota. It was a bright fall day and the sky was deep blue over the cornfields. With our guns crooked in our arms, we made our way methodically down the rows of corn. Every so often, a flurry of wings would break the quiet and a gunshot would bang in the clear autumn air. But I wasn't paying much attention. With every step I took, my mind was thousands of miles away, on a football field where my life was being decided. One step, I would panic and think, what if fixed games aren't even real? The next step, I would calm myself. Of course, they're real! And I'd feel confident again.

When we reached the end of the cornfield, I pulled out my cell phone and dialed a score-line service. My team, the one with the honest QB, was up, 14–0. I screamed at the top of my lungs. Yes! They heard me all the way across the field. On my way back through the field, a couple of pheasants took flight right in front of me. I was usually a sharp shot during pheasant season, but I was so distracted, I didn't even raise my shotgun.

Pokey, the former Schmitty's Regular who was also one of my hunting buddies, scowled at me. "What are you *doing?*"

"Sorry," I mumbled. "I didn't see them."

Back at the other end of the field, I placed another call. It was halftime, and my team was ahead, 28–0. With that, I knew my team was going to win. I sucked in a huge breath, feeling like a weight had been lifted from my shoulders.

I shared the news with my friends. Pokey just looked at me. "Great," he said. "Are you finally going to hunt now?"

I resumed stalking birds in the cornfield, now paying attention. We made it to the end of the mile-long field, and I dialed the score-line again, expecting to hear something like 42–0. Instead, my blood ran cold as I heard the score: 28–14. My face must've gone white because one of my hunting buddies looked at me and said, "Did someone die?"

Yes, I thought, and it's going to be me.

I called the fixer in New York and demanded to know what was going on.

"There's a little problem," he said. "That QB we paid off—he broke his arm before halftime. The second-string quarterback has the flu. The third-stringer is in there, and he's throwing touchdowns like crazy."

The *third*-stringer? Are you kidding me? Ending the call, I told my friends I had to go into town to see the end of the game. They all knew I'd probably bet huge, but the look on my face told them things weren't looking good. My pickup's tires threw up a cloud of dust as I sped toward Aberdeen. On the drive I checked the score again: 28–21.

In town, I drove past a couple of bars, hitting the brakes only when I saw one with a satellite dish on the roof. I pulled up and ran in. Inside, a handful of locals were watching the Nebraska game.

Out of breath, I said, "Hey, guys, I've got $25,000 on a different game, and my life is over if I don't win. Can I buy you all drinks if we switch the channel, just until the end of the game?" Due to the panic on my face, they all agreed. Or maybe it was the offer of free drinks.

The score was still 28–21, with my team up. Eleven seconds were left on the clock. The third-string QB on the team that was supposed to lose was under center at midfield. He took the snap. He backed up to throw. The defense swarmed the backfield. It looked like they had him.

But the QB scrambled and slipped free. A linebacker gave chase, and I *willed* him to tackle this guy. The linebacker wrapped his arms around the QB's legs, but the guy popped out again, drew back his arm, and threw a long bomb. The ball arced downfield. I stopped breathing. An enemy receiver leapt up, pulled the ball down, sprinted for the touchdown…

…and was tackled just short of the end zone! The clock ticked down to zero!

"I won! I won!" I shouted and danced around the bar. I'd just wiped out $25,000 in debt. Another miraculous escape! What are the odds?

Then a guy with a free beer in his hand said, "You do realize they stop the clock in college to move the chains?"

I stopped celebrating. Of course I knew that, but I was so delirious, I'd forgotten. I peered up at the TV and saw the officials moving the chains. One of them stood next to the ball, faced the end zone, and extended his right arm. First down. The head referee then faced the camera and said the last words I wanted to hear at that moment: "Reset the game clock to two seconds."

Suddenly, I felt sick. I watched in disbelief as they punched the ball in for a touchdown. The score was 28–27. My team was now up by one.

Okay, don't panic, I thought. You've got a two-point spread. They'll make the extra point, and this thing will go into overtime. If your team wins by even a field goal, you'll still make the spread, and this will all just have been a nightmarish close call.

The teams faced off at the 3-yard line. The long snapper hiked the ball. The holder took the snap and placed it. The kicker booted it for the extra point—

No good. The kick went wide.

The kick went wide.

My team won by a single point. They had not covered the spread. I had lost.

Everyone stared at me in stunned silence. I turned and walked out of the bar without saying a word. Outside, the cold South Dakota air hit me in the face. I felt completely helpless. I had no idea what I was going to do. I now owed over $50,000.

Back at our hotel, I pretended to my friends that things weren't as bad as they really were. I didn't want to ruin their trip. The next day, Sunday, I called Ed and tried to place bets like it was no big deal. But he immediately started asking where his money was. At that, I broke down and told him I didn't have a dime to my name.

"Mike, it's time you quit betting on the games," Ed said. "If you promise me you won't bet on sports anymore, I will help you."

I almost did a double take and looked at the phone.

As I hung up with Ed, I had never felt so much relief. I had been given grace. What are the odds that I would lose a *fixed game*? And bookies? Bookies make their money by sending leg-breakers when you owe them that much. But somehow, I'd gotten myself in debt to a tiny Asian bookie with a heart of gold.

I knew it was some kind of divine intervention. And because of that, the fixed-game fiasco was the last sports bet I ever made.

After losing that bet, I didn't let Karen know how bad things were. As we headed into the holidays, pillow sales were steady, and we also had regular income from a distribution deal I'd made with a man named Wayne Belisle.

By the spring of 2005, the whole MyPillow operation consisted of about 10 people. Seeing the potential in my product, Jim Furlong and a friend named Bruce Johnson joined the team, along with some of Charlie's friends in manufacturing.

Capital was still scarce, and we were living show to show. I would usually take whatever money I had made from a show and head to the blackjack tables in Wisconsin or Laughlin. It was a lot of pressure every week, especially when I had to come up with the money to buy fabric.

Then came a chance for stable income. I met Wayne's son, Tom, during a home show. Intrigued by our product, Tom called his dad to tell him how busy we were. I met Wayne soon after and he proposed the distribution agreement: I would keep doing my own shows while he would buy a monthly supply of pillows at wholesale. His son would then resell them at a profit. This sounded good to me, because it meant Karen and I would receive guaranteed income every month. At least that's the way I understood the agreement.

And we received that income—until November. When Wayne didn't buy product as scheduled, I called him to ask what was going on.

"Tom has enough pillows on hand, Mike," Wayne said. "We don't need any more right now."

The problem was that sales didn't go as well for Tom as Wayne or I had expected. I didn't really know why, but I did know I was expecting and relying on Wayne's money, and I told him so.

"We have a contract," I said.

"Yes, we do," Wayne said. Then he pointed out the wording of our distribution agreement didn't require him to buy pillows monthly; he only had to buy a certain number *annually*. Technically, he could wait until August of the next year to buy the rest of his year's allotment of pillows. I knew I should have had a lawyer look at the contract, but I didn't have the money for that at the time.

I panicked. I needed that income stream. But I had another problem. Wayne brought to my attention that the deadline for applying for a patent on the pillow was coming up in the month of November. Applying for a patent is a complicated and technical process. It also requires hiring a patent lawyer, and those guys don't come cheap.

Wayne really believed in MyPillow's potential. He found a good patent attorney and loaned me the money to cover the attorney and fees. We got the application in just in time and began the long wait to see if the U.S. Patent and Trademark Office would approve it. I now owed Wayne tens of thousands of dollars.

The holidays arrived and MyPillow sales continued climbing. That was good. But I still wasn't earning enough to pay Wayne, my mortgage, and my bookie. I was just praying we could grow home show sales enough to keep us afloat. That's when Wayne suggested another deal: He would buy MyPillow outright.

I hated the idea of giving up the company. On the other hand, I was broke and tired of being broke. Wayne told me to give it some serious thought and talk to Karen. It meant I would still be an owner, but he would have the controlling interest, and he wanted to make sure I would be okay with that. He gave me until the end of the month to decide. Reluctantly, in December 2005 I agreed to sell a majority of MyPillow.

CHAPTER

23

"You Can't Stop Me"

Wayne Belisle's offer to buy MyPillow included wiping out the patent debt I owed him, along with $100,000 in cash. He would also make Karen and me salaried employees. As I contemplated the deal, I thought about that a lot. Regular income and a clean slate. The idea appealed to me.

I told Wayne I would meet him on December 22 to sign the deal. That afternoon was bitter cold and overcast. I jumped in my pickup and drove east on I-494 toward Bloomington to meet Wayne as agreed. When I pulled my truck up to the Sofitel, a low, sprawling hotel not far from the famous Mall of America, I didn't see Wayne's car in the parking lot. Maybe he was already inside, waiting to take over my company. Part of me hoped he'd changed his mind.

I was a little early, so after cutting the ignition, I sat in my truck for a few minutes, thinking. On the one hand, signing the deal would mean a fresh start for Karen and me. On the other, the second I signed, MyPillow would belong to someone else. Forever.

My reluctance wasn't really about the money. It was that strange dream that was nagging at me—that "out-of-body essay," or whatever you wanted to call it. I hadn't looked at those six pages since putting them behind the album cover. Now, I tried to recall what I had written.

There was something about a platform. I remembered that much. Then there was that weird phone call from Cindy with the story about her pastor. That part was still perfectly clear—me standing in my garage, holding my cell to my ear.

"The dream said I'd know when the time is right," I'd told her.

"And when that time comes, you have to do it," she'd said. "You promise me that."

That essay hadn't had anything to do with MyPillow, but now I was beginning to feel the two were connected. On the other hand, I had to be practical. Card counting wasn't working out so well, and I was spending so much money on coke and crack that I needed money again for Christmas presents. And to be completely honest, for food.

The truck engine ticked. The temperature outside was somewhere in the 20s, and frigid air had seeped into the truck cab, pushing out the residual warmth from the heater. Finally, I sighed heavily and headed for the hotel restaurant.

Wayne was already seated inside. He greeted me warmly and gestured toward the opposite chair. On the table in front of him sat the purchase contract, a notebook, and a pen.

We made small talk for a few minutes. Wayne spoke with the relaxed rhythm of a man comfortable with doing business, but my nerves jittered. Finally, he smiled across the table at me, picked up his pen and asked, "Well, are you ready to get this done?"

After my long internal wrestling match about this decision, I thought I would hesitate when the moment came, but I didn't. Instead I said straight out, "I'm sorry, Wayne, but I've been thinking a lot about this, and I just can't sell my company."

Wayne's face flushed, and he stabbed his ballpoint pen into his notebook so hard that the tip came out the other side. He started yelling. I started yelling. Soon hotel security appeared and insisted we depart the premises. Wayne and I argued all the way across the parking lot until we both got in our vehicles, each slamming the doors.

I sat in my truck red-faced, my heart beating fast from the adrenaline of the argument. I was frightened but elated. I had no idea how we were going to survive, but I still had my company. I had no idea then how hard I would have to fight to keep it.

In late 2005, I borrowed money from my dad to keep the business going. But by the spring of 2006, we were out of cash again, and my solution was to refinance our house. It was the middle of the subprime mortgage boom, and we could get more money than our house was worth. Even at that, we'd only get $20,000 cash. Still, it felt like a fresh start. I promised myself I was going to do better this time. Once again though, crack got in the way.

Karen and I drove to Milwaukee for a show at the fairgrounds. We'd learned there was an office in town where we could sign the closing papers for our refinance. On the drive, we ran through our remaining cocaine supply and, with only $200 to our names, knew we would have to get more when we got into town. That's how twisted our priorities were: Here we were, on our way to borrow the last bit of cash we could, but our first objective in Milwaukee was to get more drugs.

As we made our way to the hotel, I suspected we were driving in a pretty bad neighborhood. I called my dealer Joe, who confirmed it. "Get out of there now," he said.

I didn't. Instead, after dropping Karen off at the hotel, I made a series of addict moves that ended with me surrendering my wedding ring to one thug and—when some guy pulled a pistol from a Fritos bag and pointed it at my head—my truck to another. By 5 a.m., I was being held captive in a hotel room. It's all a blur now, but somehow I got everything back. And somewhere in there, I got my crack. It was always about the crack.

That morning, I convinced Karen to do the pillow show by herself. Lying in bed after she left, I asked myself the same question over and over: *What has crack done to us?*

Karen had been a captive to all the craziness. For years, she'd had more confidence in me than anyone on the planet. By this time though, everything was crumbling around her. People now whispered in her ear constantly: *I can't believe you put up with him.*

Most of the time, despite our financial mess, I felt no fear. I was a survivor, a Houdini who somehow always managed to beat the odds. Now though, worry simmered underneath my calm exterior. With each new low, I thought that maybe my miraculous supply of luck had run out. I was terrified of letting my wife and kids down once and for all.

Still, I didn't let Karen know how worried I was, just like I never let the pit bosses know I'd just lost my last chip.

After I backed out of selling Wayne Belisle the company, it struck me that maybe he had been trying to take advantage of my financial desperation. But I soon realized that he was just a businessman who saw an opportunity. His plan had been to acquire a potentially valuable product while also offering Karen and me some financial security in exchange. He had been offering me a win-win.

Very quickly though, another man came along who did not have Wayne's integrity. I'll call him Barry Price.

Tall, with a feather-duster moustache and thick, salt-and-pepper hair, Price was a multimillionaire businessman of national prominence. Sometimes featured in business magazines, he presented himself as both an ethical man and a patriot. Price had learned about MyPillow the same way Wayne did, through the home shows, which I had continued doing.

I was encouraged when he called me in early 2006. After several friendly conversations, I felt that if we could arrange a fair distribution deal in one of the retail chains Price owned, I could really get MyPillow off the ground. I set up a meeting with Price, an investor friend of his, and Wayne. As an investor in the MyPillow patent, Wayne still had a substantial interest in my company.

By April 2006, spring rains had come and Minnesota was turning green again. The day of the Price meeting, which happened to be the day after my trip to Milwaukee, I drove to the corporate headquarters of one of the companies he owned and found my way to a conference room. I was wearing jeans and a polo shirt. When I sat down at a table full of suits, I instantly felt inferior.

If only these guys knew where I was yesterday, I thought. In fact, looking around at the suits, I felt like I was in an episode of *American Greed*. I'd felt safer with the Milwaukee guy who pulled a gun on me. At least he was up front about his agenda.

Over the next couple of hours, Price and his investor friend put forth various propositions that would have cost me some measure of control or ownership of my company in exchange for an infusion of cash. I declined them all. Finally, Price proposed selling a private-label version of my product in his stores. It was the arrangement I'd been hoping for and I said yes. Then he made another offer.

"Mike, with my resources, I can make pillows cheaper than you can," he said. "If you'll let me have your foam-producing machine, I'll pay you for it, and then I'll sell you quantities of pillows when you need them for your shows at less than it costs you to make them now."

He had my attention. With little manpower and no capital, the high cost of manufacturing had cut deeply into potential profits ever since I made my first pillows. At this point, I had little choice if I wanted to keep my company alive.

Reluctantly, I signed a one-page contract selling him my machine. Soon after this meeting, Price sent a panel truck to collect the machine, which was really that converted hammer mill I'd found on the Olson farm. As my landlord, Dick, used a forklift to lift the machine onto the truck, he turned to me and said, "Mike, are you really sure you want to do this?"

His question irritated me, but I understood why he asked it. My foam-producing machine was proprietary, and it was risky turning it over. But by partnering with a businessman of Price's stature, I felt I could take MyPillow to the next level.

"Just put it on the truck," I said. "I know what I'm doing."

But, as I watched the truck disappear down the road, my machine in its belly, I knew deep down that I had made a terrible mistake.

That same April, we got some awful news: My Uncle Butch had died. The news saddened me deeply. For about a month after rehab, he'd done so well. But he relapsed badly and drank heavily for the next two years. Finally, Uncle Butch succumbed to the effects of alcoholism in a hotel room in Wyoming, all alone.

A few days later, a small congregation gathered for his funeral in Fairmont. After the service, I stepped outside the church to have a cigarette with my dad, Jim, who had come to the funeral to honor his former brother-in-law. We were standing together, exhaling smoke streams into the cool spring air, when a clean-cut man wearing a suit walked up to me.

I'd noticed him sitting in the pews with us earlier, but hadn't paid much attention to him. Now, I was shocked when he gave me a hug and said, "I've got to thank you. You saved my life."

"Okay...?" I said, and took a step back to put some space between us.

"You don't remember me, do you?" the stranger said.

I shook my head. "No, I don't."

"Remember a couple years ago, that snowy night? Do you remember a guy with long hair sitting in the corner of your uncle's place?"

That gave me another shock. "That was you?"

"The stuff you said," the man went on. "Well, that night I quit using and found God."

Like Uncle Butch, he'd gone immediately to a rehab center. A doctor there told him that if he didn't quit drinking, he'd die within a month. Unlike Uncle Butch, he hadn't taken a drink since. He'd been sober for two years, he told me, and was doing great.

My heart warmed at his story, and I smiled. "Congratulations!" I said.

Then a question occurred to me, one that had bugged me for all the years I'd talked other people into taking a chance on sobriety. "What did I say to you back then?" I asked. "And why did you believe me when I was doing drugs and drinking myself?"

"I don't remember what you said, but it made a lot of sense."

With people like Tony in Tunica and Michael in Vegas, I'd talked about how being an addict is such hard work. About how being an addict isn't something you *are*, it's something you *do*—and about making the choice to do something else, something higher and better. I was disappointed that this man didn't remember what I said to Uncle Butch because I needed to know for myself.

As we agreed, Barry Price began manufacturing and selling the private-label pillows while I continued doing shows and fairs. Very quickly, the stock of pillows I'd already made ran low, and I called Price to place an order of his new, lower-cost version. He did not return my call, so I called again.

And again.

And again.

I had to telephone Price many times before he finally answered. "I need some pillows," I said when I had him on the line. "We've got more shows coming up."

"I can't give them to you," Price said. "My people are having problems with your machine."

Well, why didn't you say so sooner? I thought. "Let me come out and see your people, Barry. I can show them how to use it."

"The machine's not here. I sent it to a manufacturer in North Dakota." He hung up.

North Dakota?

We had already signed up for several shows and paid the deposits. How was I going to get more pillows and fulfill those obligations? After some digging, I learned the exact location of the hammer mill and drove five hours to a medium-sized city in North Dakota. I took Charlie with me. Together, we found my machine in a small, run-down building in the middle of town. It wasn't even plugged in.

"Why aren't you using it to make fill for the pillows?" I asked the owner of the building, who had begrudgingly unlocked his property to let me in. The man was in partnership with Price.

"We tried it, but when we put the foam in a tick and washed the pillow, the foam swelled up. Something must be wrong."

"You can't use just any foam," I said. "I brought some of the right foam with me. Can you just let me make foam for some pillows?"

The owner gave me an icy glare. "No," he said. "This isn't your machine anymore. Get off my property."

All the way home, I pondered what I was going to do next. Price had bought my hammer mill fair and square and then quarantined it, put it on the bench. It was late July. The Steele County Free Fair in Owatonna—the largest county fair in Minnesota—was coming up in mid-August. This was one of the biggest sales opportunities of the year for me, and I had nothing to sell. Then it came to me: I'd made one foam-shredder. I would just have to make another.

The money from the home refinance in Milwaukee had come in. I used it to buy another hammer mill and got the help of an engineer friend to adapt it for making my pillow fill. With rewiring, the new machine ran like a dream—better than the old one, in fact.

Soon, MyPillows were stacking up in the bus shed again. Then, two days before Steele County, I got a call. "I know you're doing the fair," Barry Price said. "I've got pillows for you."

I scowled into the phone. "What do you mean you've got pillows for me?"

"We made some pillows. How many do you want?"

I didn't need his pillows, but now I was curious. "How much?"

He named a price that was double what he'd told me earlier. Suddenly, everything became clear. All along, Price had wanted to control my manufacturing, because he knew he could gouge me for my own pillows.

"Barry, I don't need your pillows," I said with satisfaction. "I'm making my own again. I invented that machine you have, you know. Did you really not think I could make another one? The new one is state of the art, too. Yours is obsolete."

"How could you afford to do that?"

"Money's never stopped me in my life, Barry," I said. "And when you didn't make pillows for me when I needed them, you broke our agreement. From here on out, you are to have nothing more to do with MyPillow."

Price's tone turned dark. "Mike, I'm a millionaire, and you can't stop me."

CHAPTER
24

Millionaires and Billionaires

I was quickly learning that it's much easier to maneuver your way into ownership of an existing product than to invent one yourself. But Price didn't scare me. He had said I couldn't stop him, but he couldn't stop me either. The fair season went well for us that year, and MyPillow seemed to be taking off. Our family business was small but growing and that gave us hope. On the family front, though, things were different.

With crack you start losing things. Karen and I had lost something. She and the kids had been my number one priority. Now crack was number one. Increasingly, the drug was coming between us. We began hiding our crack from each other—or at least each of us thought the other was hiding it. I remember getting into yelling matches about that, accusing each other of holding out. As trust leaked away, anger and suspicion began to replace softness and respect.

It was also becoming harder to hide our drug use from the kids. More and more, I canceled activities with them. Even when I would try to be a good dad and go to one of the boys' ballgames, I would sneak off to the park restroom and do cocaine off the ceramic toilet tank lid. Afterwards, my sons would come up to me and ask, "Did you see that, Dad?" I made up half-truths and outright lies, knowing all the while that time was slipping through my fingers. I knew it and felt powerless to stop it.

And yet, as strange as it sounds, many who were closest to us had no idea we were addicts. When Jim and I weren't doing home shows, we were team-counting to support our families and subsidize the business. That meant Jim and I in particular spent a ton of time together, and yet he had no idea I was a crackhead. In fact, our adventures in card counting were forging a very close friendship.

Once, the two of us, with Nick and Corey, drove two hours to Jackpot Junction Casino in Morton, Minnesota, to bring in some badly needed cash. But when we got there, we couldn't find a place to play. Most of the tables were too crowded. Then when we found a good table, we couldn't get a positive deck.

Jim, Corey, and I were watching from a distance, sipping cocktails and soft drinks, as Nick played spotter at a table with a four-deck shoe. I was drinking a beer and Jim was drinking a Mountain Dew. Nick hit a big deviation, losing every hand when he should've been winning. The cards just would not fall and the advantage stayed with the house. After a whole day of bad decks, Jim had finally had enough.

Keeping his eyes on Nick's table, Jim said to us quietly, "Hey guys, watch this."

And here's what happens next: He walks over to the table, his cup of iced Mountain Dew still in his hand. Jim stands there watching for a moment as if deciding whether to sit down and join the game. Then he fumbles his drink. The cup falls from his hand and lands right in the middle of the table, soaking all the cards on the felt, as well as the ones in the dealer's shoe.

"Oh no!" Jim says, the picture of embarrassment. "I can't believe I did that! I'm so sorry!"

Nick's got Mountain Dew on his shirt and pretends to be annoyed. Corey and I crack up. And the dealer has to change out all the cards in the shoe.

Still "embarrassed," Jim sits down and starts counting—with a new deck. Now the cards are finally falling our way, and he signals our jumper, Corey. Jim leaves the table. He and I have to get lost so that the casino won't know we're all together. We decide to go wait for Corey in a nearby men's room. At this point, Jim is really nervous. The deck has gone positive but the cards have been terrible all day, we're already deep into our bank, and Corey is now betting $300 a hand.

It seems like forever before my brother rejoins us, and when he does, the news isn't good.

"I lost it all," he says, hanging his head.

Jim loses it, just goes absolutely nuts. Corey takes it for a minute or so, then cuts him off. "I was just kidding," he says with a grin. He pulls out a thick stack of hundreds and waves it in our faces. "I won big!"

Corey and I crack up again. Jim looks like he can't decide whether to hug Corey or punch him in the mouth.

And that's how 2006 unfolded: card counting, home shows, and fairs. Then, that August at the Minnesota State Fair, Wayne Belisle walked up to my booth and said, "Mike, I want you to buy me out."

The Belisles weren't selling nearly as many pillows as they had expected. Also, I still owed him $84,000 for the MyPillow patent. In an effort to make good on the loan, I offered to add Wayne's name to the patent as collateral and he accepted. I had every intention of paying Wayne back. I just didn't know how I was going to manage it.

Meanwhile, the Barry Price situation simmered in the background. He still had my original machine. If he ever got it up and running, he could copy my product and compete with me. The whole thing was bugging me, especially Price's arrogant threat that he would use his millionaire status to bully me. I could not have predicted that my next card-counting trip would present a solution.

After fair season ended, I flew to Laughlin, Nevada, where I planned to count at the Riverside Casino to raise more cash. I had been flying to Laughlin as often as every other month between 2004 and 2006. Recently, I had been getting to know the casino owner, Don Laughlin, on a personal basis. Don was a business visionary and I admired his drive and innovation. He had started in 1966 with an eight-room hotel and three employees, and used to deal blackjack himself. By the time I started getting to know him, it would take Don half an hour just to walk across the gaming floor of the Riverside. The power bill alone at his property had gone from $170 a month in 1966 to $360,000 a month in the 2000s. And he could afford it.

While visiting with Don at the Riverside in October 2006, I mentioned my problems with Barry Price, hoping Don could give me some advice. "He lied to me, then tried to gouge me, then threatened me," I complained. "I don't know how to get rid of him."

"I think I can help you with that," Don said. He took one of his business cards and wrote on the back, "Mike is a friend of mine. I have an interest in MyPillow."

Smiling, I put his card in my pocket. I flew back to Minnesota and couldn't wait to get off the plane.

I called Price. "Let's meet," I said.

We got together at one of Price's offices, each of us offering fake pleasantries. Then I asked, "Do you know Don Laughlin?"

"Of course I know Don Laughlin…know *of* him." Don, an Owatonna, Minnesota, native, is famous in the state.

"Well, I do know Don," I said. "You may be a millionaire, but Don is a *billionaire* and here's his card."

I watched Price's fake smile flatten as he read the back of Don's card. "Effective immediately," I said, "you will stop selling MyPillow."

"Well, I guess this is where we part ways," he said evenly. He shook my hand and walked away. I headed for my truck and drove home smiling. Barry Price never bothered me again.

While I was happy to get rid of Price, I was still eager to take MyPillow to the next level. I wanted to hire more salespeople and take my product to more shows. I also wanted to film an infomercial, which I felt would multiply our direct sales far more rapidly than doing individual shows. But all those goals required money, so I went in search of investors.

My brother Corey suggested I talk to a man named Jack Colby, who owned a successful supply business that catered to the hospitality industry. I first met Colby at a bar in Chaska. He had a wide, jovial smile and seemed to be a down-to-earth guy. Coming with Corey's recommendation, I felt I could trust him. A little later, Colby introduced me to his friend, another businessman named Shelby Bates.

I couldn't get a read on Bates, who was very quiet. But along with Colby, he expressed interest in buying stock in my company. I developed a business plan that projected double-digit growth, as well as a marketing plan that included the infomercial.

In November 2006, after a series of discussions, I sold Colby and Bates 38 percent of the stock in MyPillow. The money from the sale would enable me to expand. As part of the deal, Karen and I would become employees of MyPillow and receive a salary. That did not mean I was giving up control. Under IRS rules for corporations, a person can be an owner/board member and draw profits and also be a salaried employee. The arrangement meant that the Lindell family could stop living from show to show for the first time since we'd started the company. Also, I stipulated that I would keep the Minnesota State Fair, always the most lucrative show of the year, for myself.

At this point, MyPillow did not have a board of directors. To comply with the tax code, Colby and Bates advised we create one. Of course, they wanted to be on it and since they were major investors, I agreed. So, we set up the board with just three members: Colby, Bates, and me. To raise more capital, we then sold common stock to a number of smaller investors.

Part of me felt good about this. MyPillow was growing, becoming more formalized and less fly-by-night. On the other hand, I very quickly started getting the impression that Colby and Bates cooperated with me on the surface but were really laughing at me behind my back. It was worse than that as it turned out. They were actually moving methodically to stab me *in* the back.

The turnaround happened quickly. For about three weeks, I felt I was in the driver's seat. The board rules stated that stockholders possessing 60 percent or more of the shares could vote off members of the board. I figured that if Colby and Bates became a real problem, the other stockholders and I could kick them off. But they had moved quickly and quietly to eliminate this possibility. Between them, Colby and Bates bought 3 percent of the company from another stockholder. That gave them a combined 41 percent. Now they were invulnerable.

Securing their positions on the board was just the start. Colby and Bates began storing pillows in their own warehouse in Inver Grove Heights, about an hour's drive away. They began to insert themselves between my employees and me, convincing them I was a liability and that they were the ones who would take MyPillow national.

The takeover took only weeks. I'd only sold them that initial block of shares in November, and by our December shareholders meeting, it all came to a head. Out in the parking lot before the meeting, which was being held at their offices. I did a big line of cocaine in my car. Then I walked into the conference room jazzed up and confident. Colby and Bates sat with the other stockholders, with official-looking papers and portfolios in their hands. From the start, the tone of the meeting was contentious.

Colby and Bates tried to convince me to put the money I'd earned at the Minnesota State Fair back into the company's coffers. I refused. They didn't push it. We'd already made an agreement about that. They then outlined a new strategy that focused on selling MyPillow through retail outlets.

I objected. "We're doing shows and an infomercial. Didn't you read my business plan?"

A stockholder—who was my cousin, actually—said, "Just a minute, Mike. We want to know what these guys have to say." With that, I could feel that I was losing control of the shareholders' group, the board, and my company.

There was more discussion and several more items of business. When the meeting concluded, everyone filed out except for Colby, Bates, my brother Corey, and me.

Colby looked across the table at me and said, "Mike, we're moving the company to Inver Grove Heights. Also, you and Karen are fired."

CHAPTER

25

The Feds

Y ou read that right: I was fired from my own company. I was shocked, as was Corey. You could argue that when Neff tried to hijack the Schmitty's contract, I should have seen it coming. After all, my bookie's nephew had warned me. But now two respected businessmen had taken over MyPillow within weeks of engineering a majority on a board they had urged me to create.

Looking back, I realized that their initial buy-in of 38 percent may not have been a random number. Instead, it seemed calculated: high enough for me to raise a lot of capital, while low enough to seem nonthreatening. And it was Colby and Bates who urged that the corporate rules require a 60 percent shareholder majority to kick someone off the board. From the beginning, all they needed was another 3 percent of stock to drive me out. Maybe they even had that 3 percent lined up from the start. In business, a great product is much rarer than money. I've since learned that entrepreneurs without money have their products stolen or copied all the time.

After this, and my experience with Barry Price, I was beginning to think I couldn't trust a guy in a suit.

What happened next only reinforced that opinion. It had been more than three years since I declared a shady bankruptcy to avoid that shady dram shop lawsuit. Since then, a team of lawyers had been looking into my finances. Now we finally had a court date. In January 2007, Karen and I appeared before a bankruptcy judge in a courtroom at the Minneapolis U.S. District Court, an imposing tower of beige and glass. In addition to the lawyers sitting at tables normally reserved for the prosecution and defense, there were a few spectators in the gallery. Two of them seemed a bit out of place. They had closely clipped haircuts, and wore jackets and ties. Great, I thought. More suits.

"All rise," a bailiff said, then announced the arrival of the judge, who took his place at the raised bench.

"Be seated," the judge said.

I had gotten us into one heck of a mess, and it was all on the line right here. I'd lost more than $50,000 card counting in Vegas. I still owed Wayne $84,000 for the patent. I owed my friend Bob over $100,000, more money I'd borrowed against the Schmitty's contract in order to develop the pillow and build the company from which I'd just been fired. If the judge clawed back the Schmitty's contract, the lawyers would sell it, pull the assets back into the bankruptcy, and we'd be left with nothing. Prior to our hearing, I had cut a deal with the court. With money borrowed from my dad and more I borrowed from Bob, I handed the court $105,000 to pay off the bankruptcy. I projected that I would get at least half of this back.

The judge read our case aloud, then rendered his verdict: My Chapter 7 bankruptcy was granted. But there was a catch. The entire $105,000 I had already paid was to be used for attorneys' fees.

My temper erupted. "Objection!" I yelled at the judge. "This is wrong! They doubled their fees at the last minute!"

When I made the deal with the court, attorneys' fees were only $50,000. This was crooked and I knew it. But I also knew I'd gotten myself into this mess by declaring a fake bankruptcy. Now it was as though I'd been caught bringing illegal dice to an illegal dice game. I had put myself completely at the mercy of a crooked system.

The judge banged his gavel. "Mr. Lindell, you are out of order." He also confirmed that the lawyer's fee was allowable.

I pointed at the judge sitting up high on his bench. "Are you in on it, too?" I shouted.

He banged his gavel again. "Do you want to go to jail, Mr. Lindell?"

I then suffered a complete meltdown and started calling the lawyers in the court room every name in the book. This is it, I thought. End of the line. Before my "bankruptcy," I wasn't bankrupt, but now, ironically, I was. Furious with the judge, the lawyers, and with myself, I turned to leave the courtroom and Karen followed. I fully expected to be arrested on a contempt charge before I even made it out of the room.

Sure enough, as we neared the courtroom door, the two suits who had been sitting at the back of the gallery intercepted us in the aisle and grabbed me by the elbows.

"Mr. Lindell," one of them said, "FBI."

FBI? Are you kidding me? It was just a little fake bankruptcy. Why would the FBI be here?

The two feds hustled us out of the courtroom. As we walked down a tiled corridor, one of them said, "Your bankruptcy has been under investigation for the last three years. We've been waiting for the conclusion of your case."

The agents told us that these particular bankruptcy attorneys had a history of pooling the assets in bankruptcies, then matching their attorneys' fees to the value of the assets. When the cases concluded, the only ones getting any money were the lawyers. Apparently, though, the judge I'd just accused of corruption wasn't in on it.

Karen and I continued toward the elevators with the two agents. "Would you like to be a witness for us if you are needed?" one of them asked.

"Absolutely," I said. "But right now, I think I'm about to go to jail for what I said to the judge back there."

"Don't worry," the agent said. "We'll get you out of here."

The four of us took the elevator down to the lobby where several uniformed officers blocked our way. The FBI agents flashed their badges. "They're with us."

One second I was about to go to jail in a fake bankruptcy case for cursing out a judge. The next, officers of the law parted like the Red Sea and I walked out the door a free man—courtesy of the FBI!

What are the odds?

I may have been free, but I hadn't gotten off cheap. The money that I owed my dad and Bob still hung over my head, along with everything else. The FBI asked to see my financial records. Very quickly I handed them over, hoping the records would somehow prove the government's case against the bankruptcy lawyers. Then, about a week later, I got a notice from the Internal Revenue Service. Karen and I had been selected for an audit.

An audit? Now?

When I contacted the IRS, I told a bored civil servant that the FBI had all my records. She sounded skeptical, but said she'd check out my claim, which of course turned out to be true. Not long after that, I got a notice on

FBI letterhead stating that I was exempt from tax audits for seven years, beginning three years prior to the current year and stretching three years into the future.

The FBI letter was a silver lining, a breather in what for the past two years had been a very bumpy and mostly negative ride. It seemed the Feds also smoothed over the contempt charge because I never heard another word about that. And now, Karen and I needed a break.

In the film *The Shawshank Redemption*, actor Tim Robbins plays Andy Dufresne, a man serving prison time under a cruel warden for a murder he didn't commit. After making a secret decision to execute his plan of escape, Andy asks his friend Red, played by Morgan Freeman, "You know what the Mexicans say about the Pacific?"

"No," Red says as the two men sit against a wall in the prison yard.

"They say it has no memory. That's where I want to live the rest of my life. A warm place with no memory."

Andy Dufresne's plan sounded perfect to me. In February 2007, the month after the bankruptcy hearing, Karen and I, with Skelly and his wife, escaped to Mexico on that trip I told you about at the very beginning of this book.

In case you forgot, here's a little rewind: We land and check into our resort. I immediately go out and find the Greek to get free cocaine. On the fifth day, I'm about to run out of coke. In the middle of the night, I walk to that lonely place where the drug dealer Clean Cut calls in some coke to be delivered from the next town. Things go sideways and his enforcer, Eyes, lays his machete against my neck.

Remember him asking me for a cigarette, and me reaching into my t-shirt pocket to pull out my last one?

Remember the little packet of cocaine slipping up from the cellophane pack wrapper and into full view?

I will never forget it. My blood absolutely ran cold. Clean Cut had already suspected I was the gringo who was somehow connected with rival drug dealers. If he saw that I was here in the middle of the night trying to buy cocaine when I already had cocaine, he would decide I had set him up and his enforcer would kill me on the spot, 100 percent.

Nothing I had faced in my life—not jumping out of a moving bus, not faulty parachutes or motorcycle wrecks or bookie leg-breakers—had ever filled me with such terror.

This was the difference between *thinking* you're going to die and *knowing* you're going to die.

When that teener came up out of my pocket, all those thoughts blinked through my mind in less than a second. My right hand was still at my shirt pocket, pulling out Clean Cut's cigarette. Had he seen the teener of coke?

I had never practiced magic tricks but now I employed sleight of hand, using my right hand to slip the cigarette from the pack, crumple the cellophane wrapper around the teener, and tuck it back down into my pocket. Still terrified, I handed Clean Cut the cigarette and offered him a light, again with the same hand. My nerve endings screamed as I watched his eyes for any flicker of danger.

"*Gracias,*" he said with a small smile. There was a deep drag and a slow exhale. "Ah, here it comes."

He pointed toward a single headlight approaching from down the street. A young guy on a scooter slowed down just enough to toss Clean Cut a small package, then turned the throttle and disappeared into the night.

"There you go, *amigo,*" Clean Cut said, handing me a hundred bucks worth of coke. "I told you he would be here. Now you can go back to your wife."

Willing myself to stay calm, I took the packet. "Thanks," I said. As I walked away, I muttered a few more complaints about how shabbily they had treated a good customer such as myself. I hadn't even gone half a block when I found a picnic table on the sidewalk outside of a deserted bar, laid out a line of coke, and inhaled it like oxygen.

The next day, Skelly and I chartered a fishing boat. We had the whole boat to ourselves, a 35-footer, the same one we'd hired a couple of times before. It was the kind where you were supposed to catch big trophy fish, like dorado, sailfish, and marlin, but in previous years we had caught almost nothing. Being from Minnesota where the fishing is great, and being a guy with almost zero patience, I found this unacceptable.

The last time we came down, in 2006, I said to the captain, a middle-aged Mexican man, "Hey, we're tired of paying $450 to go out on these excursions and never catching anything. Tell you what, let's go double or nothing. If we catch a fish over a hundred pounds, we'll pay you double. But if we catch nothing, we pay nothing. Deal?"

The captain sized me up from under the bill of his ball cap and grinned. "*Sí, señor,* you have a deal."

He motored away from the pier and into a 6-foot swell that pitched the deck up and down like a carnival ride. Skelly and I both got seasick. Hours passed without a bite, and both of us were so green at the gills we were ready to puke. But the captain didn't care. He just stood at the wheel, smiling. I remember looking at Skelly and saying, "He's going to keep us out here until we catch a $900 fish."

Finally, we broke down and told him we'd pay him $450 just to take us to shore. He smiled again. "*Sí, señor,* you have a deal."

He came about and we were headed in when Skelly's line jerked. After a brief battle, he hauled in a 120-pound sailfish, and not long later, I landed a sailfish north of a hundred pounds, too. We forgot all about our seasickness, paid the captain his $900, and everybody went home happy.

On this trip though, I was not happy. We sat in the stern of the same boat, miles offshore, the deck rocking gently as we watched our lines. Sunlight sparkled off the calm, blue waters of the Pacific. Suddenly, I just started talking. I had already told Skelly a lot of my problems, but I had never told anyone how bad things really were. Now, I had to tell someone, but not Karen because I didn't want her to panic. Instead, I laid it all out in living color for my best friend.

I wasn't asking Skelly for money. For one thing, I didn't think any ordinary amount of money would help. I'd gotten us in so deep that only an amount in the hundreds of thousands would have made a difference. And the money I was wasting on drugs and on this vacation? To me, that was like saying that breathing was wasting effort on air. Karen and I *needed* this break, I rationalized. We never missed our vacations.

The fishing boat rocked and a gentle swell slapped against the hull as I spilled my guts. I told Skelly everything: My house was approaching foreclosure. Two guys had taken control of my corporate board. They had fired Karen and me from our own company. Wayne Belisle owned my patent and I owed him $84,000. I was in debt to the tune of more than $200,000…

As I ticked off all my problems, I watched Skelly's expression grow more and more grim. I finished my story and said, "If you were me, what would you do?"

My best friend looked at me. I could see that a large tear had formed in the corner of his right eye. He turned his gaze to the rail that ran along the edge of the boat, and to the deep ocean beyond.

"I'd jump," he said.

CHAPTER

26

Psyching Out the Suits

I'll tell you the truth: When Skelly said, "I'd jump," it rattled me. He wasn't the type of guy who got overly emotional. That my best friend would say that to me—and mean it—really took me by surprise.

More surprises waited back home. One Thursday in March 2007, soon after we returned from Mexico, I was sitting on my deck in Carver when Jack Colby and Shelby Bates showed up. It was about 9 a.m. We hadn't had much contact since they fired Karen and me in December. I had been brainstorming ways to take back control of my company. Colby and Bates had tried to get control of the MyPillow website, but I had set up the hosting account under a friend's name and she wouldn't give them access.

That morning, the duo knocked on my front door. Shocked that they had the gall to show up at my house, but also curious about what they wanted, I let them in and offered them beers. When they declined, I opened one for myself and we all took a seat out on the deck.

"Hey, Mike, we know you're under a deadline to make enough pillows for the next show," Bates said. His voice was strangely loud. "Can we get into the factory and help make some?"

The factory he referred to was the old bus shed across the street, where I kept the new hammer mill that produced my foam fill, which was still patent-pending. My sewing machines were in there, too, along with the foam and the custom-printed fabric we used to make the pillow ticks. This was the first time Colby and Bates had expressed any interest in the manufacturing side of the business. I looked at their clothes. These guys had not come dressed to work.

I took a sip of my beer. "No, sorry. You're not getting in there."

I had already been down this road before, with Barry Price. There was no way I was letting them in there. I didn't know what they were planning, but it certainly wasn't to help make pillows.

Now Colby spoke up. *"So, you're saying you're not letting us in your factory? Is that right?"*

He, too, was speaking very loudly, and in a weird, unnatural rhythm. It was so weird that I mocked Colby, echoing his volume. *"Yes. That's. What. I'm. Saying. Why. Are. You. Talking. So. Loud?"*

Both men kept pressing me with raised voices. It was like they had walked into an old folks' home and were trying to speak to the hard of hearing. Finally, Colby took a folded sheet of paper from his pocket and handed it to me with a smirk.

"I've got a court order requiring you to surrender your manufacturing equipment," he said. "As I told you in December, MyPillow has relocated to Inver Grove Heights, and we are moving the factory there."

I waved the court order away. By then, I didn't care what they had on a piece of paper.

Then, abruptly, Colby and Bates stood up and left. Even though I'd kept them out of the bus shed and away from my machine, their faces said they'd won the round. What was going on? I called a lawyer friend, Javier, and told him about the confrontation. "What would it take for these guys to force me to give them my equipment?" I asked.

"They would have to have in writing or on tape that you denied them access," Javier said.

That explained the bizarre meeting. Colby and Bates had been taping me. Now their hambone acting job made sense.

"Javier, you have to do me a favor," I said into the phone. "Find out if a judge has ordered law enforcement to let them into the factory. And find out when they're coming."

"I can't tell you that, Mike. I might be disbarred."

I begged a little, and we hung up. Fifteen minutes later, Javier called back. "Let's have lunch at 11:30."

"Okay, see you then," I said, and hung up again.

I didn't need to know where we were having lunch. We had never had lunch in our lives. Colby and Bates were coming to seize my machine at 11:30 a.m. That was just over two hours away.

I might not have had much money or clout, but I still had a lot of really great friends. I called up a bunch of them and told them what was going on. "Meet me at the bus shed as quick as you can," I said.

Four or five guys rushed over, all of them driving pickups. We loaded up the foam and fabric and all the equipment, and my friends distributed it to barns and other locations across Carver County, places where Colby and Bates would not know to look. Next, I cleaned and swept the factory space until it was spotless. There was not a fleck of foam or fabric scrap left anywhere. The big space looked spanking clean, as if it were ready for a new tenant. I locked the building and left, grinning so wide my face hurt.

Dick Lenzen, the bus shed landlord, told me what happened next. At 11:30, Colby and Bates showed up with a truck. Dick used his key to let them in. When Colby and Bates saw the empty, gleaming space, their mouths dropped open.

"Where is everything?" Bates wanted to know.

"It was here last night," Dick said, genuinely surprised. "I was here, talking to Mike."

He was telling the truth. I hadn't told Dick what I was doing because I didn't want him mixed up in any legal trouble.

At home across the street, I waited for a knock on the door. Very quickly, Colby and Bates appeared on my stoop. They had reinforcements: two Carver County police officers who stood back a little, on the lawn. These men who had fired me now pulled out another court order and shoved it my way. This one, they said, gave them the right to seize my equipment and documents.

I could see that the new order did not list specifics. "Which equipment and documents?" I said. "I don't know what you're talking about."

Furious, Colby jabbed his finger at the court paper. "You also have to surrender your corporate books," he said.

But I had a piece of paper for them, too. It was the letter I'd received saying that my financial records were in the custody of the FBI. One of the police officers stepped up and read it.

"We don't want anything to do with this," he said, handing the letter back to me.

He turned to leave and told Colby and Bates to do the same.

I tucked the FBI letter into my back pocket, then stood in my doorway, smiling and waving goodbye.

That day, I had the last laugh, but Colby and Bates weren't finished. In March 2007, I learned that they had struck a deal with Wayne Belisle to buy my patent. I still owed Wayne $84,000 and had put his name on the patent as collateral. Now, he wanted his money back.

I went to see him. "You're not going to sell them this patent, are you?" I said.

"Yep. We made a deal. They have until May 5 to come up with the money," Wayne said.

I was upset, but I didn't blame him. It had been a year and a half since Wayne loaned me the money for the patent application. I could tell he felt bad about selling the patent out from under me, but $84,000 is a lot of money and Wayne Belisle was not a bank.

"Maybe they'll make a mistake and miss the deadline," Wayne offered.

"If they miss the deadline, will you sell it to me?" I asked.

"Yes," he said. "If they miss the deadline and you come up with the money, I'll sell the patent back to you."

It was a sliver of hope. But the odds of them not only missing the deadline, but me coming up with 84 grand were slim to none—and slim had already left the building.

CHAPTER

27

Countdown

That spring, I noticed something odd going on with Karen. We had a mutual friend, Steve, who had been as much a friend to one half of our couple as the other. But lately it seemed the friendship scale was getting out of balance. When the three of us were together, it seemed to be two against one, as if Steve and Karen had some private pact. I figured he had been whispering in Karen's ear, along with all those other friends who wondered why she put up with the chaos. By now, some were telling her straight out to leave me.

But Steve worried me in a different way. He was one of those guys who considered himself a ladies' man, and the ladies he liked the most were married. I was suspicious of him, not my wife. Even when he took her side right in front of me, I thought to myself, *Steve, the last thing you're getting is Karen.*

I had so many other things to worry about—the bankruptcy judgment, the money I owed Ed, and most of all, the patent fight. There was one bright spot: My brother Corey, the cautious engineer, had saved up money for retirement. I pleaded with him to put up the money to buy Wayne out. "You've got to believe me, Corey. When MyPillow catches on, it's going to be big."

I really needed Corey to trust me in spite of my track record—and he did, when no one else would. He agreed to tap into his retirement to write Wayne Belisle a check for $84,000. That was great news, but if Colby and Bates came up with the money before the May 5 deadline, it wouldn't matter. MyPillow, like many other products invented by penniless entrepreneurs, would be snapped up by people who had more money than passion for innovation.

Karen and I had converted one of our bedrooms into an office, and I spent days and nights in there playing through—smoking crack and trying to figure out how to dig out of the mess I'd created. At the age of 46, I couldn't even imagine my financial situation going back to square one.

But we were actually back to far worse. Counting our house and the bankruptcy judgment, which was now underwater due to our subprime refinance, we were over half a million dollars in debt. I had poured the mortgage loan money into manufacturing, but also into drugs and gambling. Now we were behind on the mortgage again, and I had begun to receive foreclosure threats in the mail, as well as red-lettered notices from the electric company threatening to shut off our power.

Every waking moment, I obsessed over all this. But my biggest fixation was the patent. All I wanted was a reset button, a way to turn back time. All Colby and Bates had to do was pay for the patent and everything we'd worked for would be gone at the stroke of a pen.

One day in early April, I was sitting in our bedroom office running the numbers like Rain Man, high on crack and in a dark, hopeless mood. Karen and Darren were out in the living room packing pillows in boxes to fulfill internet orders from the stock we had left. To them, it was just another day in our family business. They were hand-addressing the boxes with Sharpies when Karen got frustrated with the process. She poked her head into the office and told me so. It was time-consuming, she complained, and besides it made our product look cheap.

"I think we should get one of those automatic label-maker things," she said.

Her statement was the tiniest thing—perfectly reasonable. But I couldn't bottle up my fear any longer and I exploded in anger. *"Don't you get it? It doesn't matter how the boxes are labeled! It's too late! We're losing everything! They're taking it all!"*

Karen winced as if someone had snuck up and hit her from behind. And in a way, I had. She knew about the patent fight, but I had told her we would win.

She knew about the bankruptcy judgment, but I had told her the FBI was going to get us out of that. And she had no idea we were behind again on the mortgage. I hadn't told her about that at all. But now I laid into her as if it were her fault she didn't have all the facts.

"An 'automatic labeler?'" I said, mocking her. "Why are you bothering me with something so trivial? Don't you understand? *It doesn't matter!*"

My fear for our future was all over my face, and it was the first time I'd let Karen see it. I couldn't hide how serious things really were. No matter how many times I'd backed us into a corner, Karen had always put her faith in me. Though it sometimes wasn't pretty, I'd always found a way out. But now I'd played all my cards. We were no longer in control of our own destiny.

CHAPTER

28

Lights Out

A pril 29 was Karen's 50th birthday, and I paid to throw a big party for her at the American Legion hall in Chaska. A lack of money had never stopped me before and, true to form, I somehow scraped together enough to make it happen. I was still spending a lot of time locked in my office and I hadn't slept in days, but with the help of friends and family, we decorated the party venue and put out a home-cooked spread of burgers, ribs, and barbecue beef with all the trimmings. I bought a big cake, and relatives drove in from all over the place to honor Karen. Our coke/crack friends came too, taking advantage of the open bar and sneaking off to the bathrooms more often than everyone else.

To all but a few of our friends, Karen and I looked as normal and happy as we ever had. But in the days leading up to the party, I had been noticing in her a strange defiance. I can't remember why the three of us were in the car together, but Karen, Steve, and I were running around Carver a couple of days before the party. I had gotten a fresh supply of cocaine, and Karen was holding onto it. Then, when I asked her for the coke, she wouldn't give it to me. She had never done that before.

We got into a mild argument and Steve sided with Karen. Their united front was even more obvious than before, like they were a team, and I remember thinking, where do I fit in here? But I did not suspect her of cheating with Steve. In fact, I had become so obsessed with the patent problem and so intent on staying high to block the pain of our coming financial collapse, that I was blind to everything else.

After the party on the 29th, a bunch of us wound up at Steve's house, a fancy rental that was considered a historical landmark in Chanhassen. It was a Sunday night, and we partied into the early morning hours, but our finances and the patent never left my mind for long. In fact, I spent much of the night listing all the frightening details for a friend of ours, Meri Lee. As the crowd thinned out, Karen spent the evening talking to Steve.

Monday morning came and reality set in. The kids would be waiting for us. Karen's birthday was over and it was time to go home. As the few stragglers still at Steve's headed for the door, I said to Karen, "We have to go."

She gave me that defiant look again. "I'm not leaving."

That stopped me. I didn't know quite what to say to persuade her. I mentioned that she had the company cell phone.

"Your phone is coming with me," I said, trying to get her to leave with me.

Karen just looked at me and handed over the phone. I stood there for a minute, feeling powerless. I certainly couldn't force her to leave. An eerie feeling crept over me, a sense of impending doom. Unable to process what was happening, I walked out of Steve's house and drove home alone.

By this time, I hadn't slept in several days. Maybe that's why, when I walked in my own front door, I saw things with a new set of eyes. My house was in shambles. Not just because the kids had spent much of the weekend there alone. It was much more than that. Our belongings were strewn everywhere. I saw piles of laundry and stacks of dishes caked in dried food. The house obviously hadn't been cleaned for a while. Karen had always been meticulous about these kinds of things.

It was as if an invisible hand ripped a blindfold off my eyes. In a flash, I realized that my house had been falling apart around me for a long time. How had I missed it? What else was I not seeing that was right in front of my face?

That feeling of dread swept over me again. I yelled at Lizzy, who was now 19, "You have to help me clean up this house! Something terrible is going to happen!"

"What are you talking about?" she said.

"I don't know. Something's going on with your mother."

"Well," she said, "we *are* a very dysfunctional family."

Blood rushed to my head, and I felt a pulse in my neck. "*What?* I don't even know what that means, but don't you ever say it again!"

"I'm leaving," Lizzy said. And she did.

Karen hadn't come home with me, and now Lizzy was leaving, too. I ran downstairs to get Charlie. He would help me clean up the mess. But when I reached his room, I saw that it was 2-feet deep in trash. Also, I noticed flood damage. Our basement had flooded some time before, and I had not repaired the mess. Charlie's bedroom door was warped, the ceiling sagged, and the closet doors wouldn't close. I suddenly realized that I'd let my son live in his room like that. I was angry with myself and took it out on him.

"You're 18 years old and you're living like a pig!" I yelled. I glanced around wildly and noticed items we'd been missing in the household for months. "You are going to get trash bags and sort this mess out!"

I don't remember what else I yelled, but Charlie started yelling, too. He began picking up items from the pile on the floor and throwing them into random piles. When he threw a baseball trophy I felt should be treasured, I flipped out.

"Don't you dare throw that!" I yelled. "*That means something to our family!*"

Darren came running down the stairs. "Leave Charlie alone!" he shouted.

I yelled at Darren to stay out of it and kept shouting at Charlie to *clean this place up!*

I was now completely unglued. "Something terrible is going to happen," I kept repeating out loud. My world was collapsing—my marriage, my family, my house, my business. Deep inside, some twisted logic drove me: If I could just get the house cleaned up, those other things would fall into place too. I could hit the reset button. I could hold off disaster.

Charlie wouldn't cooperate with this fantasy, however, and Darren was still screaming in his brother's defense. I noticed a huge ceramic pot pipe in the shape of a dragon. I grabbed it, smashed it on the floor, and started railing on Charlie for smoking pot.

"*What?*" he screamed, bursting into tears. "Who are you to talk?"
That's when I kicked him out of the house.

After the meltdown with my boys, I shut everything and everyone out. I locked myself in the office and returned to my crack pipe, as well as the countdown that had plagued me since March. I told myself that the patent was everything. Charlie would be fine. Darren would get over it. Karen would come home and so would Lizzy. If I could save the patent, I could save everything, and they would all forgive me.

It was April 30. Colby and Bates had five days left to make their move for patent ownership. I knew that one of them—I couldn't remember which—was overseas. It was my understanding that he wouldn't return until the second week in May. I could only pray that the other one would wait until his partner got back to pay Wayne.

I had reason to hope. The two had approached a previous transaction involving the patent with huge hesitation because they were having trouble getting the rest of the company from me. Also, I had sent them crazy emails hoping to scare them off. Reading them, they'd told Wayne they thought I was certifiable.

"If you think he's certifiable, why would you try to take his dream?" Wayne had said.

My behavior was by design. I hoped that Colby and Bates would underestimate me. I hoped they would see me as an unemployed, bankrupt addict without the financial means to challenge them. If they thought I was also literally nuts, maybe they would be as lackadaisical about this deadline as they had the first one. If they missed it, Corey and I could swoop in and buy the patent back from Wayne.

It was a long shot, but it was all I had.

I had now been up for five days and was still locked in the office when Karen finally came home. It was about 10 p.m., and I was relieved when I heard her walk in the door. The feeling didn't last long. Charlie had been waiting outside and told his mother everything. Karen went ballistic. When she banged on the office door, I threw it open. We had an epic fight, screaming and yelling until I finally said I didn't care, Charlie could stay. Then I retreated into the office and locked the door again.

I smoked more crack and fantasized about Corey writing a check to Wayne Belisle. Around midnight, Kevin Chase came over and sat with me in my office. I told him how bad things were. Hours passed. I swung between hope and despair.

Kevin and I had been shut in the office for a very long time when I looked at the clock. It was now well toward dawn. I was a little surprised that Karen hadn't come in to say hello to Kevin. We'd had blowout fights before, and one or the other of us usually came forward to make peace. It was her turn to make the first move, I felt, since she was the one who had stayed at Steve's. But she didn't.

I went downstairs and found Charlie. We greeted each other stiffly. "Where's your mother?" I asked.

Charlie looked at me sadly, accusingly. "She left."

"What do you mean, she left?"

"I mean she packed a bag and left."

"With who? Steve?" I said.

"Yes," Charlie said. "She's gone."

An hour later, the lights went out.

1994 My sister Cindy and me.

1995 With Wayne Hilk—
whereabouts unknown.

1997 With my dad Jim,
arriving at the Las Vegas airport
on one of the "Schmitty's Goes
to Vegas" trips.

1997 At the Stardust on a "Schmitty's
Goes to Vegas" trip.

1999 Making it "snow" at Schmitty's.

2000 Showing off my "Schmitty's Goes to Vegas" winnings.

1999 Left: A friend came into my bedroom and snapped this "cracked out" photo in the dark. Right: Peeking out a window, paranoid.

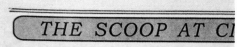

2000 Darren and me with the walleye he caught while fishing on Father's Day.

THE SCOOP AT CI

Pull Tabs on Hold at Schmitty's
"The waters have been muddied"

Schmitty's Tavern has been without pull tabs for several weeks now, awaiting continued discussion on December 10th, date of the next regularly scheduled city council meeting. Adoption of an ordinance regulating charitable gambling is under consideration.

Mike Lindell, owner of Schmitty's, has asked that the Children's Fund of the Minnesota Licensed Beverage Association be the designated pull tab charity at his establishment rather than the Victoria Lions because, he said, the change would be more financially beneficial to him. He has also pointed out to councilmembers that the City of Waconia has been sued for attempting to further control charitable gambling.

Stated Councilmember Tim Amundsen on November 12th, "If there is any threat of my name appearing on a charitable gambling lawsuit, as has happened in other communities, none of this is worth it."

He added, "Personally, I'd like to go without charitable gambling in Victoria and use other methods of fundraisers. Other cities have ordinances with similar wording and they've still been sued. The water has been muddied. The City of Victoria received a threat. I am not comfortable."

Stated Councilmember Dave Lindgren, "Seems we've lost our sense of charitable gambling and what it's supposed to be for – charities."

He added, "It makes me uneasy to think we'd have to go somewhere

Lindell says his expenses incurred due to the gambling operation are greater than 50%.

Victoria city councilmembers are considering adoption of a resolution that would establish conditions that applicants must meet in order to obtain a Lawful Gambling License within the City of Victoria. As allowed by law, the conditions would be stricter than state guidelines.

Stated City Attorney Tim Keane, "It's common in small towns to only allow one [charitable gambling] group in town." In the City of Waconia, for example, only one licensed organization may conduct lawful gambling. In Chanhassen, at least fifteen members of the licensed charity must be residents of that city.

Referring to past conversation, Councilmember Paulsen commented, "I get the feeling that pull tabs are a life or death issue."

Mike replied, "It is. Without them, I'd have to close my doors."

Asked Jim, "Why make waves when everything was going so well?"

"To maximize," said Mike. "For better efficiency."

Said Jim, "I see you shooting the golden goose for just one part of your business. Gambling should be only an adjunct, and you talk as if it's the key."

Concluded Mayor Mary Meuwissen, "Since the last council meeting I've thought about this, and I want you to know that I don't see this as a fund for you and your kids. This is charit-

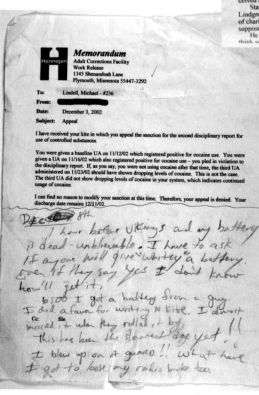

2002 Memo documenting failed urine analysis at Hennepin County Adult Corrections Facility. We were not given any paper to write on, so I repurposed this so I could journal.

NAME: Mike Lindell   **INMATE ID#:** 00944658   **CELL#:** 236   **DATE:** 12/03/02

RESIDENT REQUEST: PLEASE BE SPECIFIC

Could I please review my out date with you. I'm hoping you will consider giving me 2-days of my good time back. I feel I have earned it.

thanks for the consideration

(signature)

RESPONSE: I have reviewed your file + case. Your request is denied.

Other Side

NAME: Mike Lindell   **INMATE ID#:** ...58   **CELL#:** 236   **DATE:** 12/07/02

RESIDENT REQUEST: PLEASE BE SPECIFIC

Mr. Schmaltz, thank you for considering Monday for my outdate. I'm writing again because I did work for 2-supervisors to possible get back 2 of my 10 days.

If this isn't possible can I have my lawyer bring my Tavern closing papers to sign here on Monday afternoon.

Please let me know by 12:00 on Monday

RESPONSE: Your request for a return of good time is denied. Your lawyer is a profession visitor + he can visit with you at any time.

thank you _(signature)_

-SLC 12-9-02

HC11455 (1/1/02)

KITE/REQUEST SLIP
HENNEPIN COUNTY ADULT CORRECTIONS

acred.#3-1A15,3-4B-03,3-4B-06,
3-4F-03,3-5A-02

ACF PROBATION OFFICER'S
☐ Bobbi
☐ Dennis
☐ Julie
☐ Lisa
☐ Pat
☐ Deb D. (Case Mgr Asst)
☐ Deb S. (Women's)

PSYCHOLOGIST
☐ Dr. Heggem
☐ Stress Management

EDUCATION PROGRAMS
☐ GED
☐ Computer
☐ Parenting

TELESIS
☐ Coordinator

WORK READINESS
☐ Coordinator

CHEMICAL HEALTH PROGRAM
☐ Coordinator (Lynn A.)
☐ Altamese
☐ Carol
☐ Rosalino

PROGRAMS & SERVICES
☐ Booking
☐ Canteen/Reparation
☐ Cellblock Supervisor
☐ Chaplain
☐ Classification Team
☐ Engineering
☐ Food Services Supervisor
☐ Industry Coordinator
☐ Library
☐ Medical Department Supervisor
☐ Nursing Staff
☐ PSWP Payroll
☐ Residents Accounts*
☑ Shift Supervisor 7-3, 3-11, 11-7 (circle one)
☐ Other Schmaltz

SUPERINTENDENT
☐ John S.

BUSINESS SERVICES MANAGER
☐ Dan D.

PROGRAMS & SERVICES UNIT SUPERVISOR
☐ Roger P.

WOMEN'S/WORK RELEASE/HOME MONITORING UNIT SUPERVISOR
☐ Jill S.

MEN'S UNIT SUPERVISOR
☑ Roger G.

PRODUCTIVE DAY WORK PROGRAMS UNIT SUPERVISOR
☐ Dennis G.

* ONE SELECTION PER KITE*   * SEE BACK SIDE TO MAKE REQUEST*
* RESIDENT WILL PAY A 25 CENTS FEE FOR EACH COPY OF ACCOUNT REQUESTED*

Hey Schmaltz - I bet I could eat 50 Hard boiled Eggs. Have a nice life.

(signature)

2002 I sent a blizzard of request slips, called "kites," to Warden Schmaltz of Hennepin County Adult Corrections. He said he had never received so many from one prisoner.

2002 Pull tabs vote passes for Schmitty's Tavern in Victoria, Minnesota.

2003 God Against Crack: Part of the out-of-body message I received—from somewhere or Someone.

2003 Materials from Vas Spanos' card counting course.

The term "Exact Normalized Count" is defined as the result of multiplying the running count times 100 and then dividing by the number of unseen cards.

$$\text{E.N.C.} = \text{Exact Normalized Count} = RC \times 100 \div N$$

where RC = running count, and N = number of unseen cards.

Example 1. Suppose running count = +4; N=30. Then ENC = 4 x 100 ÷ 30 = 13

Example 2. Suppose running count = -8; N = 95. Then ENC = -8 x 100 ÷ 95 = -8

THE APPROXIMATE VALUES OF THE NORMALIZED COUNT.

Number of unseen cards	Appr. Normalized Count
312 - 261 (6-5 decks)	Count x 3/10
260 - 209 (5-4 decks)	Count x 4/10
208 - 156 (4-3 decks)	Count x 1/2
155 - 106 (3-2 decks)	Count x 3/4
105 - 76 (2-1½ decks)	Count x 1
75 - 56 (1½ - 1 decks)	Count x 1½
55 - 36 (1-¾ deck)	Count x 2
35 - 26	Count x 3
25 - 21	Count x 4
20 - 11	Count x 5

I have calculated all of the above using methods employed in statistics and I have found the answers to be:

(1st) The % advantage for the <u>overbet</u> changes by 0.685% every time the normalized count changes by one

(2nd) The % advantage for the <u>underbet</u> changes by 0.655% every time the N.C. changes by one

(3rd) The % advantage for the <u>Blackjack hand</u> changes by 0.10% every time the N.C. changes by one.

Now, we are all set to make a complete chart of how the advantages change as the N.C. changes (increases or decreases) of the three bets (i.e. <u>overbet</u>; <u>underbet</u>; <u>regular Blackjack bet</u>).

2003 Celebrating a big win.

1990 – 2000s Players' cards from my two favorite casinos.

2004 The train ticket I bought for Michael to go home to his family.

2004 MyPillow kiosk at Eden Prairie Center.

2004 The first official logo for MyPillow was designed by my oldest daughter, Heather.

2005 This is the old bus shed that I converted into our first MyPillow factory in Carver, Minnesota. Originally, we only occupied the garage on the left.

2005 With my son Charlie, grinding foam.

2005 I built this bin and added it to the foam grinder to capture the shredded foam.

2005 Sewing together MyPillows.

2005 Heather working our first MyPillow booth at the Minnesota State Fair.

2005 DAC (Driving After Cancellation) of License Offense in Hennepin County.

2006 With Skelly in Mexico on a fishing boat excursion. We both got seasick before landing two big sailfish, each over 100 pounds.

2007 Pictured left to right: Jenny, Skelly, me, and Karen on our Mexico trip, the day before a drug dealer laid a machete to my neck.

2007 With friends and family at Schmitty's on Karen's 50th birthday.

2008 MyPillow's proprietary fill was patented on December 9, 2008.

2011 With Don Laughlin at the Steele County Free Fair, Owatonna, Minnesota.

BOOK

3

JESUS

CHAPTER

29

Breakdown

I'd only ever punched two people in my life, but I was about to hit the trifecta. Over the next few days, I drove to Steve's house four times. I was sure I could talk Karen into coming home.

It broke my heart, the look on Charlie's face when he told me his mother was gone. I'd been so caught up in the storm of our financial problems that I hadn't thought about the fact that my kids' lives were unraveling, too. But I knew something that maybe Charlie didn't: Karen would never leave her kids for long.

When the lights went out and the computer screen in my office went dark, I realized the power company had made good on its shutoff notices. *Are you kidding me?* I thought. *My wife leaves, and the house goes black?* If you were looking for a better metaphor for my collapsing life, you couldn't make one up. The only thing left now was for the bank to show up and slap the promised foreclosure notice on our front door, which I knew wasn't far off. After the sun came up the next day, I fast-talked my way into having some guy from the power company turn the electricity back on. Then, blood boiling, I drove to Steve's.

The first three times I went over there, I took one of the kids with me, trying to remind Karen that she was a mom and a wife who was wanted and needed at home. Each time, she stayed out of sight. And each time, Steve would walk out front and say, "She doesn't want to see any of you. You drove her away." I knew Karen would never say that, and him saying it in front of my kids infuriated me.

But deep down, I knew he was right about my part in it. I had driven Karen away. The truth was, I was rarely home anymore, out indulging my addictions instead. I had been using my marital faithfulness to justify not being there for her. I had a business to run, and I wasn't cheating on Karen, my thinking went. Wasn't that good enough?

Of course it wasn't. And Karen's departure exposed my excuses for what they really were. But that didn't give Steve the right to insert himself between us, and his words enraged me. I was convinced that while Karen was seeking a place to hide from our chaos, he had a different agenda.

The first time Steve met me on his lawn, it struck me that all his whispering had brainwashed Karen against me. Pain and anger burst up inside me like a volcano. I marched up the grass, put my fist through Steve's front bay window, and yelled into the house, pleading with Karen to please come out. Always efficient and proud of his historic-register home, Steve had the window fixed by the next day. I drove over and smashed it again.

On my third visit, I stormed into the house and searched for Karen. In one of the lowest and most painful scenes from my life, I ran from room to room in another man's house, calling out my wife's name. I didn't find her and later learned she was hiding in a spare bedroom between a bed and a wall.

Each time Karen refused to come out, my confidence slipped. On some level, I had been hoping that this was just a particularly bad fight, that she would see reason and come home. But as my hope faded, disbelief, confusion, and rage replaced it.

The fourth and last time I went to Steve's, he happened to be outside. I came roaring up the driveway in my truck, this time by myself. As soon as he saw me, he raised his cell to his ear. Stalking up the sloped yard, I could feel my pulse pounding in my temples. When I got close, I heard Steve talking.

"The criminal is back," Steve was saying into the phone. "It's Mike Lindell."

My rage boiled over. I roared at him, "You're interfering with a 20-year marriage! You're interfering with my family!"

Steve was in mid-sentence on his call when I punched him in the face. He fell over backwards and rolled down the slope of his perfectly cut lawn. I felt a surge of triumph, of *justice*—followed by the realization that when I hit him, he had been on the phone with the police.

Not good.

I hurried back to my truck and jumped in, still flushed with fury. I raised both fists and brought them down on either side of the steering wheel. A spiderweb of cracks opened on my dash. It looked the way my heart felt. I threw the truck in drive and sped off.

If the cops hadn't been after me before, they certainly would be now. At first, I steered the truck aimlessly, then ended up on Highway 5 driving west toward Victoria, my mind blank with shock. Finally, I wound up at my friend Randy Vanderlinde's house.

"I have problems," I said when he met me in the driveway.

"I see that," he said, gazing at the wreckage of my dash. Randy was the quiet, reserved type. He wouldn't pry for more information unless I volunteered it.

Suddenly, a strange calm swept over me. I looked at Randy. For some reason, I felt I shouldn't tell him what had just happened. Instead I told him, "The next time you see me, things will be very different."

I backed out of the driveway without another word.

After leaving Randy's, I found myself back on Highway 5, this time headed east toward Steve's house. Conflict warred in my head. I needed to get Karen, but knew if I went back there I might get arrested for assault. My mind was so frantic I had to pull over. I searched my brain for a way to find out what was happening. Finally, I came up with a name: Rachel.

Rachel Moore was in her 40s and never married. I'd met her recently in passing and I thought she was a friend of Steve's. I hardly knew her, but sitting in my truck on the side of the road, I felt desperate. I opened my cell and dialed friends until I found one who had Rachel's number. When I got her on the phone, she said yes, she and Steve were friends.

I spilled out the painful facts about my situation, then asked, "Do you think you could do me a favor and call Steve and see what's going on over there?"

"I can do you one better," she said. "I'll just drive over there."

"No, I don't want you to have to go out of your way, and plus wouldn't he think that's weird if you showed up there?"

Rachel said it was no big deal. She didn't live far from Steve and besides, she'd recently attended a party at his house and had left her sunglasses there. "I'll just tell him I stopped by to pick them up."

Perfect, I thought. I offered to pay Rachel a hundred dollars in return for this errand, but she refused. "I'll go right now," she said. "It won't take long."

While I waited for Rachel's report, I sat in my truck and thought about my life. Exactly 20 years before, God had given me the woman of my dreams. He gave me four wonderful kids. I had developed a number of successful businesses, including the lunch wagon and the bars. I had worked my butt off day and night and thought I had everything I wanted. But crack had chiseled away at my marriage and then, like a wrecking ball, accelerated into mass destruction. Every now and then, I'd caught a glimpse of the growing damage. But each time, my addictions and the pace of life quickly blotted out my concerns.

Now my life had collapsed from under me, the way a house can when eaten through with termites. I sat on the side of the road waiting for Rachel to call me back, wondering if it was too late.

Finally, my cell phone rang. "The cops were there talking with Steve when I pulled up," Rachel said. "He told me to go inside and grab my sunglasses."

"Did it look like my wife was there?" I asked.

"I didn't see her, but there's a big bouquet of roses, and it looked like Steve was about to leave because there were a couple of suitcases sitting by the door."

My heart did a slow, dizzy roll and I felt sick.

"Thank you so much for checking for me," I said, crushed. "I still want to pay you." I'd always had a hard time accepting something for nothing. "Can we meet somewhere?"

"Well, you aren't going to pay me anything, but you can come to my house and hide out from the cops if you want."

In that moment my mind flashed to the only comfort I had left: cocaine. If Rachel had partied at Steve's, it was almost certain she used it.

"Yeah, sure," I said. That one decision launched my life in directions I couldn't have imagined.

Less than five minutes later, Rachel greeted me at her door. I offered her money again but she still refused. I then asked her, "Do you want to do a line?" That began a seven-hour conversation, in which I stood in Rachel's kitchen and spilled my guts. I told her everything, stopping often to share more lines of coke. I felt accepted, listened to, *heard*.

For the next three days, Rachel and I did cocaine, smoked crack, drank, and talked. I was almost certain that Steve had just whisked Karen away on some kind of romantic trip, and the time I spent talking to Rachel was an escape from that reality. Completely self-involved, I never even thought to check on the kids.

I had now been up for seven days straight. My wife was gone, and I was about to lose my house. The only shred of hope I still held onto was the patent. Colby and Bates had three days left to buy it out from under me. As of this moment, it was the only hope I had left.

I stayed at Rachel's, enjoying a steady supply of drugs and sympathy. I watched the calendar tick down and kept in touch with Wayne to be sure the patent was still up for grabs.

Kevin Chase came over, and the party continued. I called a dealer I knew, a guy named Tiggs. The three of us drove Tiggs nuts, calling at all hours for more drugs. He would come out to the suburbs with a couple of his lieutenants and a fresh batch of cocaine. We'd all pile into their car and head for the drive-through at a local bank, pot smoke billowing from the rear windows as Tiggs' men got high. After withdrawing enough cash to pay for the coke, we would spend the change on booze and cigarettes then circle back to the house.

May 5 came, the patent still unbought, and my anxiety grew. Was the impossible becoming possible? Were Colby and Bates really about to let their deadline pass?

For me, the MyPillow patent was like a little sprout. Over and over, I had let my addictions conspire with unscrupulous people who tried to pull it up by the roots and take it from me. Rachel, Kevin, and I had a serious talk. I vowed to them that this time would be different. I would buy back the patent, quit drugs completely, and make MyPillow huge. The three of us made a pact: We would all quit together. We would quit everything. Today would be our last day.

I only have to make it until midnight. That's what I kept thinking as May 5 passed, the minutes ticking by so slowly I felt I could almost hear them. I didn't want to risk getting paranoid from smoking crack, so I scraped cocaine into neat white lines, inhaled them, and watched the clock.

11:59 p.m.

12 midnight.

12:01 a.m.

I called Wayne. Had Colby and Bates come through?

"No," he said. "The patent's yours if you can pay for it."

I felt an explosion of joy and relief as I called Corey.

"I don't have enough money," my brother said. My heart sank.

To get the total amount, Corey would have to borrow money from his 401k and he was now hesitant to do so. I panicked. We had to act now, I told him. *Had* to. I tried to reassure Corey that MyPillow was going to be big and that borrowing this money would be one of the best decisions he ever made.

Finally, he agreed. Within a couple of hours, we had made the deal with Wayne.

We did it! I thought. Until that moment, the MyPillow dream had seemed to flatline. Now it had a faint pulse again.

I had now been up for eight days, aided by Tiggs' coke, some of which we had converted into crack. But as I'd told Rachel and Kevin, I was finished with all that now. By the evening of May 6, I was absolutely exhausted. It seemed my whole life had been thrown into a hammer mill and chopped into pieces. I needed to rest.

It seemed like perfect timing since we had just run out of cocaine. I went upstairs to lie down in the guest room. Not even 20 minutes later, Rachel came upstairs. She looked at me and smiled. "Can I get some more money? I already called Tiggs."

I was so disappointed because we'd made the pact to quit. Begrudgingly, I handed her some cash. After she left the room, I lay in bed staring at the ceiling and getting angrier by the minute. Finally at about 5 a.m., I marched downstairs. Kevin was lying on the couch, and I found Rachel in the kitchen. Her back was to me, but I could see smoke rising above her head, sifting out into the room.

"I thought we were quitting," I said.

Rachel turned to face me, crackpipe in her hand. Her face wasn't the face of the woman who had been so supportive and understanding. Instead, it had twisted into something I knew all too well: the face of addiction.

"You might be quitting, but I'm not!" she snapped. Her anger hit me like a slap in the face. In my grief over Karen, I had thought I found a refuge. I thought Rachel and I had bonded as friends. Suddenly, that false reality burst as I realized it was all about the drugs.

I ran from the kitchen, found my keys, and scrambled out to my truck, which hadn't moved in four days. It was all crashing down on me now, and it hit me all at once. I suddenly realized that my focus on the patent had been a distraction, like putting my finger in a failing dam to hold back a flood. When I was high, I'd felt like the king of my own destiny. I thought saving the patent would save my world. But now, sober and with the sun coming up, I knew the truth: Everything I held dear had turned to dust. Without Karen and my family, nothing else mattered.

I cranked the ignition and pointed my truck toward home. Foot on the gas, I drove like a maniac. All the way there, I could hear this blood-curdling screaming like someone having a complete breakdown. I was halfway home before I realized it was me.

CHAPTER
30

Walking Coma

Miraculously, I made it home. Charlie was there but we didn't talk much. Instead, I found an empty bedroom and collapsed. With my entire soul, I yearned for a total reset, for everything to return to the way it was before.

Somewhere in there my mind must have cracked because, against all reason, I picked up the phone, dialed 9-1-1, and told the operator that Steve was holding my wife against her will.

"He's brainwashed her!" I raved.

The operator did her best to understand what I was saying and assured me the police would try to find Karen.

Thirty seconds later, I called back. "Have you found my wife yet?" I said.

This time, instead of trying to assure me, the operator started asking questions that quickly began to sound like an interrogation. I hung up the phone. *Idiot*, I thought. How stupid did I have to be to call the cops when just a few days prior, I'd punched Steve in the face and smashed his window—twice?

Pretty stupid I guess, because the cops showed up at my house minutes later. One officer looked me over. "You look like you've been up for about nine days," he said.

That was exactly how long I'd been up. His accuracy astonished me.

While he questioned me, a second officer took Charlie into another room. Whatever Charlie said convinced the cops that, however crazy I sounded, I really was desperate to find my wife. One of the officers made a call. Not long after, a voice squawked from the radio receiver that was attached to his uniform: "We've located her. She is refusing to go home." There was nothing they could do, the police explained to Charlie—they couldn't force his mother to come back.

Outraged all over again, I started to argue when I realized I'd probably better shut my mouth or risk going to jail for my behavior at Steve's. I pulled back my emotions, thanked the cops for looking into it, and watched them drive away. Suddenly exhaustion consumed me, and I crumpled onto the couch. I drifted off to sleep, certain Steve had told the police everything and wondering vaguely why they hadn't arrested me.

Six hours later, I woke up to a new reality. Karen was really gone. The depression I felt was as if the whole house were sitting on my chest. Then it got worse as I realized that during all the chaos, I'd neglected MyPillow for days. Wearily, I reached for my phone and dialed my voicemail. It was completely full of customer requests. They wanted a pillow, or more pillows, or to find out which fairs we'd be at next, or, or, or…

I felt overwhelmed. How was I going to handle all that when my life had just burned down? As I let the messages play, the lyrics to an old Elvis song crept into my head.

> *Lord, this time you gave me a mountain,*
> *A mountain I may never climb…*

I was about to flip my phone shut when one of the voicemails caught my attention. I heard a friendly voice say, "Hey, Mike, it's Rachel." After listening to me talk about my problems over the past few days, she wanted to help, the message said. She offered to help with bookkeeping, making pillows, whatever I needed.

Instantly, the scene from the previous night in Rachel's kitchen vanished. I forgot her anger and the look of addiction on her face. Instead I felt relief. Not only that she would help me, but that she seemed to truly care. At that moment I really needed someone to care. Immediately, I called Rachel back. I would love her help, I said. I forgot to offer her money this time, which was good because I didn't have any left.

The divorce was excruciating, but lightning fast. I punched Steve on May 1. Just three weeks later, I met Karen in a parking lot, where we signed the papers I'd had drawn up by a lawyer. The meeting was horribly matter-of-fact—surreal, really—almost like we were ordering a pizza.

After all we had been through, her main goal seemed to be to halt the chaos, to finally just have peace of mind. I told her I would assume all our debts—the house, the bankruptcy, the money I owed my bookie, everything.

"I'm going to give you money every month," I told her. A thousand dollars a month was all I could promise at the time. There wasn't much left of the company, I explained, except that Corey had been able to save the patent. If MyPillow did someday become what I hoped it would, I promised her I would take care of her for the rest of her life.

"You deserve every bit of it," I said.

Despite having a house that was now in foreclosure, I was able to buy another one on 4 acres, using a contract for deed. I moved into this house in the woods and invited Rachel to live with me because, by then, we had become more than friends. Lizzy moved out of our family home, leaving Charlie and Darren to stay there alone. I didn't invite them to move in with Rachel and me. I justified this with the rationale that the boys were better off not being around me since I was a full-blown crackhead.

I had told Randy that the next time he saw me things would be very different, but I had never expected this. It seemed that one minute we were celebrating Karen's 50th birthday, and the next we were divorced and living in different places with different people. The before-and-after was as stark as changing from one channel to another on TV.

By now I had learned that Rachel was almost as much of an addict as I was. We both took turns trying to rescue each other, the blind leading the blind. Our relationship was volatile—a constant storm of drugs and arguments. Trying to manage this new relationship in concert with addiction, paranoia, and running a company was like being a one-man pit crew in a 12-car race. It still did not occur to me that such chaos seemed normal to me.

The summer of 2007 passed into fall, and by the holidays something had taken hold of me—a massive, debilitating fatigue of body and mind. Rachel had moved out after one too many fights, and although I had the big house all to myself, I isolated myself in my bedroom. I didn't eat. I didn't do drugs. I didn't watch TV. I didn't read. I didn't work. I didn't do anything except lie in bed and stare at the ceiling. Once in a while I went to the bathroom, and when I was in there, I drank water from the faucet over the sink. Other than that, I have absolutely no recollection of that time.

When they didn't hear from me after Christmas, Cindy and her husband Bryan came over to check on me. They later told me I was so zombie-like and haggard that they called my doctor and convinced him to make a house call.

"He has a condition we sometimes call a 'walking coma,'" the doctor told Cindy and Bryan after he examined me. My brain, he said, had executed a kind of emergency shutdown to protect itself from the stresses I had been subjecting it to. The doctor assured my sister that I'd come out of it eventually.

What brought me out of it was my good friend Jim Furlong. A few weeks earlier, he had given me some terrible news. His doctors had diagnosed him with incurable stomach cancer. "They say I only have a few weeks left," Jim had said then.

I didn't believe it, because I'd seen him in my future. All my life I'd had these premonitions, and they almost always came true. This time, I had seen Jim far into the future, still with MyPillow. To me that meant he wasn't going to die, and I'd told him so at the time.

Now, Jim showed up at the house in the woods, stood outside my bedroom door and called out, "Mike, if you get your act together, I've got something for you."

He then set a canister of chocolate-covered popcorn, my favorite, outside the door and left. To this day, I don't know why, but his kind and simple gesture woke me from my trance-like state. Others had come to visit me and I hadn't reacted. But when Jim visited, the machinery of my mind clanked into motion and started working again. I could almost hear gears inside my head, moving slowly at first, then faster and faster as my brain went back into operation.

Though I hadn't believed Jim was dying, he believed it. And when he came to see me, his diagnosis hadn't changed. But instead of spending what he thought were his last days with his family, he had dragged himself all the way out to my house just to let me know he cared. His sheer selflessness shined a light down through my darkness.

After shaking off my walking coma, I turned my attention back to my company once again. A couple of years before, I had appeared on Channel 6, a local public-access channel, to talk about MyPillow. The station manager,

Gay Jacobson, whom I'd met at an early home show, really believed in my product and kept after me to stop by and visit the station again.

One day back in early 2006, I had been on my way to see one of my drug dealers in Minneapolis when Gay called to ask me to stop by. Since it would be another hour before I could meet my dealer, I reluctantly agreed. When I got there, Gay showed me around then told me there was a live show starting in about half an hour.

"It's a local human-interest show, and I would like you to go on and be interviewed," she said.

I knew she was trying to help me, but my fear of speaking to people landed on me like an anvil. "No," I said. "Absolutely not."

Gay tried to encourage me. "You'll be fine!" she said. On camera, I should just say the same things I had when she met me at the home show.

"Can I come back in an hour?" I said. My plan was to dash over to my dealer's house and grab some cocaine. Then I could come back and do the show just fine. Of course, I didn't tell Gay that.

"No," she said. "It has to be now. The show is live."

Somehow she managed to talk me into it. Within 10 minutes I was on-set live and overwhelmed with fear. Just absolutely terrified. I fumbled through the interview, hoping every question would be the last and that the whole thing would just be over. If I make it through this, I thought, I will never, ever go on TV again.

To this day, I have not watched that interview in its entirety. I cringe every time I try. And it wasn't one of those things where it wasn't as bad as I thought, either.

People who didn't know I was an addict saw the interview and said, "What? Were you on drugs?"

People who did know said, "You didn't have any drugs, did you?"

That interview was two years before my walking coma. To help me out—and maybe to plug holes in programming—Gay was still running that interview every couple of weeks in the middle of the night.

One night in February 2008, I was sitting alone in the house in the woods. My cocaine and crack use had escalated, and I was working fewer and fewer home shows. Because of the paranoia, I rarely left the house. When I did, I half-heartedly conducted MyPillow business out of a room Corey and I had rented in the old Carver schoolhouse. I was also getting two or three calls a day from people ordering pillows on the cell phone number I kept for business.

That night in February, the MyPillow phone rang. I looked at the clock. It was about 6:30 p.m. I pushed the talk button. "MyPillow, Mike speaking."

"Yes, is this the guy I've seen on Channel 6?" a woman said.

"Yes, it is."

"Well, I don't want to buy a pillow right now, but I was praying, and God let me know that what you're doing is so important. You can't give up. I'd like to pray with you."

I didn't have a problem with that. "Sure," I said.

For the next half-hour, the woman prayed for me and MyPillow while I did lines of cocaine off the desk in front of me. Finally, the woman wrapped it up with, "...in Jesus' name, amen."

"Thank you," I said. And we hung up.

About 90 minutes later, I was on my computer reading a website about crack addiction called The Devil's Candy. I often visited this site, always plotting my escape from addiction. The MyPillow phone rang again, and this time the caller introduced herself as a boutique owner in Minneapolis.

"I've seen you on Channel 6, and God's called me to pray for you," she said. "What you're doing is very important and you can't give up."

"I believe MyPillow will be a platform someday," I ventured. I said this somewhat cautiously. The woman was a perfect stranger after all.

"Yes, exactly! A platform," she said. "It's very important to God." She offered to pray for me, and I'm not kidding you, this woman prayed for the next hour-and-a-half. Every now and then, I'd say a few words about the company. Other times, I'd mute the phone and do a line. Although I didn't know what the future held or why, I was encouraged that this woman said the company was important to God.

I was wide awake now, inhaling line after line of white powder. Fast forward to 3 a.m., and the phone rang again. This time a male voice barked over the phone, "Are you that guy I seen on TV?" The caller seemed irritated.

"Yes, on Channel 6," I said.

"Well, let me tell you something, pal. I don't believe in God. But I keep having a dream that I'm supposed to call you and tell you what you're doing is important to God. I hope these dreams stop now, you a**hole!"

The man hung up and I burst out laughing. As I wound down from that though, it hit me that something strange was definitely going on. I mean, the first two calls were crazy enough. What are the odds that two people would call out of the blue with an almost identical message and offer to pray for me? Still, that might have been a coincidence. *Might* have. But now, here's a guy who doesn't even *want* to call, and was apparently passing along the same message out of his own self-interest!

Then I remembered Cindy's pastor. What had he said to her that day she called me, back in 2003 after I wrote that weird essay? The pastor had said something happened to me and that it was "important." The same thing the three callers said. I had always believed in God in a general way. Now it seemed He had singled me out. I'm sorry, but what else could this be? The odds of these three phone calls were just too astronomical.

My phone rang again at 8 a.m., so I picked it up and said, "Let me guess. You don't want to order a pillow. You want to pray."

The woman on the line made a little noise of surprise. "How did you know?"

"It seems to be the thing," I said, and the woman started laughing. When I told her about the other callers, she echoed their story. During prayer she had received a powerful message that she should call me, she said.

"You have a 'platform'?" she said tentatively. "But I don't know what that means."

It was the second time I had heard that word. After chatting for a few minutes, we hung up. I'd been doing lines for about 24 hours straight and I wasn't hungry. Instead of eating, I fixed myself a whiskey and Coke. I never drank in the mornings unless I was still up from the night before. Lately that seemed to be pretty often.

Sipping the drink, I reflected on what a bizarre night I'd just had. I had a few pillow orders to fill, as well as some paperwork I was filling out for Corey that was critical for MyPillow.

At about 11 a.m., another phone rang, a line I kept only for Internet access. No one ever called me on that phone, but it was attached to an answering machine. Swirling the ice cubes in my whiskey and Coke, I stared at the phone and waited for the ringing to stop. Probably a wrong number.

Finally, a light started blinking on the machine and I played the message. The voice on the other end was female and robotic, like one of those automated recordings with unnatural, inhuman gaps between words.

"Mike, this is a message from God," the voice said. "Everything you've experienced in your life will give you the strength to get through the next month."

I took a step back. My drink fell from my hand and smashed on the floor, liquor splashing against my legs. A sob broke from my chest. The previous year, 2007, had been the worst year of my life. Then those four people had called with what seemed like positive news—what I was doing was "important." But now—*now*—some crazy robot lady was telling me things were going to get *worse*? And that whatever the next 30 days brought, I was going to need strength. The fifth caller's prediction seemed like a terrible omen.

CHAPTER

31

I'll Wait You Out

Omen or not, things went downhill fast. Rachel returned that afternoon, and we immediately resumed the argument we'd left off days before. She told me she'd called the police on me—what for, I didn't know, but it had resulted in a warrant for my arrest. The cops, she said, were on their way.

"But I haven't done anything!" I protested.

I fled the house and jumped into Rachel's car. I sped out of the driveway and drove three miles to Carver, only using her vehicle because I'd left my truck elsewhere. Once in town, I abandoned Rachel's car and ran the few blocks to my old house, the one in foreclosure, where I asked Darren to give me a ride to my truck.

Later that day, a cop called me and asked me if I stole Rachel's car.

"No," I said.

The officer changed his tactics. "Mike," he said, "if you *had* stolen Rachel's car, where would you have put it?"

"Halfway up the hill by the church in Carver on the left side of the road."

"Thanks, Mike. And can you come and meet us? We just want to talk to you."

Is he kidding? I thought. "No, I'm not going to meet you, and don't bother coming to look for me," I said. "I haven't done anything wrong."

Quickly, I hung up. Already it seemed the fifth caller from the night before had been right.

After retrieving my truck, I drove to Minneapolis to see my main dealer, Joe. A stocky, muscled-up guy who had grown up in the Chicago projects, Joe was the kind of man who might scare you if you ran into him alone on a dark street. But he really was the nicest guy. He lived in an apartment downtown, and with a warrant out for my arrest, I thought his house would be a good place to hide out for a while.

It wasn't fair season, and my salespeople, as well as independently contracted vendors, were doing shows without me. That meant I could conduct a lot of my business by phone. So, I hung out at Joe's day after day, converting cash into coke, then converting coke into crack.

I hadn't slept since the day the weird phone calls started. That day rolled into three days and three rolled into five, then seven, then 10. I was "playing through," troubleshooting my life as I continued to watch it slip through my fingers. Though I had made it through the walking coma, as the doctor called it, I knew I was still crumbling inside. I was an expert at self-sabotage, so even though I had good intentions—to quit drugs, turn over a new financial leaf, be a better parent, build my business—I always managed to dig a hole under my own feet.

I was supposed to attend to some important MyPillow business, but I avoided it, hitting the crack pipe constantly instead. If I stayed high, I could avoid the inner pain I was feeling, pain like I'd never felt in my life. Time sped by in a blur, each day fading into the next. Before I realized it, I had been awake for two weeks straight. On the 14th day, I was in Joe's bathroom when I heard the front door to the apartment open and shut a couple of times. Then I heard multiple voices. It sounded like Joe had company.

I opened the bathroom door and walked out. Two other men were standing there, and all three, including Joe, were glaring at me. I knew the other two guys. There was Tiggs, the youngest of the bunch, but a powerful dealer in his own right. And there was Ray, a black suburban professional who moved large quantities of coke to a few select clients without ever missing a day at his real job. Ray was the one who had told me never to touch crack.

I drew back and looked at them. "You guys know each other?"

"We do and we don't, and that don't matter," said Tiggs, who suddenly turned as mean and tough as I'd ever seen him. "Joe called us and said you've been up for 14 days. You need to go to bed. We're cuttin' you off."

I started to argue and Ray, who was already disgusted with me, interrupted me. "What's the matter with you? Don't even call me, man." He walked out the apartment door.

Tiggs then issued Joe some instructions, and Joe walked out, too. Now Tiggs turned to me. "How much you got left?"

"A couple of rocks," I said.

"All right. I'm gonna wait you out." Tiggs walked over, sat on Joe's sofa, and crossed his legs. Then he threw up his hand and gave me a *Well? What are you waiting for?* look. "You ain't getting no more, so you may as well finish what you got," he said.

I couldn't believe this. My own dealers were doing an intervention? I sat down in a chair across from Tiggs, prepped my pipe, and smoked a rock. As he gazed at me through a cloud of his own pot smoke, I thought, *Nah. I'll wait you out.*

Twenty or 30 minutes passed between rocks. In the intervals, I got on my phone and ignored Tiggs. After loading my pipe a few times, I finally burned through my last rock. Tiggs was still gazing at me from the couch. He had a small, secret smile on his face that I didn't quite understand.

Another 20 minutes passed. I could feel myself coming down. With the number of days I'd been awake, I knew it was going to be one of the worst come-downs I'd ever had. Also, I did not want to come down because I hadn't figured out my future yet. I hadn't found a way to escape the pain. I scraped my pipe for residue and smoked that. When it was gone, I farmed on the floor and smoked anything I found that resembled crack. After a few hours of this standoff, I was dying for my drug. It was unbearable. That's when I looked over at Tiggs and saw that he'd fallen asleep.

Hah! I thought. I won. Twisting the knob quietly, I slipped out Joe's front door, took the stairs two at a time, and headed for the street.

I was out there for only an hour, winding my way through the dark. Dealers and addicts buzzed at the corners like bees around hives. Each time I approached someone, the reaction was different. Some turned and walked away. Others said, "Naw, man, can't sell to you." It was like I had some kind of disease.

In desperation, I started offering 50 bucks for $20 worth of crack, but it didn't take me long to realize I could've offered $500 with the same result. That's how quickly and thoroughly Joe had gotten the word out. It turned out that

Tiggs' instructions to Joe were simple: Pass the word in the street that if anyone sells to a crazy-looking white guy with a moustache, they're done.

Confused and angry, I climbed the stairs back up to Joe's place and walked in to find Tiggs awake and still sitting on the couch. He gave me a small smile. "How'd that work out for you?" he said.

I lost my cool. "What's the *matter* with you guys? All I want is more stuff! You've sold to me all this time and now you're cutting me off?"

Tiggs ignored my outburst. "Give me your phone," he said. "I'm gonna take a picture of you."

I don't know why, but I obeyed, and Tiggs snapped the photo.

"You've been telling us for years that this pillow thing is some kind of 'platform,' and that you're gonna come back here and help us get out of this drug life," Tiggs said. "Well, we're not gonna let you die on us. You're going to bed. You ain't got no choice."

He tossed my phone and I caught it. "There you go," he said. "Put that picture in your damn book."

Tiggs was right: I didn't have a choice. I'd been up for 14 days and without more crack, I was done. Shooting him an irritated look, I trudged back to Joe's spare bedroom and shut the door behind me. There wasn't even a bed in there, just a blanket. It was about 2:30 in the morning when I curled up on the floor and finally fell asleep. When I opened my eyes, it was dark. The sun had already risen and set again. For the next dozen hours or so, I drifted in and out of consciousness, not because I needed more sleep, but because I didn't want to wake up and face what was out there.

On the second full morning, I jolted awake and sat up. Somehow my subconscious had dredged up a reminder: that important MyPillow business I'd been avoiding. It was that critical paperwork I'd been working on for Corey the night of the weird phone calls. Those papers would seal a deal with a company that had committed to a huge wholesale buy from MyPillow. This deal was crucial to keeping the company afloat, and today was the deadline.

It was about 25 miles back to Carver. I didn't want to go back there because I knew there was still a warrant out for my arrest, but Corey had to get those papers. When I opened the bedroom door, the apartment was empty. Once outside, I jumped in my truck and headed toward home. Calling ahead, I learned that Corey was at our schoolhouse facility, so that's where I went. But just as I pulled into the parking lot, I saw a police cruiser pulling out. The cop U-turned, flashed his lights, whooped his siren, and pulled me over.

Immediately, I flipped open my cell phone and called Rachel. "I'm getting arrested right now." I pleaded. "*Please* go down to the courthouse and withdraw these false charges."

Rachel agreed and I hung up. Grabbing the MyPillow papers, I jumped out of my truck. I absolutely had to get these papers to Corey, and there was no way I'd make the deadline if I was sitting in jail. The police officer was exiting the cruiser, and I recognized him as someone I knew—Officer Larry.

My mind raced: I can run, I thought. I'll get the papers to Corey, then come back and surrender. I turned to make a break for it—

"Mike, stop right now!" Larry yelled. "I have a warrant for your arrest. Whatever that is in your hands, I want you to put it down."

I put up my hands, holding the papers in my right one. "Larry, I know I've got a warrant, but these papers need to get to my brother or it's going to change the course of history. MyPillow's going to be gone if I don't. And MyPillow is a platform for something so important in the future. Something to do with God. So many people will be affected if my brother doesn't get these papers."

I know that sounds crazy and grandiose, but that's what I had dreamed, and it wasn't just me. That's what Cindy told me. That's what those weird callers had told me, too.

Officer Larry just stood there staring at me.

"You know what, Larry?" I went on. "Rachel's down at the courthouse straightening all this out right now, and the charges are going to be dropped. I'm going to be found innocent and if I'm not, I promise you can arrest me any time, and I promise I'll have cocaine on me when you do."

Larry looked at me for another moment and sighed. "Call your brother," he said.

In the end, it was a compromise. Larry showed me to the back of his squad car, and I called Corey. Not one for confrontation, Corey didn't want to come out. He sent my brother-in-law Bryan out instead. Bryan came out to the parking lot and Larry gave him the papers before arresting me. And the following Tuesday, I was found innocent.

CHAPTER

32

Death Spiral

One definition of a miracle is something that defies the laws of science or nature. In my case, the laws of probability and mathematics seemed constantly at odds with actual events. As one event piled on top of another—Cindy's warnings, the phone calls, the dealer intervention—I found myself really coming to grips with the idea that God was trying to send me a message.

This all hit me one Saturday in March 2008, about a month after the dealers turned downtown Minneapolis against me. I was holed up in a friend's apartment in the city with another friend, Dale Wind, smoking crack. I told him about what my dealers had done and how I kept meeting people and convincing them to quit. I shared the whole story of Michael, the guy I'd smoked crack with in Las Vegas before putting him on a train back home to his family. I also told Dale about Tony, the guy I'd met in Memphis on that card-counting trip. How Tony had come to Memphis to visit his uncle, who owned a chicken restaurant. How he'd spent all his money on drugs. How he spent all that time smoking crack with Gary and me, then rescued us when the cops picked us up in Memphis. How I gave him a few hundred dollars and told him to quit crack and go home.

"I never found out what happened to Tony," I told Dale, "but this has happened so many times. It seems like I can convince other people to quit, but I never can."

Dale and I got into a deep conversation about God. I shared my "what are the odds?" way of looking at things and confided that I felt God was sending me a message. I also said I was ready to quit and, once again, found myself giving the same lecture I had given to many of my friends over the years. Dale said he was ready to quit, too, and we made a pact: We'd quit together.

I picked up my cell and called Cindy. "I'm quitting," I told her when she picked up the phone. Cindy knew I was an addict, but not how deeply I was into drugs. She thought I was only into cocaine. In any case, she'd heard me vow to quit many times before.

"Well if you're quitting," she said not quite sarcastically, "why don't you come to church with Bryan and me tomorrow?"

I'd always felt like Cindy was a spiritual gateway for me. Not that she had some special pipeline to God or anything. But it seemed like she had long been close to God, and I could see that her faith was strong and steady. Maybe Cindy's kind of faith was what I needed to finally break free. She and Bryan were still going to Living Word, the church they drove an hour to reach each Sunday. Since Dale and I happened to be in Minneapolis, the church was only about five miles away.

"Okay," I said. "I'll have a friend with me. He's quitting, too."

Since we had committed to quitting in the morning, Dale and I agreed it would be a good idea to head downtown and get one last batch of coke. We started looking for a dealer—somebody besides Joe, for obvious reasons. It was after 2 a.m. and all the bars that served liquor were closed, but we saw the lights on at a show club, so we parked and went in. Inside, I started sizing up the crowd, trying to spot somebody who would sell to me. We hadn't been standing at the bar 30 seconds when a guy walked up and said, "Hey, are you from here?"

"Yeah," I said.

"Do you know where Fridley is?" He'd come into town on a red-eye flight, the stranger said, and got lost while trying to find this other town.

"Yeah, Fridley's north of here. Where are you from?"

"Memphis," he said.

"Really? I was just telling my friend here a good Memphis story," I said. I gave the stranger a 15-second version of that crazy trip.

He drew back his head and gave me a weird look. "Is your name Mike?"

"Yeah…?" I said.

"And you're a gambler?"

"Yeah, why?"

"Do you know a guy named Tony?"

My neck tingled. "Yeah."

The man's eyes grew wide. "After that trip, Tony got clean and now he owns a bunch of chicken restaurants. He said you saved his life. He calls you 'the angel from the north.'"

I didn't know what to say. I was blown away. And my friend Dale? He was completely freaked out. We had just been talking about God, about odds, about all the "coincidences" that kept happening to me. I had told him the Tony story not more than an hour ago. And now we walk into a random bar in downtown Minneapolis and learn from a complete stranger what happened to the guy?

Dale shook his head slowly in disbelief. "I'm done," he said. "I'm out of here." He hurried out of the club.

The stranger and I compared notes. I told him a more complete version of my Tony story, and he said it matched what Tony had told him. When he got home from Memphis, Tony had turned his life over to God and married his fiancée. He now spent a good part of his time and money helping other people get off drugs, the stranger said.

"I can't believe this," I said. "Do you know what the odds are that we would meet?"

I didn't know myself. A million to one? A billion to one?

It was impossible that this guy was here.

It was impossible that I was here at the same time he walked in asking for directions.

It was impossible that he knew not only my story, but even my name.

It was impossible.

Despite this miraculous encounter, you will not be surprised to learn that I did not go to church with Cindy the next day. Since Dale had abandoned me, I used it as an excuse to find more cocaine. I wound up in a Minneapolis crack house where I hit the pipe hard for the next two days. Instead of quitting, my crack use escalated. I began segregating myself from a lot of my non-crack-using friends and family, especially Cindy.

Shortly after my run-in with Officer Larry, she had called me at the house in the woods. "Mike, the pillow company is just a platform for a bigger thing," Cindy said.

She added that God had revealed this to her in prayer. By now I was used
to people claiming to have weird messages for me from God, and Cindy's
statement triggered a memory. While I was packing up our family home
in order to move in with Rachel, a notebook had fallen out of a picture
frame when I pulled it off the wall. It contained the six-page "out of body"
message-to-self I'd hidden behind the album cover. That was the first time I'd
become aware of this whole idea of a platform. Now though, I had this internal
sense that I was losing everything—not just material things, but losing myself.
At this point, I didn't see how I was ever going to be able to help anybody.

"I know," I told my sister simply.

"Well, okay," she said. "But God also showed me that if you don't quit
smoking, you're going to die."

I laughed. "Cindy, smoking is like my fifth worst vice." I knew she meant
cigarettes. "I think I'm going to be okay."

About a week later, my phone rang again. The shouting began as soon as I
picked up. "It's not cigarettes, it's crack cocaine! You're smoking crack cocaine?"

It was Cindy again.

"Are you kidding me? I'm not smoking crack!" I said. I went a few verbal
rounds with my sister.

"I know you're lying," Cindy said. Again, God had spoken to her in prayer.
"If you keep doing it, you're going to die." Abruptly, she hung up.

Suddenly, I realized that I'd somehow woven God's messages to me into
my rationale for continuing to indulge my addictions. I'm no theologian, but
it seemed to me that if God was all-powerful, and if He had destined me to
do great things with MyPillow, then nothing could stop that—including me.
That meant that until the time came for the platform, whatever it was, I could
do whatever I wanted, including drugs. But Cindy's words helped me begin to
realize the error of my thinking. Maybe it was a two-way street. Maybe I had to
cooperate with God.

Shortly afterward, I received an undeniable reminder of my mortality. In the
summer of 2008, medical testing revealed I had precancerous growths. A surgeon
removed them, and I was fine, but if I'd found them later, they could have been
fatal. That was the day I started talking to God.

"I'm going to quit," I told Him. "I'm not going to quit today, but I'm
definitely going to quit."

After I made that promise, things began to unravel quickly. In August, I had to
deliver pillows to Jim and others who were manning my booth at the Minnesota
State Fair, my biggest event of the year. I drove to the fairgrounds with a

truckload of pillows, but I couldn't make myself go in to deliver them. I had been up all night smoking crack and felt so sketchy and paranoid that I backed my truck into a pole in the parking lot.

Then, I found out that the numbers coming out of the fair were down—way down. Usually, the fair proceeds were enough to inject badly needed cash into my company. But this time, receipts were so low that I wouldn't be able to cover expenses. I decided to take the fair proceeds to Laughlin and multiply the money by counting cards. Instead, I lost hand after hand, hour after hour. The 1.5 percent advantage I should've had seemed permanently suspended.

I decided to abandon Laughlin for Las Vegas in search of greener pastures—and cocaine, which I had never been able to find in Laughlin. I caught a ride with a Riverside blackjack dealer and his girlfriend. It was September 12, 2008. How do I remember the date so clearly? Because of what happened next.

Halfway to Las Vegas we got pulled over for speeding. The cop asked us all to show our I.D. I didn't sweat it: For once, I had a valid Minnesota driver's license. I also had zero warrants out for my arrest. We'd been stopped on the highway for almost 20 minutes when another highway patrol officer pulled up.

I looked at the other two in the car. "I know this drill," I said. "One of you is going to jail."

But the next thing I knew, officers appeared at my window with guns drawn. "Out of the car! Out of the car!" they yelled.

A thorough frisking and a pair of handcuffs later, I found myself in the Clark County Detention Center in downtown Las Vegas, at the beginning of a nightmare.

I didn't know why I'd been arrested, and kept asking, "Why am I here?" But no one would answer. I was not given a phone call. I was not allowed to contact a lawyer. Instead, they placed my possessions in a Ziploc bag, snapped a mugshot, and took my fingerprints. Next, I was hustled to a small holding cell crammed with at least 20 people. The biggest guy in the cell was using the only roll of toilet paper as a pillow, and another big guy was using the toilet as a chair. Neither man seemed inclined to share.

A long night began. I became thirstier and thirstier, but the water fountain was behind the Toilet King, and he wouldn't let anyone near it. Meanwhile, the jailers gave us almost nothing to drink.

At least 24 hours passed. A guard pulled me out of the holding cell and took me to another confinement area. It was nearly pitch black, but I could make out the shadows of bunks everywhere. I still didn't know why I was there.

The officer told me that the jail was on lockdown and gave me my bunk number. "If you make any noise," he said, "lockdown will be extended."

I had no intention of making any noise. All I could focus on was how thirsty I was, so I asked to use the bathroom. When permission was granted, I sprinted to a water fountain, sucked down what seemed like a gallon, and worked my way to my bunk in the dark.

I was just about to climb up when the guy in the bottom bunk said, "You touch my bunk, I'll kill you."

I basically had to do a chin-up to get into my rack. I had just made it up there when I heard a whisper. "Hey, fool, you just drank all that water. You better pee your pants, because if you ask to use the bathroom, you're going to get us all more time in lockdown."

A third voice came out of the dark. "You pee your pants, I'll kill you."

That night seemed eternal. When the lights finally came on and the inmates started moving around, I climbed down and the pain from my bladder seared through me. I had started to crawl to the bathroom when a guard came and kicked me in the gut.

"What do you think you're doing?" he snapped. "Get off the floor."

I spent three days in that jail without knowing why I was being held. During that time, I saw a mentally disabled man beaten by other inmates. I saw the guards call the prisoners names and withhold basic humane treatment. I reflected that this was where my choices had brought me: I had arrived in hell.

Finally on Tuesday, I appeared in shackles before a judge via video feed. He informed me that I was being charged with a felony because I had stolen from a casino. I was stunned. As it turned out, he was talking about the $100 marker at the Stardust casino, the one I had signed for seven years before when I'd taken the Schmitty's Regulars to Vegas. The guy had never paid the marker, and the Stardust reported it as felony theft. Years earlier, the Stardust had given me a letter absolving me of this debt, but the property had since closed permanently. Then, in 2006, developers demolished it in a spectacular nighttime explosion. Apparently, the Stardust bosses had sold their unpaid debt for collection, and my marker was somehow still on their list.

Video Judge set my bail at $1,300, but I still sat in jail for three more days. First, Corey hesitated to send bail money because he heard I got busted with a drug dealer instead of a card dealer. Then, even though I'd made bail, the jailers let me sit for another 24 hours, saying, "We'll let you out when we feel like it."

That's a direct quote.

I'd had it. My annual duck hunting trip with Darren was the next day, and I exploded in anger at the meanest guard in the jail. Years of pent-up rage blasted out all at once, and words stampeded from my mouth as I called him every name I could think of. The entire jail went silent as the inmates waited to see what this guard would do to me.

But all he did was smile, happy he had finally broken me. Without saying a word, he walked over, picked up a phone, and ordered my release. Later on, the charge against me was dismissed. The Stardust marker had indeed been forgiven years earlier. It had all been a huge mistake.

Or had it? Looking back, I think it was God, still trying to get my attention. And He wasn't finished.

Darren was 18 now and had been living with Rachel and me for about five months. I had congratulated myself for moving him in with me, but now I have to admit the truth: I was so deep into drugs at this point that his presence in the house was almost an afterthought.

Still, we did have this hunt planned, and I was looking forward to it. I had been taking this annual trip since I was a kid and never missed it, no matter what else happened during the year. It was like an anchor in the chaos of my life. I got home from Nevada just in time. Darren and I packed our gear and headed down to Iowa, where we hunted Sturm's Pond. Dick and Cathy Sturm had trusted me on their land for more than 40 years, even through the times I was in trouble and people wondered why they didn't ban me. That always meant a lot to me.

Sitting in a duck blind under a brilliant autumn sky, Darren and I brought down bird after bird. When we pulled into our driveway a few days later, 20 ducks and geese lay in the truck bed, cleaned and dressed. It was twilight as I braked to a stop in front of the house in the woods and cut the engine. After my week in that hellhole jail, I was grateful for the quality time spent with my son. We unloaded the truck and I shut the garage door. I was heading around to the front porch when I noticed Darren wasn't following me.

I stopped and turned to him. "Aren't you coming in?" I noticed that his lips were quivering and he looked about two seconds away from bursting into tears. "What's wrong?" I said.

"I want to go live with Charlie," Darren said, his tone timid and unnaturally high.

It was a gut punch—not only to hear my son say those words, but to see his struggle. By now, Charlie had moved into his own apartment. I could tell instantly that Darren had spent hours, maybe days, building up his courage to say he wanted to move in with his brother. Darren knew it would break my heart. It then occurred to me that his car was probably already packed.

I looked at him steadily, hoping he couldn't tell I was holding back tears. "Well, that's fine," I said gently.

I will never forget the way Darren said those words. I know how hard it was for him, and I felt just horrible that he'd had to watch the chaos of his dad going down. And I felt guilty, too, because I realized that I'd been using Darren as my last little bit of stability, as though maybe I wasn't as bad a dad as I had been when I abandoned the kids at our family home. All my worst fears became crystal clear in that moment. I really wasn't a good father. I wasn't even a good man. I had let my addictions destroy my own family.

So that was September. And God still wasn't done. In October, Jim Furlong quit MyPillow. It turned out that while I was in Laughlin losing the Minnesota State Fair money, some people had told Jim I was an addict. To that point, I had kept my drug addiction a secret from him. He had lived through so much of my chaos, including my divorce and my relationship with Rachel. He knew I was struggling to keep MyPillow afloat. But this new piece of information gave him a different perspective on everything.

Jim called to tell me he was going to work for his brother, who was a trucker. It was a terrible blow. For three years, he had been a rock-steady source of encouragement and stability. He was on the road for us constantly, selling at home shows across the country. He had even loaned money to MyPillow on more than one occasion. With him quitting, it felt like the heart was being ripped out of my company.

But I gritted my teeth and refused to get emotional. When Jim was diagnosed with cancer, I hadn't believed he would die because I had seen him in my future, working with me at the pillow company. I didn't believe him now either. I thought he'd be back.

"That's okay, Jim," I said. "I understand. Good luck in your new career."

My life had been crumbling for quite some time, but now it seemed to be picking up speed. One by one, I was losing everyone I cared about, the people who had kept me from coming completely undone. I couldn't help but think of what Cindy had already told me twice in 2008: "You can't keep standing in front of semis, Mike. The window is closing, and God is tired of waiting. Even if you don't die, He's going to pick somebody else."

CHAPTER

33

Hope Match

That December, I was sitting on the floor of the house in the woods in a depressive trance when an old friend materialized in front of me like Captain Kirk in a transporter beam.

Christmas had come and gone. Rachel and I were on the outs again, so I was living alone. I couldn't keep up with the contract-for-deed payments on the house and was about to lose that, too. There was no furniture because it had all belonged to Rachel, and she took it when she moved out. I had almost nothing left. I'd had an iPod filled with vintage music like the songs on the jukebox at Schmitty's, but I had just traded that to a minor dealer for a tiny bit of coke. All I had left were my truck and my hunting guns.

The friend who appeared before me was Dick VanSloun. I had stayed on Dick's couch during my first work-release jail time all those years ago. He had probably knocked on the front door and let himself in when I didn't answer, but it seemed to me that he appeared out of nowhere.

"Hey, Dick, how you doing?" I said.

Dick is short and stocky and talks a little like Joe Pesci in *My Cousin Vinny*. Kind of a tough guy, but not over the top. I was very happy to see him. He and I had always been close. In fact, we'd briefly been in business together back in the day, laying cable via underground directional boring. But I hadn't seen Dick in more than four years, and the house in the woods was wildly out of his way.

"What are you doing here?" I asked. "What's going on?"

Dick crouched down so that we were at the same level. "I don't know why I'm here, Mike. I just felt like I was supposed to come out here. You tell me what's going on."

While staying at Dick's house, he and I would throw massive parties. He was the guy you would get drugs from. But in April 2004, Dick got caught dealing, and with the charges the D.A. pinned on him, he had eight years of prison hanging over his head. Strangely though, his trial kept getting delayed again and again, for so long that the lawyers in the case had never seen anything like it. A couple of years passed, and by the time he actually appeared in court, everyone in town, including Judge Kanning, knew Dick had completely turned his life around. He had quit drugs, completed addiction treatment, was going to church regularly, had gotten a steady job, and was even taking care of his ailing mother.

So, in the courtroom, Dick was standing behind the defense table, and Judge Kanning looked down at him and said something like, "What more can I do to you that would get you to a place any better than where you already are?" And he sentenced Dick to a very long probation, crediting him for time served for the one day he was actually in jail.

Now here he was, standing in my living room with a clean-and-sober track record four years long. We small-talked a little about old times, and then a little about what I was doing with my life. Dick didn't come right out and say, "Hey, you better quit or you're going to disintegrate," but he did communicate his concern.

I looked at him, at his face, at how healthy he looked. He seemed calm, happy, and confident. There was a question I needed to ask him, though, something I'd wondered about for a long time.

"Is it boring?"

Dick knew exactly what I meant. Sobriety. Was it boring?

"No, man, it ain't boring," Dick said.

When it came to drugs, Dick was my peer in every way. We were about the same age, started cocaine around the same time, had lived as functioning addicts, switched to crack in the late 90s, and smoked ridiculous quantities. Dick was also the only person I knew who had done all that and then quit for good. There wasn't another soul on earth who could have walked in my door and painted that picture for me.

There is a term I wouldn't come up with until much later: hope match. A person's hope match is someone who has been through what they've been through and come out clean and sober on the other side, with their heart restored. That's why none of the treatment programs I'd been in had worked for me. I felt that professional counselors meant well and that they really wanted to help. They had the right degrees and certificates hanging on their walls. But to me, they were teaching a theory class. When I sat in a room with them, I would think, *You have absolutely no idea what you're talking about. Really and truly, you don't.*

I didn't want to hear from someone who had read about addiction. I wanted to hear from a former addict who had experienced *my* addiction.

Dick and I stood and hugged, and I walked him out. He hadn't said much, but he'd said all he needed to. He knew me. He knew I was incorrigible and that he wasn't going to talk me off any ledge. But he also showed me something I absolutely had to see.

Dick VanSloun was my hope match.

On the last day of 2008, I surrendered the house in the woods to its previous owner. Meanwhile, the foreclosure on our former family home was complete, so I was literally homeless. Darren was now living with Charlie, so I didn't need much. The first place I went to was the Hole in the Wall Casino, the place where I'd dropped my pants when the pit boss accused me of wearing a wire. They comped me a room for a week.

When my time was up, I returned to the Chaska area and asked my friend Bruce if I could sleep on his couch until I found other accommodations. Bruce was a private cab driver who drawled like Forrest Gump. He had the kindest heart. Maybe that's why he welcomed me in when few others would have.

It was January 2009. I did a little crack. I drifted in and out of bars. At one bar in Carver, I met a man in a cowboy hat named Jake. I told him about my (failing) pillow company, and he offered to introduce me to a few investor friends. He called them mavericks.

"They'll look at anything," Jake said.

I thanked him and forgot about it. I wanted to keep my company going but I wasn't interested in meeting any more suits. Meanwhile, two of my vendors, Frank and Jack, did have 50 or so orders to fulfill and had run out of pillows. I pawned my hunting guns, bought materials to make them a few, then ran out of funds to make more. When I delivered the new pillows, I asked Frank to pay me the cash he and Jack had collected from customers. He paid me for the new pillows, but put me off for the rest.

And just like that, MyPillow came to a halt. In fact, everything came to a halt. This was a new low, and I found myself ready to change. And yet, my desire to change came from so much more than all that I'd lost. Also haunting me was what I had left to lose. I finally understood that Cindy was right. If I kept using drugs, even if I survived, I would lose whatever mission God had for me. In the wild downward spiral of 2008, I had become convinced that the platform was my life's purpose, my service to God and to people, a future that might redeem and make sense of all the craziness that had gone before. More than anything else, I didn't want to miss out on that.

From the beginning of 2008, God had impressed on me that He wasn't going to wait much longer. I lay on Bruce's couch, caught between sadness and excitement. Sadness because I was leaving cocaine, the friend I had depended on for more than 25 years. Excitement because I knew I was headed for an epic personal comeback. I was on the verge of getting my self-respect back. My family could finally be proud of me again.

My emotions that night swung wildly back and forth, like preparing for a funeral and a birth at the same time. The choice I faced reminded me of the projection booth back at the Flying Cloud drive-in, when I had changed reels between the two films of a double feature. Near the end of the reel on the first movie, as the credits rolled, the film would begin to make a fluttering sound. If you waited long enough, you would then see individual frames flickering on the drive-in screen. Finally, the screen went dark. It was time to change the reel and start the second movie.

That's the way I felt now about my future. My life was like a double feature, and the credits on the first film—one full of pain and misadventure—were rolling. Now that reel was running out, and that fluttering sound I heard was God's still, small voice telling me I could still choose the second feature. But if I didn't choose wisely, *right now*, the entire second half of my life would be the wrong movie. The one without the platform. The one where I did not fulfill my calling. I had waited until the last second of the last day when I could still make a choice.

I chose a Thursday as my last day as an addict. It was January 15, 2009. Shortly after midnight on January 16, I told Bruce, "I'm quitting today."

"Wow," he replied in his slow, friendly drawl. "We could call this chapter, 'End of the Line.'"

For years, I'd been telling Bruce and other friends about that book I was going to write someday. Every time I'd get out of one scrape or another, I'd say, "Wow! This is going to make a great chapter in the book!" And everyone would laugh in agreement. But now I was about to write what I thought was going to be the greatest chapter of all: The Comeback. I was going to come back from the disastrous turmoil of addiction.

That night, I lay down on Bruce's couch and offered what may have been my first genuine prayer. "God, when I wake up, I don't ever want to have the desire for drugs or alcohol again."

CHAPTER

34

Comeback

O
n Friday, January 16, 2009, I woke up on Bruce's couch and checked in
with myself, kind of like someone who takes a long fall, then lies there
for a second to be sure they're all in one piece.

Yes, I was all in one piece. And I could feel, without question, that my desire
for drugs and alcohol was gone. I jumped up and ran to Bruce's tiny bathroom
like a kid running to the tree on Christmas morning. I leaned toward the mirror
over the sink. I looked pretty good, or at least not too bad for someone who just
came off a 30-year bender. To me, that was a little bit of a miracle.

But the greater miracle was how I felt inside. I felt calm and refreshed
and peaceful. It was a new kind of peace I had never experienced before. I also
felt an urgent sense of calling. I thought it would have been normal to feel
overwhelmed by responsibility, but instead I felt relieved. That new movie I'd

hoped for—the second part of my life's double feature—had begun, and I was ready for whatever was coming next.

Later that morning, I jumped into Bruce's taxi and he drove me to Cindy's house. When she opened the door, I said, "I quit."

My sister, who had been with me through so many ups and downs, who had seen so many of my vows come and go, must've seen a new conviction in my eyes. She opened her door wide and welcomed me in. (Of course, she also hid her baking soda and spoons immediately.)

One of the first things I asked Cindy to do was take me to find Rachel. I had promised Rachel that if I ever quit, I would come back and help her quit, too. Cindy was fiercely against this, which was understandable, as she certainly didn't want me around anyone on drugs. But I insisted. I had to keep my promise. Reluctantly, my sister grabbed her car keys and did as I asked. Rachel wasn't hard to find, since she was staying with two other user friends of ours. But when I told her I had quit and that she could, too, she dug in her heels and told me to go away.

On my second morning of sobriety, I was lying on the bunk in Cindy's basement when a phrase I'd never heard before kept going through my head: "Run, baby, run." I was again in that same sleep/dream state that had come over me just before I'd awakened and written the strange essay about quitting crack.

Over and over again: Run, baby, run. Run, baby, run. Run, baby, run.

I sat up in bed and now fully awake, yelled up the stairs. "Hey Cindy, have you ever heard the phrase 'run, baby, run'?"

She called back down, "I think it's the name of a book."

Soon after, I found a copy of *Run Baby Run* in the Minneapolis Public Library and read it cover to cover in a single day. It's the story of a New York City gang leader, Nicky Cruz, who was converted to faith in Christ through the work of evangelist David Wilkerson in 1958. Cruz went on to work with Wilkerson in the ministry Teen Challenge, helping people overcome substance abuse and other problems.

I thought about the way Cruz helped many other gang members leave that lifestyle behind and knew instantly why he was so successful: He was their peer. He'd been where they were. He understood them. He was their hope match.

After reading the book, I began to sense that my future work might involve addicts. By no means did I think my story was as powerful as Nicky Cruz's. But I was so excited about the potential similarities that I paid a librarian the required fee so I could keep the book.

On my third day of sobriety, I went to church—willingly this time. Dick VanSloun had told me that God, faith, and church attendance had been a big part of his sobriety. I hopped in the car with Cindy and Bryan, we drove an hour to Living Word, and I didn't complain even once. It was the same church where the pastor had told Cindy that something important had happened to me on the morning I had that strange dream. It was also the same church where Dale Wind and I had planned to go when we vowed (and failed) to quit.

Up until now, I had mainly resisted church, feeling alternately that it was boring, a waste of time, or that I was somehow unworthy. Now, I sat through the service and actually listened to the message instead of just hearing it. I didn't understand all of the preaching and wouldn't for a long time, but I knew I had come to a place of peace and healing.

That Monday, Jim Furlong called me. What are the odds? I hadn't heard a single word from Jim since he quit MyPillow the previous fall. Now, he had something to tell me.

"Frank and Jack are taking over your company, Mike," he said.

At the state fair the year before, Jim said, he learned that Frank and Jack had a scheme underway to copy MyPillow, take all of my shows, and bring their copy to market. At the time, Jim thought maybe they were justified in doing so, since as a crack user I wouldn't be able to keep my company running anyway. Since then, Frank and Jack had hijacked every one of my home shows. After the fair season ended, it was easy to do. Because they had sold at these shows before, they simply approached organizers and said something like, "Mike's on drugs. He's out, and we're MyPillow now."

The show organizers had been dealing with these guys for a while and had no reason to ask questions. The really insulting thing was that Frank had come to me just after the new year and asked for more pillows. I'd hocked my hunting guns to buy the materials to make them.

"They're at the point now where they're ready to manufacture and sell pillows and force you out of business," Jim said. "I know we haven't talked in a while, but I thought you deserved to know."

I later learned that as soon as Jim finished delivering this news, he held his cell phone away from his ear. He'd expected me to start screaming. That's just what I would have done, too, had he told me this news just a few days earlier, when my rage problem was still fully intact. Now, though, with this newfound peace, I calmly replied, "Okay, Jim. It's going to be okay."

"What do you mean, 'it's going to be okay'?" he said, taken aback.

"I quit crack, Jim. This is all going to be okay."

I spent the next half-hour telling him why I was so excited about the future.

I wasn't sure why Frank and Jack had decided to backdoor me. I had never let them down or broken a promise, no matter what I was going through. I'd ensured they had pillows for their shows even when I didn't have the money to do so. As addiction goes, my track record on that score was a bit odd, actually. Even in the depths of my drug use, I never broke promises to show promoters or customers. Looking back now, I can see that God was protecting my future from my past.

The sad thing with Frank and Jack was that nothing had changed in all the years we did business together—until they found out I was an addict. When Jim found out, he quit. When Frank and Jack found out, they went after my company.

One of the big lessons I've learned is that, like Neff, some people see nothing wrong with preying on addicts. Many are easy targets and don't have many resources to use in a fight. Other people fall into the same category as Barry Price, who found it easier to snap up an entrepreneur's good idea rather than invent his own—and for similar reasons. As Price had said, he was a millionaire, and there was nothing I could do about it.

Later on, I would make it my mission to help both addicts and entrepreneurs. Now though, I focused on what was in front me. In spite of everything that had happened in the years since I'd launched MyPillow, I always viewed every customer as if he or she were my only customer. Now, newly sober, I was about 10 days behind fulfilling outstanding website orders. To fill these, I needed fabric to make pillow ticks. I had used up everything I had to make Frank's pillows a couple weeks prior, so I called my fabric supplier, John Anderson.

John was a middleman. He ordered fabric for me from a specialty house that delivered rolls of material printed with the MyPillow logo. John then sold the rolls to me at a markup. Throughout our business relationship, he would never reveal the identity of this specialty house, but I continued using him because the supplier was giving him credit that he passed on to me.

Because MyPillow was such a small operation, John also stored the fabric for me and sold me quantities as I needed it. I called him and told him I needed some now.

"Bad news, Mike," he said. "My supplier says you gotta pay up front from now on. It's gonna be $30,000. Cash."

I had never had to pay up front before, and I had never left John hanging. I knew he already had the fabric and that it didn't have anything to do with his supplier. I also knew that John knew I didn't have $30,000. That's when I suspected he was in cahoots with Frank and Jack. With my logo plastered all over the fabric, there was only one use for it. He was going to sell my fabric to them.

I kept these thoughts to myself. "Wow. Thirty thousand dollars is a lot of money, John," I said. "When do they need it?"

"Now. Today."

There was no reason in the world for John to say that, since he'd had no idea I'd be calling. All I could think was that he was about to close a deal on the fabric with Frank and Jack. John had to find some way to put me off long enough to pretend that I had been too late.

"Could I at least have until next Friday?" I said. "Come on, John. It's our only chance to keep doing business together. I know it's a long shot, and I don't know how I'll ever come up with the cash, but can you please check?" As with Neff, I played it as if we were still friends.

"I'll check," he said reluctantly. What else could he do?

A few minutes later, John called back. "Okay, you've got until Friday at 1 p.m. If you don't get the money by then, the fabric is gone."

The stakes were high and I had several problems. One, I couldn't make pillows without fabric. Two, without pillows I couldn't fulfill orders. Three, Frank and Jack had taken all my shows. And four, now I was sure John was in on it, too.

On top of all that, where on earth was I going to get $30,000? I'd already hocked everything I owned and was sleeping on a spare bed in my sister's basement. I was wrestling with this issue, trying to come up with some last-ditch idea, when I suddenly remembered that guy I met at the bar in Carver a week or so before. The one who'd told me about his "maverick" investors. But I hadn't written his number down. And if I did find him, would he even remember me?

That afternoon, I drove to the bar and asked the bartender if he remembered a guy in a cowboy hat who had been in about a week ago.

"Yea, that's Jake," the bartender said. "But he only comes in about once a month, and he was just in here last week."

My face fell. "Oh." But as I turned around to leave, guess who walks in the door? Seriously: You can't make this stuff up. I rushed right over to Cowboy Jake and wasted no time telling him what I was after. "Do you have a way you could get me in to see your investor friends?"

He pulled his phone out of his pocket. "Sure. I'll call them right now."

Five minutes later, I had an appointment to see the mavericks at 10 a.m. on Friday morning, three hours before John Anderson's deadline.

That morning, I walked into a conference room in an Eden Prairie office building, wearing blue jeans and a T-shirt, and carrying a pillow and three jars of foam. I took a seat at the head of the table, facing eight businessmen in suits. There was a CIO, a CFO, a CEO, maybe even a C-I-E-I-O. In the past, I would never have faced a situation like this without cocaine. But those days were over.

I was nervous, but also strangely confident. Why? Because this had to work. This was Plan A. As usual, I had no Plan B.

I plunged in, telling these men the story of MyPillow. I showed them the foam in the jars. I demo'd the pillow, how you could shape it and it would stay. I was also brutally honest about my circumstances, about the people who were trying to copy my invention and why I needed $30,000 to buy fabric immediately.

Then I told them how my company came to be in this mess. "I used to be a crack addict," I said. "I'm broke. I don't have a penny to my name. But if you invest $30,000 in my product, I will sell MyPillow at shows, where it has been very successful, and I will pay you back $40,000 in three months."

One of the C's had a question. "When did you quit crack?"

I didn't skip a beat. "Last Thursday," I said.

Immediately, four of the mavericks got up and left.

"Well, now there are four of you," I said when they were gone. "That's $7,500 apiece, and I'm going to pay each one of you back ten grand."

I got out a piece of paper and scribbled down some numbers to show them how I was going to do that with money I'd make at upcoming shows.

Finally, one of the men said to the others, "What do you think?"

Another said, "I'll do it if the rest of you will."

A third man said, "Well, go get him a check."

I cleared my throat. "Uh, guys, it's gotta be cash."

I walked out of there with $30,000 in three $10,000 bundles, each made up of hundred-dollar bills. They didn't even write up a contract. When one of the C's suggested it, another one said, "A contract? If he defaults, he doesn't have anything to take. Just write up an I.O.U."

By now, it was 12:30 p.m. With 30 minutes left until my deadline, I thanked them from the bottom of my heart, ran out to my truck, and called John. I'd already told him I had a line on some investors.

First words out of his mouth: "Do you have the money?"

"No, I don't have any money on me, but I need to come see you."

This was technically true since I'd laid the cash on the passenger seat. "I went to see those investors, and I think they could really help us in the future. But I'm not sure they believed I really even have a product or that I can get all this fabric. What I need to do is come up and take a picture of the fabric with the MyPillow logo on it."

"What?" he said. He was thoroughly confused because I meant to confuse him. "What in the world are you talking about?"

"John, I'm serious. I just want to show them my word is good. If I text them a picture of me with the fabric before 1 p.m., they'll know I was telling them the truth in our meeting. You've got to send the fabric back now anyway, but I want to get a picture before you do. Besides, I have something else I need to talk to you about."

Again, what could he say? John reluctantly agreed to meet me right away.

I rolled up at 12:50. Stuffing the money in my pants pockets, I got out of the truck. John took me behind his house to the white tin shed where he stored the fabric. I rushed him along, as though I were frantic.

"What did you want to talk to me about?" he said.

"Let's take the picture first. We can talk about it then."

The truth was, I wanted to make sure he still had what I wanted. Together, we slid the shed door open, and there it was, roll after roll of MyPillow fabric.

I reached into my pockets and pulled out the cash. "Surprise!" I yelled. "I got the money. I just wanted to surprise you. Are you surprised?"

Stunned was more like it, judging by the look on his face.

"It's a miracle, John. We're still in business!" I wrapped him in a big bear hug as if he were as pleased as I was that I'd beaten his phony deadline. The poor guy looked like he was ready to cry.

"Help me load up the fabric, John. Isn't this great?" I said. "It's a beautiful thing! Oh, come here. Give me another hug!"

CHAPTER
35

Living Free

As I fought to regain control of my company, I was so driven that I didn't even stop to realize what sobriety felt like. All I knew was that I woke up every day with this amazing sense of hope, and I didn't want to lose that feeling. My former dealers and fellow users were the first to believe I was sober for good. None of my dealers smirked and said, "You'll be back." Not once did anyone ask me to do crack or drink with them ever again. I had told them all many times that I was going to quit, and now they could see in my eyes that it had really happened.

The people closest to me took a little longer to trust me, and I believe that's true for most addicts. You aren't going to get trust right away. Eventually, though, even Cindy stopped hiding her baking soda and spoons.

I began going to Living Word church regularly and attended a couple of different Bible studies. They ran a faith-based substance abuse recovery center at the church called Living Free. Even though I had been completely free of the desire for drugs for two months, I felt led to go there. I wasn't sure why, except that maybe some part of me hoped I would find out why I had become an addict in the first place.

When I told Cindy I planned to attend Living Free, she said, "I guarantee you're going to find out that the reason you're an addict has something to do with our parents' divorce."

I was immediately angry. "You don't know what you're talking about," I snapped. "We had a great childhood. I wouldn't change anything."

I was sure Cindy was dead wrong. In addition to Willmar, I had been to at least a half-dozen other treatment centers in the 80s. All of them had emphasized the money I'd wasted on drugs and how much I hurt the people around me. What did those things have to do with divorce? I thought. Nothing, that's what.

When I signed up for Living Free, I met my counselor, Rafe Ronning. Rafe had curly blond hair and looked so young that I couldn't imagine what he had to teach me. In our first meeting, I spilled out my story with excitement: I was an alcoholic and crack cocaine addict and I had been completely freed from these unhealthy desires more than two months ago. "For some reason, I feel like I'm supposed to come here," I told him. "I have a pillow company that's some kind of platform for God. I'm going to write a book and help millions of addicts."

Rafe told me later that he went home that night and said to his wife, "I've met a lot of delusional addicts, but you wouldn't believe what walked in today."

On that first day, Rafe facilitated a group session. In group discussions at Willmar and other places, I'd enjoyed bragging about my colorful past, like my narrow escapes from death and the "almost" mafia. Now I had a new story that I couldn't wait to tell: those Mexican drug dealers who had threatened to chop off my head.

Instead, I had to sit and listen. I fidgeted in my seat as other people shared about their painful childhoods and how that affected their self-worth, and blah, blah, blah. I was self-involved and without empathy. *Wait until they hear my story*, I thought. At my second group session, I finally had my chance to share. I was a couple of minutes into my tales of death-defying stunts, casino enforcers, and ingesting mass quantities of drugs while running a business, when Rafe shut me down.

"Mike, I don't care how many drugs you did or all your big stories," he said. "I want to hear about your father."

I stopped and looked at him, confused. "What do you mean? I had a great father. I just didn't live with him because my parents divorced when I was seven."

That got Rafe talking. He spoke for quite some time about the role of fathers in children's lives, especially in the lives of sons. About how a break or breach in the family unit, as in my case, or the abuse of a child by an adult, particularly a parent, can produce a wound that the child doesn't even know is there. Rafe talked about how these wounds can plant the seeds of addiction, which don't sprout until later, as that young man or woman begins to feel deep down that something is missing. That they are somehow different or not good enough. That's when they begin seeking ways to mask that pain.

Rafe's words began to open my eyes. His simple summary of the roots of addiction may not have explained everyone's inner struggle, but it explained a lot about mine. I began to think that maybe Cindy had been right. Maybe the divorce did have something to do with it.

On my third day at Living Free, those realizations deepened as Rafe had us write out our life stories. He asked us to pay particular attention to turning points, to important events that had altered our lives. When I really looked closely at these, I could again see the connection between my childhood and my addictions. There had been sudden, invisible earthquakes that I hadn't thought of in that way before. Like when my mom suddenly moved us out of the house by the lake and into the trailer court. As a child, I had simply ridden out these shocks, not understanding or even being aware of their impact on me. But now, forced to put my story on paper, I could see how really painful those things were. Suddenly, I didn't feel so condescending toward the people who had shared about their painful childhoods on the first day.

I continued at Living Free for a couple of months in a strange and unfamiliar state of peace and patience. After the other treatment centers I had been to, when I got back into the world I would feel like a ticking time bomb of shame. And I wasn't alone. Friends from home and friends I met in treatment had similar experiences. We got back out in the world and maybe our girlfriend or wife or husband didn't wait for us. Or we didn't get our job back or some tragedy struck—somebody died, we went bankrupt, we lost our house.

Every one of us relapsed. Every single one.

In the past, it hadn't mattered how long the treatment was or the specifics of the program. I was just looking for that first excuse. Sometimes my excuse was that things were going *too* well. Although I didn't know it, I craved drama and chaos because that felt normal to me. As I have mentioned, being an addict is extremely hard work, and I had been working so hard for so long that I didn't know how to be at peace. So, I would go in search of that familiar adrenaline rush, trying to turn up the noise and run so fast that my pain couldn't catch me.

Now at Living Free, I had slowed down enough to listen to someone else for a change. Seeds were being planted. I now had an idea where my addictions may have come from. But to be honest, I still didn't like talking about it. I remained a little defensive about my family. In group sessions and alone with Rafe, I felt compelled to share the good things about my childhood.

Meanwhile, with Frank and Jack lurking in the wings, I had a company to save. I had quit drugs, I reasoned, and gotten some useful information that would help me move forward. That was good enough for me. After about 10 weeks, I left Living Free. It would turn out that I'd also left behind some important unfinished business.

In February, I took my new stock of pillows to the Des Moines Home and Garden Show, held at the Iowa Events Center. At first, it seemed the show would be a total bust. With just two hours left, I had only sold about a dozen pillows. I called Cindy and told her I needed to make another $1,200 just to keep the company going.

"You need to pray for favor," she said.

"What's that?" I'd never heard the expression.

Right there on the phone, Cindy prayed that God would show His favor and kindness to me by sending me more customers. She also asked specifically that God would help me come up with the money I needed. In my newfound faith, I hung up confident that everything would work out. But when the show ended, I hadn't sold a single additional pillow. I was disappointed, of course, but I also felt bad for Cindy. I didn't know how I was going to tell her that her prayer hadn't worked.

The venue was now almost empty of people, except for a few vendors and security guards. The organizers were starting to shut down the lights. I slid the cover over my booth, planning to come back and tear it down the next day. Feeling down, I joined the trickle of other people on their way out.

A man walking next to me noticed the MyPillow logo on my shirt and said, "Hey, we saw one of your pillows go by."

What are the odds? I thought grimly. I'd only sold those few.

But the man was still interested. He wanted to know what made MyPillow different. I explained a little and asked if he'd like to see one. Yes, he said, and followed me back to my booth, along with eight other vendors and a couple of security guards. Removing the cover, I explained how I'd invented MyPillow and how it worked, and even told them I'd recently quit doing crack. They seemed fascinated, both by the pillow and my story. We talked for an hour, and when it was done I'd sold them $1,210 worth of MyPillows—$10 more than I needed to stay alive.

Wow! I thought. Maybe this "praying for favor" thing really does work. I couldn't wait to tell Cindy.

I closed down my booth again and was the last one leaving the event center when I passed a 17,000-seat arena. That was when I was struck forcefully with one of my premonitions, a kind of waking dream.

Standing at the door of the empty arena, I saw the seats fill with people, dreamlike but as real as the people I'd just left. I saw myself speaking to the dream people—thousands of them. I don't know what to call these incidents, but as I mentioned, they almost always came true. That's why this one terrified me. Talking to people in a home-show booth was bad enough. But talking to an arena full of perfect strangers? I'd take a failed parachute, a mob enforcer, or a machete-wielding drug dealer over that any day of the week.

After getting sober, I slept in my sister's basement and spent my days working hard to drive MyPillow sales higher, while also learning how to run a business without the chemical confidence of cocaine. This kept me busy, but in my free time I sometimes felt very lonely. After a 20-year marriage, I felt incomplete on my own. I don't know quite how to describe it. I felt *too* free somehow, like a train running downhill with no brakes, or a hot-air balloon cut loose from its mooring.

Over a period of several days in 2009, Cindy told me she had a vision. She had seen a woman with long, dark hair wearing a teal-green outfit. She also felt God impress upon her that this woman was my match in every way. At God's insistence, Cindy shared this with me. My sister had been right about so many things that I tended to believe her about this woman. I just didn't know what I was supposed to do about it if I didn't even know who she was.

So I concentrated on my company. I began rebuilding by bringing on more employees. I started with Rachel Moore. I hadn't been able to persuade her to quit drugs at first, but she soon broke free of the two guys who had been holding her back and got sober on her own. To encourage her to keep moving in a positive direction, I gave her a job doing shows. Neither of us wanted to rekindle our romance, but we managed to be friends again.

At church, Cindy introduced me to an older gentleman, Thom Clapp. He was an experienced businessman, and I was looking for someone like that to bring wisdom to our operations.

"Well, young man, I can help you," Thom said after learning about my company. "I don't want any money, but I do need the title of CEO." I didn't care about titles, so I gave it to him. Thom is still involved with MyPillow, though now we call him our CPO—Chief Praying Officer.

After Jim Furlong watched me stay sober long enough to trust that I might really be done with crack, he asked to rejoin the company. Hearing that Thom was going to be CEO, Jim suggested that he serve as chief financial officer.

I said, "Sure, why not?"

Later Jim asked to see the company's checkbook.

"Who ever said the CFO gets to see the checkbook?" I said.

A bit later, Rachel introduced me to David Behr, who quickly became one of the best MyPillow salesman I had ever seen. David then introduced me to Tonja Waring, a single mom who began setting sales records herself. Other key players joined the team—Jennifer Duneman and Ted Rogers, as well as Mitch and Becky Aspelund. These people would form the new core of my company and become critical to our future success.

My battle with Frank and Jack intensified as they began to use my addictive past against me. They circulated stories of my involvement with drugs among show organizers, even as they stayed one step ahead of me, applying to shows and paying the required fees before I could scrape up the money. There were shopping mall shows every week, as well as larger home shows, and I went to see the organizers myself. One told me that even though Frank and Jack had already booked a booth, she'd let me into the show. But given her new knowledge about my drug use, she insisted that I pay two years of fees up front.

After the Des Moines show where I sold $1,210 worth of last-minute pillows, I decided to check in with other Iowa venues on my way home. In 2008, Frank and Jack had represented MyPillow at two large fairs in Iowa, and I wondered if they'd caused any problems. At the first fair office, I learned they had not paid the required fees. When I tried to explain that I had two rogue salesmen on my hands, the fair organizer understood but said MyPillow was still responsible. I agreed and promised to pay up. At the second fair office, the director was livid, having received almost a hundred complaints from customers who had ordered pillows but never received them. Translation: Frank and Jack had run out of MyPillows, but still took people's money. Again I tried to explain, but the director would have none of it.

"I don't care what happened," she said. "You will not be allowed into this fair ever again."

I asked her to at least let me make it right, and she agreed. She supplied me with the names, addresses, and phone numbers of all the customers who had complained. I contacted every one of them, apologizing on behalf of MyPillow and offering each a pillow *and* a refund. I really couldn't afford to offer refunds, but I didn't care. I felt terrible that this had happened and borrowed money from my nephew Ben in order to make good on my word.

After that, I drove all over Iowa delivering the promised pillows. Many people were shocked that I would go to all that trouble to make things right. Though I never asked them to, dozens contacted the fair director and asked that MyPillow be let back in. I felt blessed and relieved when the director called me.

She not only let me back in the fair but gave me a prime spot for my booth.

By May 2009, my war with Frank and Jack hit a boiling point. Every year, the Minnesota State Fairgrounds hosted other events in the run-up to the fair. At a horse show in August, my two rivals set up their booth. Their product was an exact copy of mine, right down to the now-patented foam fill. Rachel and I were assigned a booth nearby but not in the same building. During the course of the show, Frank and Jack called the State Fair police and claimed that I had confronted them at their booth, cursing and threatening them. This was an outright lie designed to get me kicked out—which I was. Fair police literally put me in their squad car, drove me off the grounds, and said I would be permanently banned from the state fairgrounds.

This was bad. Very, very bad. That meant I would lose the Minnesota State Fair, which scared me to death as I still relied on the fair to keep MyPillow afloat.

The day after I was ejected, I went back to the fairgrounds police station. The officer there delivered the bad news that a detailed report on my alleged behavior had already been prepared.

"But I was never at their booth!" I protested. I had definitely visited that building, but it was a gigantic, high-ceiling place with at least 10 rows of exhibitors. I had stopped in at a friend's booth on the opposite end. He was selling tree trimmers.

"They have witnesses," the officer said.

"Really? Who?"

The officer named Frank, Jack, and everyone working for them. It was my individual word against the word of about a half-dozen people. How was I going to argue against that?

Suddenly I had an idea. "What time did they say I was at their booth?"

The officer checked his records. "The harassment occurred at 1:04 p.m.," he said.

Only one customer had visited the tree-trimmer booth when I was there. There had been a problem with her credit card so I remembered her name. I gave the officer the name and said, "Check and see what time her purchase went through."

He called my friend's booth and learned that the receipt had been time-stamped at 1:04. Exactly. What are the odds?

The booth worker informed the officer that I had been there for at least 15 minutes. That meant I couldn't have been harassing Frank and Jack as they claimed. Angry that he'd been lied to, the officer urged me to press charges. I told him being proved innocent was enough. I had no desire to hurt Frank and Jack. I just wanted them to leave me alone. But these guys would not give up.

In 2010, I was walking down an aisle at the Minneapolis Home and Garden Show, where I'd gotten my start as an exhibitor five years earlier, when I heard

Frank's voice over a loudspeaker. I turned to see him working a microphone like a carnival barker.

"Hey, everyone, there's Mike Lindell of MyPillow! We've sold thousands and thousands of pillows, but Mike ruined his business because he was a meth addict!"

I looked at him and laughed. "It wasn't meth, it was crack!" I yelled back. "Get it right!"

36

Turnaround

W hat you might call the "Minnesota Pillow Fight" would last for two years. Frank and Jack tried to destroy MyPillow by destroying me personally. It didn't work. Ultimately, I was able to get back all my shows while their business would fade from view.

I spent those years both rebuilding my business and experimenting with ways to make it grow. I didn't have an MBA or any other business degree. I was a blue-collar guy from a blue-collar town, flying by the seat of my pants just as I always had.

By now, my staff had grown to about 25 people, with about 10 selling at shows and the rest working in manufacturing. For a while, that included my son Charlie and a bunch of his friends, with Charlie supervising the whole thing. I was very proud of him.

To get the word out about MyPillow, I hired a marketing firm to build a website. Here's what I told the guy: "What Amway did in 20 years, I want to do in three."

I had already built MyPillow's web presence organically so that in a Google search our name was the number one hit. I wanted to take that to the next level, but that's not how it went.

Instead, MyPillow disappeared from the Internet.

Well, from the search engine anyway, which is practically the same thing. For a newer company with a limited marketing budget and no storefront or retail sales, this was catastrophic. When I complained to the firm that had built the website, the woman in charge of our project was dismissive.

"Well, it's not like you have a registered trademark on the words 'my pillow,'" she said with a touch of sarcasm.

I looked at her and replied, "Actually, I do."

Her mouth fell open. Suddenly she realized the impact of her firm's error. As she set about fixing it, another rep there suggested the additional strategy of trying to get local press coverage. Years before that, I'd had another one of my premonitions: I'd seen a newspaper article accompanied by a somewhat goofy picture of me hugging a pillow teddy bear style. I thought, why not? I gave the rep the go-ahead for a local story, and he reached out to the Minneapolis *Star Tribune*. But I also tried to think bigger. And that's when I hit on what I thought was a great idea: hotels.

In the spring of 2010, Don Laughlin gave me permission to try an experiment. If I could get a sample of 300 people to try a MyPillow in their Riverside Hotel rooms overnight, how many would actually come back and buy one to take home? It took over three weeks to recruit my 300 volunteers, but when we did, 130 came back the next day to buy my product. It was an incredible conversion rate. If I could put MyPillows in every room, that would mean sales of $14,000 a day!

Again, Don gave me permission to try. Raising $80,000 from a small investor group of friends and family, I replaced every pillow in the Riverside. On every nightstand, I placed a small novelty pillow and sales brochure so that interested guests could call in or order online. Then I sat back and waited for the sales to roll in.

They didn't.

On the first day, only $200 came in and the next couple of days were the same. I was sick to my stomach. I had made a critical error. The 300 people in the test already had a big interest in trying MyPillow, which skewed the conversion rate. Also, the website and search engine problems had not yet been fixed, making it harder for potential customers to find us.

I went to talk to Del Newman, the Riverside general manager, about setting up a booth where I could actually sell MyPillows directly to customers. It would be very time-consuming—eleven hours a day sitting in a booth—but I was determined to get my investors' money back.

For three months in the summer of 2010, I literally lived at the Riverside Hotel and Casino. Every day was the same. I got up at 4 a.m. and counted cards until 9 a.m. Then, I left the blackjack tables and went to work in the MyPillow booth until 8 p.m. After playing some craps to relax, I would head up to the Gourmet Room, eat a comped steak and lobster dinner, return to my room, and go to bed by midnight. At 4 a.m., I would get up and start all over again. By the end of 90 days, I had earned back all the MyPillow investors' money while also making a lot of money for myself by counting cards.

During this time I became friends with almost all the Riverside employees and many of them became like family to me. Don Laughlin and I got to know each other better, too. Don was someone who had turned a lonely patch of desert into a profitable town that bore his name. I looked up to him as a man with a daring vision and the drive to turn that vision into reality.

One day, he invited me on an aerial tour of Laughlin and the surrounding area. It felt surreal, flying along the river and over the desert alongside Don as he piloted his own helicopter and answered all of my questions about how he'd built the town. Speaking through headsets over the thrum of chopper blades, I told him about my dream of growing my company and using it as a platform to help others.

"You're going to have all that," he said.

Coming from Don, those words meant the world to me. High up in the clean air over the Nevada desert, I felt I could almost see my future.

Six months later, I was back at the Riverside, playing one-on-one with a dealer on the graveyard shift. By 6 a.m., several stacks of chips had multiplied on the felt in front of me. Rob Laughlin, Don's grandson, was working as the pit boss that morning. Every so often, my phone made a strange beep. After a while, Rob asked me why.

"That's an order," I said. "Every time somebody buys a MyPillow, I get notified on my phone."

"How many orders do you get a day?"

"Right now, a dozen or so," I said. Then I looked at him and smiled. "But someday, Rob, my phone is going to beep so fast I'll have to turn it off to be able to concentrate on anything else."

Those words were still hanging in the air like a speech bubble in a comic book when my phone beeped twice. Then it beeped three times. Then it wouldn't stop.

Beepbeepbeepbeep..beepbeepbeepbeepbeep…beepbeepbeepbeepbeepbeepbeep…

Rob and I stared at each other. Was it a phone malfunction? I checked my phone and grinned. Nope, not a malfunction. Instead, MyPillow sales numbers had shot off the charts, and I knew exactly what had happened. The *Star Tribune* article had hit.

That article, a simple human-interest story, appeared on the front page of the business section. All it did was tell how I invented MyPillow, and how I was manufacturing it myself and selling it in Minnesota. Alongside the piece, the paper ran that geeky picture I'd seen in my premonition years before: me hugging a MyPillow as if it were a teddy bear.

We sold more pillows that one day, January 3, 2011, than we had in the previous three months. And it didn't stop there. My kids were running a booth at the Burnsville Mall that week. They called to say they had people lined up through a long hall and around the corner. Word was, almost all of them had read the article.

The next day, I was driving in the mountains north of Laughlin when I got a call from the Better Business Bureau. My new corporation, MyPillow, Inc., was not a BBB member, but the young man on the phone told me that when the *Star Tribune* ran its article, BBB had gotten more website hits from people checking out MyPillow than any other company on a single day.

My understanding of the Better Business Bureau was that it functioned as an independent group that objectively evaluated companies, then assigned them with ratings—A+ through F. Consumers could turn to the BBB if they wanted to know more about a company's reputation.

"Would you like to join?" the young man said.

"What's my BBB rating now?"

"You're a C+, but if you join you'll be an A."

"Why am I a C+?" I said. "Do I have complaints?"

"Oh, no, no. We just don't have enough information on you. If you join, we will." He then quoted me a steep price for membership.

Instantly, I became upset. "Why do I have to pay to get an A rating if I have no complaints? That makes no sense." In no uncertain terms, I insisted I would not be blackmailed. About an hour later, a sweet-talking woman who was apparently more senior called me back. "We just wanted to let you know, you don't have to join. We've done a little research on your company and updated your rating to an A."

Done a little research, I thought. *I'll bet.*

The woman quoted me a lower price for membership. Grudgingly, I joined since I felt a BBB membership would be expected of a company like mine. It would not be the last time I tangled with the BBB.

A couple of weeks later, I was filling in at a stock show in Denver for an employee whose mom had passed away. The employee had already been out for a week, but he was still grieving and needed more time to get his mother's affairs in order. His request was the beginning of the commonsense employee policies that are still in place at MyPillow today.

Back when I worked at Cooper's as a teenager, the manager once told me that if I didn't like company policy, I should go out and get a company of my own. Well, I had done that. And I decided that MyPillow would not make judgments on whether employees' bereavement requests were legitimate. We would honor bereavement leave whether the deceased was an immediate family member, a grandparent, a great-uncle twice removed, or a favorite neighbor. My employees would be paid during bereavement whether it took three days or three months, and their job would be waiting for them when they got back. That's still our policy today, and not one person has ever abused it.

The Denver stock show was slow. Sitting in my booth amid the smells of animals, hay, and feed, I had time to think. How could I replicate the advertising success we'd achieved with the *Star Tribune* article?

The answer came to me: Don't advertise. Just tell your story.

I called Tonja Waring and we began writing miniature versions of the *Star Tribune* story over the phone. We started placing these "advertorials" right away, again with the geeky photo. When these ads began to drop, advertising firms started calling me to say how terrible they were, and how they could write much better ads for us. But since I was doubling my money, I took great pleasure in ignoring them.

Not long afterward, I learned about another incredible advertising opportunity: remnant ads. Remnant ads are basically column-fillers. Newspapers will drop them in when they have empty space and not on any predetermined schedule. Compared to other display ads, remnant ads are incredibly inexpensive. I began buying them, first in the Midwest then expanding from there. Very quickly, these ads also doubled our money in sales. It felt a little like winning at gambling, and I went all in, even borrowing money to widen our reach.

MyPillow was finally going national.

Despite all my door-knocking between the time I invented MyPillow in 2004 and the spring of 2011, not a single box store, retail chain, or shopping channel had been interested in selling my product. Fine, I thought. I decided to take my product directly to the people. MyPillow is a "spiel" product, I thought, a demo product. I'd long thought an infomercial would be the perfect way to show people how it worked.

Retail experts I spoke with thought I was crazy. First, infomercials don't really work, they said. Second, the only reason to do one at all is to get into the box stores. As usual, I didn't listen, but instead talked my friends and family into investing in yet another idea. I told them we were going to make the best infomercial ever. Even my kids invested everything they could.

I hired an experienced production team to write a script, but it turned out to be awful. I mean just horrible, with cheesy lines like, "Look! The phones are lighting up like Christmas trees!"

I talked to the production team. What I wanted, I said, was something authentic and natural. Maybe me just talking about my product and demo'ing it. Maybe me telling a little of the story behind MyPillow as I had done at so many shows and fairs. I felt the storytelling part had proven itself with the *Star Tribune* response, and I wanted to stick with that.

"No, no, no!" they said. "You can't be *in* it. You need professionals and an actor!"

The more we discussed it, the more it became clear they thought I was an idiot. I fired them all and started over.

One day while I was between infomercial production teams, I was mopping floors at our manufacturing facility, the old Lenzen bus shed. I used to mop the floors back at the Flying Cloud drive-in and always found it helped me think. My cell phone rang. It was a radio station in New York City wanting to know if I'd like to advertise. I had tried one ad on a local radio station for a few days and it hadn't worked. I politely declined and hung up.

Just then, a MyPillow employee named Jill Green was walking by. Jill had come aboard a couple of months before. "Who was that?" she said, having happened to hear me turn someone down.

"WABC in New York."

She stopped in her tracks. "What? That's the Imus station!"

"What's an Imus?" I said.

"*Don Imus*. He's a huge star on the radio." Imus had something like 15 million listeners on a hundred stations. "You've got to call them back."

By then, Imus had been on the radio for more than 40 years. But since I had been in a cultural coma for most of that time, I had never heard of him. Jill filled me in: He was quirky, often controversial, and the most influential person in radio. Don Imus knew *everyone*.

We did call WABC back. They said if we flew out to New York City, we would also get to meet Don Imus. I wasn't super excited about wasting money on plane tickets and couldn't have cared less about meeting this Imus fella, but Jill insisted. We also sent Imus some MyPillows. A few weeks later, I flew to New York, bringing Jill along for moral support. The first thing on the schedule was to meet Imus. At a studio overlooking Central Park, a big guy—at least 6 foot 4—escorted us into a waiting room. I pegged him as some type of security.

"You can sit down," he said, indicating two couches that formed an L. "But I'm telling you, you're only gonna get about five minutes with Mr. Imus."

Fine with me, Mr. Bodyguard Guy, I thought, having no idea how much the next hour was going to change my life.

We had been waiting a while when a skinny, long-haired cowboy, grizzled with years, walked in. Recognizing him from photographs, I stood and extended my hand. "Mr. Imus, I'm Mike Lindell. It's an honor to meet you."

Imus scowled. "I don't shake hands. Now what am I here for?"

I had been warned that Imus could come off as a little gruff. A *little?* I thought. But aloud, I said, "Did you get the pillows we sent you?"

"No. What are you even talking about?" Imus took a seat on one of the couches. His expression was that of a man who had received thousands of gadgets, gifts, and trinkets from people all over the world. And now a pillow? He looked bored. And impatient.

Deciding it was time to improvise, I grabbed a decorative pillow off the couch I'd been sitting on and launched into my spiel. "Pretend this pillow is MyPillow…"

I stood in front of Don Imus and explained my invention in animated fashion, my arms swinging wildly. He stared up at me and when I stopped talking for a second, he said, "You're f-ing crazy."

The security guy jumped up to end the meeting, but Imus motioned him to sit back down. "I want to hear some more from this guy."

I then talked for the next 50 minutes, telling him my whole story, from addiction to quitting crack to inventing MyPillow. Imus listened patiently, then left as abruptly as he'd come in.

The security guy was dumbfounded. "I have never ever seen Mr. Imus listen to anyone for that long," he said.

A few weeks later, people called to tell me they'd heard Imus on the radio talking about my product and this crazy guy he'd met. It turned out that Imus had finally tried the MyPillows we sent him and had begun giving on-air testimonials about how they changed his life. (His words, not mine.) From 2011 on, Imus would talk about me or MyPillow on his program nearly every day, sometimes even when we weren't paying for ad time. With his trademark big talk, he'd tell listeners that MyPillow was one of the best inventions in history, on par with fire and the wheel. That always made me laugh. I don't know if I'd go that far, but Imus' endorsement was certainly as important to our company as those inventions were to mankind. During some seasons when other forms of marketing failed us, Don Imus single-handedly carried my company. I'll always be grateful for that.

I ended up doing a weekly talk show on WABC—basically an hour-long live radio infomercial—with Laura Smith for almost two years. From Laura, I learned that listeners really like it when the folks they hear on the radio are just real people. I learned that I didn't have to be perfect and that it was okay to mess up. Each week, my nervousness faded a little further into the background.

I was also still very interested in making a television infomercial. In July 2011, I sat down with Mark Jones, a producer Jill Green had suggested. Tall and muscular with a goatee and a ruddy complexion, Mark was a principal in a marketing firm called LifeBrands. "Just tell him your story," Jill said.

In our first meeting, I did. Mark and his business partner, Jeff, agreed with my infomercial concept: an interview-style format with a live audience. Since we'd already burned time and money with the production team I'd fired, they also agreed to do the project at a reduced rate and in about one-third the normal time. That was all great, of course. But if the infomercial succeeded on the scale I predicted, MyPillow was also going to have to ramp up production. And I mean by a lot.

I predicted we would go from $20,000 per week to $2 million per week in gross sales right out of the gate. In order to do this, we would need our raw materials up front. Every time we needed fabric in the past, we had to come up with $30,000. Now that figure would be in the millions. To raise that kind of cash was a pipe dream—and I wasn't even on crack.

Although my instincts told me the infomercial would hit big, I had no guarantee. But if I was serious about this, I had to move ahead as if I were sure of success. The question became, how do we prepare for anticipated demand with little money and no credit?

I decided to start with the greige goods (pronounced "gray goods") that I always ordered from New York. Greige goods are the raw materials used to manufacture products made from fabric. I had finally learned the secret identity of the fabric supplier John Anderson used before I cut him out as middleman. It was Santee Printworks in Manhattan. Up to this point, I had bought relatively small amounts of our special printed fabric from Santee, paying for it up front. Now I projected that I'd need about 50 times my usual order.

All I had to do was convince Santee's VP of finance, Leon Barocas, to give me, a small entrepreneur, hundreds of thousands of dollars in fabric on the basis of an untested infomercial that hadn't even been made yet. No problem, right?

When I stepped into the June meeting with Leon and other Santee executives in their offices in midtown Manhattan, I acted more confident than I felt. I'd put on a suit so I'd look respectable and "corporate." My confidence got a boost when Leon threw copies of that day's *Wall Street Journal* and *USA Today* on the table in front of me. Up until then, my remnant ads had appeared mainly in regional papers, and certainly not in papers subscribed to by Manhattan executives. But my ad had dropped that very day in both major newspapers. What are the odds?

I pretended this was no big deal, but was secretly thrilled about the added credibility. At Leon's invitation, I told the Santee executives what I wanted: an extension of credit more audacious than any I'd ever asked of anyone before.

One of the VP types said, "You have no credit history with us. And besides that, we wouldn't give full credit on printed fabric to anyone, even if they were Donald Trump."

Obviously, the VP's mind was made up, but Leon was still listening.

I focused on him, positioning MyPillow as a company on the verge. I told him about my infomercial idea and my projected sales figures. Never one to undersell an idea, I predicted that my infomercial would be the most successful in history.

Leon was quiet for a few moments. Then he made the call: Santee would order the greige goods based on my grandiose predictions and give me full credit.

People around Leon told him this was a crazy move. Eight years later, Leon himself would tell a reporter he still didn't know why he said yes. But his willingness to take a chance on me changed my company's trajectory.

Against all odds, our fill supplier, Federal Foam, also said yes. Now, with several hundred thousand dollars' worth of materials en route to my facility in Carver, all I had to do was produce this wildly successful infomercial I'd promised. That turned out to be harder than I thought.

CHAPTER

37

The Next Level

After Mark Jones reserved a studio at Channel 2 in St. Paul for filming, we sat down with a pencil to design the set. We also sent out flyers to MyPillow customers, inviting them to be part of the live studio audience. Finally, Mark and Tonja huddled over the script. The basic plan was for Tonja to interview me about the pillow and keep the story moving.

In late August, I headed down to Channel 2 for a read-through. We didn't have much time to pull things together—our studio time was scheduled for the next day. Mark handed me the script. "Let's try running your lines," he said. "Just say them like you do at shows. Be yourself."

Reading the script aloud, I realized it didn't sound much like me. But I kept going, telling myself they were the experts. I was a ball of nerves and fumbled every line. In fact, I made such a mess of the read-through that the producer texted Mark something like:

This guy is the worst I've ever seen.

I didn't know this at the time, of course. Mark stopped our rehearsal and tried to reassure me. "Just read the lines and give me energy like the first time we met," he said.

But the energy he wanted just wasn't there. I couldn't sound natural because I was reading lines. "I don't like this, Mark," I finally said. "It doesn't sound like me. This part here isn't even true. Who wrote this stuff?"

"Part of it came from the old script," Mark said. "I tried to recycle some of it so that what you spent wasn't a complete waste."

Waste? I didn't care about that. I was in a panic, but thankfully Mark was calm. "Mike, I'll just make an outline and we can use that tomorrow with no teleprompter."

That made me feel a little better. But I walked into the studio the next morning with a knot in my stomach. I blinked against the lights and cameras. Is this what a deer felt like when it was caught in the headlights of an oncoming car?

I found Mark and we sat down in a dressing room. He'd made an overnight decision. "Here's the deal," he said. "We have one line for you to say when you walk on the stage, and the rest will be unscripted. Tonja will have an earpiece. If you get stuck, she has scripted lines that will help get you going again."

Slowly, I began to nod. This could work. That's what I thought in the safety of the dressing room anyway. Soon, it was time for makeup and I was surprised when the artist told me she used to do makeup for Prince.

"You're kidding!" I said as the artist began using her brushes on my face. Happy to have something to take my mind off the taping, I launched into a story. "Paisley Park is right down the street from a bar I used to own…"

To set the stage for her, I had to go all the way back to Florida in 1999 and one of the annual trips Karen and I used to take. I was standing in a Panama City Beach bar called Sharky's when Skelly called me on my cell. But Karen thought I was talking to another woman. We got into an argument, which triggered another argument with a leather-covered biker who had already tried to provoke me by helping himself to an appetizer I'd ordered.

He grabbed me by the arm, nodded at Karen, and growled, "That's no way to talk to her!"

Feeling wrongly accused by both my wife and a rude stranger, I suddenly didn't care that the biker had two friends nearby. Just like that, my rage took over. I drew back my arm and punched him so hard he fell over backwards.

I came back to my senses. *What did I just do?*

I sprinted out of the bar, all three bikers cursing and chasing me, their wallet chains jingling. In a strange town and with no idea where I was going, I felt like I had run a mile by the time I spotted a bar and ducked inside.

You know those moments when everything seems to stop like a freeze-frame movie? That's exactly what it was like. First, every person in the place stopped talking and stared at me. Second, I realized why: I was the only white guy in the place. Then, just like a movie, everyone returned to their conversations.

Some guy was up on a small stage, singing karaoke. I stepped up to the bar and ordered the signature drink, which if I remember correctly, contained about 10 shots of liquor. I told the bartender that I owned a bar back in Minnesota, about three miles away from Prince's famous home and studio, Paisley Park.

Next thing I knew, I blurted, "I know him." Prince, I meant.

I don't know why I said that, other than the signature drink and my usual habit of trying to amaze people. Or maybe my nerves got the better of me as I kept sneaking glances at the door, waiting for three fire-breathing bikers to appear.

The bartender cocked an eyebrow. "Really? Well, if you know Prince, why don't you get up there and sing one of his songs for us?" He nodded toward the stage and the karaoke machine.

"Sure," I said, a bit reluctantly. Either the potent drink was giving me courage, or I needed a distraction from the guys I figured might be coming to rough me up.

Up on stage, I cued up "Purple Rain," to which I knew every word. I didn't hold back. Everyone in the place about fell over laughing at me, a white guy with a 1985 mustache singing a Prince song. I earned a standing ovation, but not because I was a good singer. The bartender had called some buddies and told them to hurry down to check out my comedy show.

After two encores for the bartender's friends, I poked my head out the front door. The bikers were waiting for me across the street. But the bartender had told me not to worry: No white guys ever came in that bar unless they were lost tourists like me. By the time I finally left my new friends at 4 a.m., the bikers were gone.

A couple of years after my trip to Panama City Beach, one of Prince's security guards came into Schmitty's. His name was Vinny, and he came in fairly often.

"Mike, Bob Seger is playing at Paisley Park tonight," he said.

I'd heard Prince had a full soundstage on his property and that he often opened it to other musicians. Not really for concerts, but more for practice sessions or just to jam. Vinny had once told me that if Seger showed up, he'd get me in. I loved Seger's music and couldn't wait.

I asked Skelly if he wanted to go with me. At about 2:30 a.m., he and I pulled into the parking lot of Paisley Park. Only a handful of cars dotted the lot, but there were a couple hundred autograph seekers standing around, hoping to spot someone famous. Feeling privileged to be there, Skelly and I walked up to the side door of a huge and boxy white building. If you didn't know that the most famous person in all of the Twin Cities lived there, you might have thought it was a small manufacturing site. Well, except for all the purple footlights.

Vinny let us in a side door and led us toward the soundstage. Already, I could hear the sound of a very distinctive guitar. We walked into a large room that was dimly lit like a night club, but almost completely empty except for a few people scattered around listening. I saw some kind of technician running back and forth to a control board. The band wasn't playing full songs. They'd jam a little, stop and converse with the tech, and make adjustments.

As excited as I was to be allowed in this place, I also felt a little disappointed. It wasn't Seger onstage. It was a different but equally famous band. Skelly and I hung back in a hallway beside the control room. I listened to the music and wondered where I could get a drink. When the sound tech, a small guy dressed in jeans and a t-shirt, came back to the control room, I asked him if there was anywhere I could get a beer.

"No, sorry," he said.

"Well, we came to see Bob Seger. Is he going to play later?"

He smiled. "What? This isn't good enough for you?"

"It's okay. I just like Seger better. Him and the Eagles and Prince."

"Oh, you like Prince, huh?" the technician said.

"Yeah, and I've got a great Prince story for you." Then I proceeded to tell him the whole Panama City Beach story—punching out the biker, hiding out in the club, drinking the signature drink with 10 shots of liquor, bragging to the bartender that I knew Prince.

"Hang on a second," the tech said, and walked up to the stage to confer with the band. When he came back, he wanted to hear the rest of the story.

"Well, a customer in the bar challenged me to sing a Prince song, so I sang 'Purple Rain.'" Now I started singing it to the tech.

I never meant to cause you any sorrow,
I never meant to cause you any pain...

"That's a long song too," I said when I finished singing the entire thing.

"I know," the tech said with a pained expression, clearly a little embarrassed for me.

The band onstage launched into another song, and I had come to the end of my story. Hoping to be invited back, I didn't want to overstay our welcome, so I said goodbye to the tech, and Skelly and I headed for the exit.

"That was a nice guy," I said when we got outside.

"You idiot," Skelly said. "That was Prince!"

The infomercial makeup artist stopped with her brushes, pulled back, and looked at me with surprise. "That was you? Prince tells that story all the time!"

Sharing my favorite Prince story had taken my mind off my nerves, but when I got on the set under the lights with cameras rolling, I became that deer in the headlights again. During every run-through, I froze or stumbled badly. Taping my lone scripted line ate up nine takes and more than an hour of studio time. On the upside, it did make a nice blooper reel. On the downside, that all happened *before* the live audience came in.

Panicking again, I asked Mark how long we had the studio. As long as we needed it, he said. This, of course, was a white lie designed to make me feel better, and it did. I could mess up as many times as I needed to.

Then came something that made me even more comfortable. Right before we started recording with the studio audience, we brought in a long demo table for me to use on the set. After we got through the scripted line, I was able to stand behind the table, and to everyone's relief I began to calm down. It was like I was behind the bar at Schmitty's again, or inside a sales booth at a show. With that little bit of protection, I began to feel I was in my element. And when the cameras rolled, the words just came.

As Tonja and I talked back and forth about MyPillow, I could tell the audience was engaged. They nodded when I emphasized a feature or benefit of my product. They laughed when I was funny. As the day progressed, I became more and more confident.

People who have seen the original MyPillow infomercial said it seemed completely unscripted, and most of it actually was. When I tossed a down-filled pillow off the stage and said down pillows were ruining America, that was ad-libbed. When I said our foam fill was so malleable you could make little balloon animals out of it, that was not practiced at all. As frightened as I had been, it seemed like a little miracle.

Finally, the crew taped my final pitch and Mark yelled, "Cut!"

A wave of relief washed over me. After all those months of worrying and hoping, the infomercial was finally in the can and I felt it could not have gone better.

****

"Hello, I'm Mike Lindell. I've invented the world's most comfortable pillow. I make them right here in the United States. Do not change that channel, because the next half-hour's going to change your life."

When the infomercial hit the airwaves, it certainly changed mine. The first airing was on October 7, 2011, at 3:30 a.m. I was living in my sister Robin's basement by then, and I sat alone in a recliner down there watching the first airing. It was a bit surreal, watching myself on the Discovery Channel. Everything in my life came down to this. All the years of hard work, all the promises I'd made, the lifetime of debt I would be in if it didn't work. I was scared, but also strangely confident.

That morning, MyPillow exploded. Orders poured into the website and the out-of-state call center I'd set up a month prior. Mark Jones went into a media-buying frenzy. With only slight additional editing, we started airing the infomercial in heavy rotation on numerous channels. In a small way, I felt vindicated—that selfish, "How do you like me now?" feeling you get when you succeed despite people trying to bring you down. But mostly, I felt hopeful. I'd caused a lot of people a lot of grief, in particular my family and friends. Now, I hoped they would finally be proud of how far I'd come.

On Day 3 of the infomercial, I decided to do a little quality control check on the call center to see how they were treating my customers.

"Hey, what's in that pillow?" I asked the guy who answered the phone.

"*I* don't know," he replied. "Google it."

Infuriated, I slammed down the phone and made an immediate decision to move our call center in-house. I was told that couldn't be done. It would take months to build out a call center in our Carver schoolhouse facility.

"We don't have months," I said. "We're going to do it in a week." In the end, it took 10 days.

Sales continued to skyrocket. Very quickly, revenues enabled us to invest nearly half a million dollars in more airtime. Instantly, people started nagging me about traditional corporate structures. I needed to take the title of CEO, they said. I needed a corporate attorney. I needed a "real" board of directors. I thought that all sounded horrible. I had one thing on my mind and that was getting pillows to my customers. Then someone said I needed a human resources department. I thought that sounded *really* horrible, but I did it anyway, along with all the rest.

In a few short months, we went from approximately 20 employees to more than 500. It seemed that everyone in my family was working at MyPillow, and many of my old friends from Schmitty's. We hired everyone in sight— sometimes, as one reporter later wrote, "literally off of barstools."

For example, there had recently been a big fight over at Cy's bar in Chaska, and a couple of the guys involved had been charged by the cops.

My manager, Jen, called me.

"Hey, Mike, a couple of those guys from the brawl at Cy's are coming down to the schoolhouse to see if they can get jobs. I just wanted to warn you," she said.

When the guys showed up, I asked them their names. Mark and Luke, they said.

"Those are nice names from the Bible," I said. "Have you committed any felonies today?" I was only half-joking.

"No," they said.

"Good. You're hired. But I'll be watching you guys."

Mark and Luke stayed with the company for three years, and we never had a problem. That was the beginning of my practice of hiring people who need a second chance. A couple of years later, long after I had taken the position of CEO and set up a human resources department, a friend of mine came to me asking for jobs for him and his girlfriend. She was a great worker, he said, and would be a good fit at MyPillow. But she had a black mark on her record: She'd been charged with embezzlement by a former employer.

I told him I would hire them both. As they left, my HR manager pulled me into her office. "We can't hire her," she said. "What's it going to look like to the public?"

"Have you looked at your CEO lately?" I replied.

It was only by God's grace that I myself wasn't a convicted felon, I told her. If this applicant was qualified for the job, I wanted her hired. We did hire her—and stuck with her even through a prison rehabilitation program she was required to attend after her case went before a judge.

That was five years ago, and today she is a model citizen. I have found that extending trust to people who have made mistakes, even terrible mistakes—a lot of them due to addiction—has resulted in some of the best employees ever. While our track record with this practice isn't perfect, I have found that second-chance trust is most often repaid with loyalty and gratitude.

I was certainly grateful for the success of that first infomercial. By Christmas, it was the number one infomercial in the world. We were working three shifts, 24/7, every day in both the bus shed manufacturing facility and the schoolhouse call center. In January 2012, I pulled into the Holiday gas station in Victoria to check the MyPillow account balance at an ATM. I was excited because I knew that for the first time ever, the balance should be over a million dollars. I inserted my card and punched in my PIN, but when I looked at the numbers on the screen my stomach dropped. The balance was only $90,000.

I called my bank in a panic. Not to worry, they said. The account balance was actually $2,090,000.

Smiling, I then dialed Tom Schrempp, a friend who had stuck with me through the very worst of times. I had figured out what the problem was.

"Hey, Tom," I said. "Do you realize that ATMs don't go out to seven figures?"

He laughed. "No, I didn't realize that."

It was a great problem to have.

The seven-figure MyPillow bank balance that launched 2012 was a bright spot in what became two very stormy years. On top of the world business-wise, I still felt lonely and empty. And with MyPillow's success, I felt I could turn part of my attention away from my company and focus on filling the hole in my heart.

I went on a few blind dates, the first two of which were disasters of uncomfortable silence. The third date, however, was different. We hit it off immediately. She talked so easily, and I felt comfortable being myself. Suddenly, I was all in, head-over-heels in love. Very quickly, we were engaged. But by November 2012, we both realized that our matching Type A personalities clashed for control. Knowing it wasn't going to work, we broke off our engagement and parted ways.

Immediately, the deep emptiness returned. I realize now that this is the way it is for a lot of addicts: Uncomfortable with ourselves, we simply cannot be alone. And that is why, not even a month later, I jumped into another relationship.

I had first noticed a beauty named Dallas dealing cards at the Riverside way back in 2008. She had long, dark hair, a face that glowed, and one of the sweetest smiles I'd ever seen. I hadn't felt such instant attraction to a stranger since Karen Dickey walked into the Statesman in 1985. Since Dallas was a casino dealer, it was easy to get to know her and we became friends. I had long wanted to ask her on a date, but the timing was never right.

In 2011, I offered Dallas a job as my executive assistant, and we kept our relationship on a professional level. After my November 2012 breakup, though, we began a whirlwind romance. Within a month, I asked her to marry me. I spent ridiculous amounts of money trying to impress her, capping this off with a million-dollar purchase: a large and ostentatious lakefront home I bought on credit. We quickly moved in together.

Through all this, Cindy stood on the sidelines waving red flags like a signalman on a NASCAR track. My sister had by then met the woman she'd seen in prayer, the one in the teal-green dress, the one she said God told her was my perfect match. During a break at a Christian conference in 2012, a woman approached Cindy and said in a soft southern Texas accent, "Hi, I'm Kendra. I don't know why, but God wants us to keep in touch." Cindy had come home and told me that Kendra was the one.

"Well, that's too bad," I said. "Because I think Dallas is the one."

It seemed to me that Cindy's vision, or whatever it was, was just plain wrong.

On the business front, I was fighting three new battles, all of them lawsuits having to do with the theft or copying of my product, brand, and persona. While I fought, my relationship with Dallas barreled ahead. My sister wasn't the only person to warn me against it. Many of my friends and family members couldn't understand why I was moving so fast again. More importantly, they couldn't understand why I was neglecting MyPillow and pouring all my time and money—*so* much money—into a relationship they could see was doomed from the start. Back then, I was certain that neither Cindy nor any of the rest knew what they were talking about. Looking back now though, it is all painfully clear.

Remember that unfinished business I mentioned from my time at Living Free? I know now that my deep insecurities had opened the hole in my heart. For years, I had been scrambling to find a way to fill it—with drugs, gambling, adrenaline, or the approval of other people. Deep inside, I was not happy with myself, and the only way I *could* be happy was with the love and approval of someone else.

I was blind to all of that then. And that was what caused me to ignore wise counsel and instead obsessively pursue a relationship that flashed so many warning signs that Dallas might as well have had "Bridge Out" tattooed on her forehead.

My board of directors insisted that we sign a pre-nup and we did. Then in June 2013, we were married in a lavish $100,000 ceremony and reception.

My first marriage lasted 20 years. My second lasted about 20 days. On the second day after the ceremony, Dallas and I got into a huge argument and she moved out of our lakefront home. A couple of weeks later, during a car ride to Chaska from the airport, she delivered the final blow.

"I'm not in love with you," my wife said. "Also, you're boring."

Her words felt like a dagger to my soul. Still, I refused to believe our marriage was over and pursued her like a lovesick teenager—which to tell you the truth, I probably was inside. At that time, I probably had the emotional maturity of a 16-year-old boy, trapped in the body of a middle-aged man.

For days, I sat in our big, fancy, empty house alternating between listening to Chris Rhea's "Fool (If You Think It's Over)" and Pablo Cruise's "Love Will Find A Way." I begged Dallas to come home, but she ignored my pleas and moved back to her mother's house in Arizona. About six months later, my lawyers met Dallas' lawyers for mediation. I sat across the conference table from Dallas as her attorney fought to get everything she could for her client, despite the pre-nup.

Dallas and I were silent while our lawyers squabbled back and forth. Then at one point, our eyes met. "Dallas, why would you do this to me?" I said.

She broke down, almost crying. "I know it was a mistake, Mike. I couldn't handle unconditional love." Her lawyer started kicking her under the table, trying to get her to stop talking. Finally Dallas blurted out, "I don't want anything."

At that, the mediator stood up. "I guess my job is over. Give her whatever you want, Mike."

Despite the pre-nup, I agreed to a settlement. At the end of the mediation I smiled at Dallas, hugged her, and said goodbye. Even today, I still think we were just two people looking in the wrong places for ways to heal our old wounds.

CHAPTER

38

The Last Wager

B etween 2011 and 2012, we sold almost $100 million in MyPillows, but wound up $6 million in debt. The truth is, God had given me a dream for a great product and a gift for selling and marketing. But like many inventors and creatives, I had no idea how to operate and scale the underlying business.

I wrote stacks of checks as I bought up more and more infomercial slots. But I really had no idea how to track the airings to find out which were working and which should be canceled. Meanwhile, I did not calculate the difference between gross sales and net profits, or figure in indirect costs. At one point, Federal Foam sent its CFO to check on our overall operation. Very quickly, he discovered that although we were bringing in millions in sales, our costs were through the roof.

To top it off, as I was sitting in my sister's basement one night, half-watching TV and wondering how to fix all this, I saw a dark-haired man on the screen. He wore a mustache and a blue shirt. This man could have been my twin, and he was selling a copy of MyPillow. I almost fell out of my chair.

I found out that the company behind this ad was called Telebrands. Lawsuits followed, and I had to make a deal with them. I didn't want to, but I felt forced in order to stay in business.

Meanwhile, MyPillow was losing $250,000 a week. Part of our expenses came from having to build a new factory. In March 2012, I had made a deal with Dick Lenzen to buy the bus shed. But right before the closing, we learned that the area was improperly zoned for my company's operations. When we applied for re-zoning, the Carver city council ruled that MyPillow had grown so big that we were now a neighborhood nuisance. The council then laid out compliance demands that would cost hundreds of thousands of dollars, and gave me until October to comply or vacate. I didn't have the money to meet the council's new demands. And I had no idea how we were going to find a new location and build a new factory before the October deadline.

But we did it. Within two months, we had designed, built, and moved into a new facility in Shakopee, less than 10 miles away. Unexpectedly, this "crash build" turned out to be a good thing. It gave me a better sense of what my employees' skill sets were. For example, when I saw what a great job the painting contractor did, I made him my head of maintenance. Like me, many of my leaders were not trained or credentialed for their positions. But they happened to be people who could get the job done. Against all odds, we were up and running two days before the Carver deadline.

When I'd walked out of that Carver city council meeting, the council's demands looked like government overkill. When I opened MyPillow's doors in Shakopee I realized that, like many unwelcome obstacles, they were instead a hidden blessing.

The Telebrands confrontation turned out in similar fashion. I knew I had made a terrible decision in making a deal with them. But the deal did function for a time as a Band-Aid for MyPillow's leaky finances. Later in the year I made a deal with QVC, even though I'd sworn I would never appear on that network because they had turned me down three times before. My first airing was in October 2012. I did an eight-minute segment that pulled in $60,000 a minute— six times the average for that time slot.

Still, these positive developments weren't enough to turn our red ink to black. During much of 2013, I had been so caught up in my relationship with Dallas that I left most major decisions to others in my company. By the spring of 2014, sales were weak in every channel and getting worse.

The infomercial was fatiguing, as they say in the business, only producing a fifth of what it once had. The problem was, we had manufactured tens of thousands of pillows in anticipation of sales that had first leveled out, then fallen over a cliff. We were still doing better on QVC than most products, but the numbers were much lower than those we'd put up earlier. Radio advertising generated some sales, but our TV ads were down to almost nothing. The box stores were now ordering fewer pillows or had stopped selling them altogether. Meanwhile, I'd incurred $2 million in judgments from the legal battles I was fighting, and now those were hanging over my head.

Some people on my leadership team were growing frustrated. One day in early 2014, I was riding in the car with my call center manager. My new director of communications, Jessica Maskovich, was sitting in the back seat. The call center manager said to me matter-of-factly, "You are a terrible CEO. You should just be the face of the company and stay out of the way, because you have no idea what you're doing."

I glanced at Jessica in the back seat and saw her cringe. I remember feeling like I'd been cut with a knife. But strangely, I didn't react at all. It was almost as if I had grown numb to the whole situation.

In May 2014, desperate to make payroll, I talked Jim Furlong into going to Laughlin with me to count cards. It was what I always did when I needed money. Most of the time, the casinos were as good to me as a bank.

By now, going to the Riverside was like going to a family reunion. There were lots of hugs and happy greetings as we sat down at the blackjack tables. And even though the pit bosses knew perfectly well we were counting cards, they let us play, dealing deep into the decks as we went head-to-head with our favorite dealers.

We played probably the best we'd ever played, with no mistakes. But through deck after deck, Jim and I kept running into a wall. The frequency and consistency of our losses began to defy mathematics. If there was one face card left in the deck along with 20 small cards, we'd hit the face card and bust. If we stayed on 18, the dealer's hole card would give her a 19. We lost every single hour, every single day. With the steady advantage we should have had over the house, the odds of this happening would be like flipping a coin 100 times and having it come up heads 90 times. The math was just impossible.

Two-and-a-half days in, Jim turned to me and said, "I'm sick of this."

"I am, too," I said. "Let's just go home."

I had thousands of dollars left. I'd never given up and gone home when I was still alive to fight another day. But we were done. We packed up and caught the next plane to Minnesota.

"That's the worst deviation I've ever seen in my life," I said to Jim on the flight home.

"Me, too."

"Well, it's making the book," I said, meaning the book I'd always said I was going to write.

"The only way it makes the book is if you were to quit forever," Jim said.

Quit gambling forever? That was a bizarre thought. I looked at Jim. He looked back at me. I could see that he was only half-joking.

On Saturday, May 31, four days after we got back from Laughlin, I decided to head down to Diamond Jo Casino just across the Iowa border to try again. I had just turned south on I-35, when I heard an almost audible message:

> *Go to church tomorrow. You are done with gambling.*
> *Four days ago, you played your last card.*

Mind you, I didn't *hear* a voice. Call it an impression, direction, or a guiding hand. Call it whatever you want, but it was clear as a bell. It was so clear, in fact, that I exited at the next southbound ramp, crossed the interstate, and turned back north toward home.

The next day, I went to Living Word and sat in the balcony. There was a group of families who sat up there, and I enjoyed the way they worshipped. The "voice," or whatever it had been, had directed me there. Looking down from the balcony, I listened to the sermon and waited. The pastor hadn't been speaking long when the voice came to me again:

> *You are done with gambling.*
> *Don't worry about counting cards to cover your company's expenses.*

The voice then came to me a third time:

> *You will meet Kendra. She is the one.*
> *Through her, you will become closer to Me.*

Tears trickled down my face, and I didn't know whether it was because I felt God's presence, because He had just set me free from gambling, because my search for love was over, or because I didn't have to worry about my company. And although I didn't really see how the latter was even possible, I believed. The feelings that came over me were joy, hope, and relief, all wrapped up in one big bow. Soon, people around me in the balcony noticed my tears. A couple of them kept repeating, "Hallelujah," while others placed kind hands on my shoulders. I felt genuine Christian love.

****

After meeting Kendra at the Christian conference in Texas in 2012, Cindy stayed in touch with her. My sister had occasional conversations with each of us, insisting that God had shown her that someday, Kendra and I would be married. That's a lot of pressure for anyone, especially for a person like Kendra who had never been married.

After a couple of years and a lot of prayer, Kendra agreed to meet Cindy and me in Laguna Beach, California. I had agreed to make a guest appearance on a local radio station to talk about addiction. I bought a gift for Kendra and carried it onto the plane, where it just barely fit in the overhead bin.

Things were bleak at MyPillow, but as Cindy and I flew west toward the sun, I had a certain peace. Against all indications, I thought, we're going to get through this. Maybe it was that assurance I'd had from God in May.

Now, it was near the end of July, when Southern California is cloudless and warm. Cindy and I arrived in Laguna Beach before Kendra and rented a car to pick her up from John Wayne Airport. I was so nervous, and knew she had to be, too. We met Kendra at her gate. She was even more beautiful than the photos I'd seen, dark-haired with a wide, beaming smile.

As we walked to the parking lot, Cindy and Kendra chatted like old friends. When we got to the car, I pulled out the gift I'd brought and showed it to Kendra. It was a very large, very plush stuffed elephant.

"Let's just put this over here," I said, tucking the elephant in an out-of-sight place in the back seat.

Kendra cracked up. She knew exactly what I meant. Cindy had been whispering wedding bells in both our ears for two years by then. We had just acknowledged—and set aside—the elephant in the room.

Throughout that weekend, I found Kendra to be genuine, kind, and easy to talk to. When we found ourselves on our own, we talked about all kinds of things, some very personal. I especially remember one moment in particular. Kendra and I were meeting for lunch. She and I each left our rooms at about the same time and met in the hotel hallway. As we walked toward each other, we felt suddenly, supernaturally transparent, as if each of us could see the soul of the other.

Kendra was not like any woman I'd ever met. She radiated a purity and joy that I found hard to describe. That fascinated me, but also intimidated me. I felt she had a close connection to God that I would never have.

When the weekend was over, I was already back in Minnesota when my cell phone rang. It was Kendra, calling to say she had lost her Bible. This wasn't just a book to her. It was the place where she had written notes, prayers for family and friends, significant events, and insights she'd gained from the Scriptures.

"I must have left it at the airport or on the plane," she said, clearly very upset. She'd used that Bible for at least 10 years.

I did what any man would do for the woman destined to be his mate: I jumped on a plane to Texas to help her look for it.

Well, we ended up finding the Bible. A janitor had turned it in to the airport lost-and-found. But while we were searching the terminal, I watched Kendra's way with people. She pointed to a man and said, "I've got to go pray with him."

I hung back, very uncomfortable with this. I mean, who goes up to random strangers in an airport and offers to pray with them? Kendra, that's who. As I watched, she went up to him and said, "The Lord's telling me I need to pray for you." And the guy just burst into tears.

As she had from the first time she spoke with my sister, Kendra seemed to have a gift of knowing. That's why something she said to me in Laguna became the first step in turning MyPillow around once and for all.

CHAPTER

39

Never Look Back

I didn't know it then, but by the time Kendra and I met she had been praying for my company for a month. In fact, I later learned that was the whole
reason she agreed to meet us in California. Not because she wanted to
pursue a relationship, but because she had something to tell me—something
she couldn't have known by any natural means.

"I sense that there's a great drain on your company from inside," Kendra
said over lunch. "It's dire. You're about to lose everything."

How does she know that? I wondered. From the outside, MyPillow still
looked like a successful company. My product was for sale in major retailers
all over the country. By then, my infomercial had appeared so many times that
people were starting to stop me in the street. But with Kendra, I felt comfortable
admitting the truth.

"You're right," I said. "We're $6 million in the hole." Then I told her that I had already replaced some problem employees with new ones.

Kendra looked at me intently. "There are people high up in your company who are not your friends. They do not have your back."

When she told me the identity of one of them, I was stunned. This person was one of my closest confidants. In that moment, I was caught between doubting Kendra and knowing deep down she was right. I just didn't want to believe it.

As soon as I got back from Texas, I started asking questions. It didn't take long to uncover the core of the problem. After a day of confrontations and with my hearty approval, two of my top managers resigned.

Both departures made me realize that if I were ever going to be a great CEO, I had to learn how to do it right. I had to develop boundaries. I had to cut out all distractions and put my company first. I had to make the most of my natural strengths and develop new strengths where I was weak.

From that day on, I dipped into every part of my business as if it were the only part. We had outsourced our email advertising. I pulled it back in-house, retooled it, and immediately generated several hundred thousand dollars. We pulled our radio advertising back in-house and overhauled it. We returned to the type of print ads we'd been running before the infomercial.

While these changes were underway, I huddled with my remaining team. What else could we do to dig out? We had a huge stockpile of pillows. Could we discount the overstock and sell it at home shows and fairs?

During this burst of change, I had another premonition. Like the one I'd had on I-35, this one was clear as a bell. In July, I shared this premonition at a board meeting. We were still millions in the hole, including the two judgments, which had to be paid by the end of the year. But with my core management arranged around a conference table, I declared that we were going to end 2014 with $8.2 million in the bank.

They stared at me in disbelief. "Write that in the minutes," I said. "I want a record of it."

On the morning of November 5, 2014, I was sitting in a deer stand in western Minnesota. Tom Schrempp owned this land, 200 wooded acres on the Minnesota River near Montevideo. I'd driven out with Tom, along with a few other hunting buddies. Fall was on its last legs, and I was bundled up in orange against a temperature of 18 degrees—pretty cold, but not the frigid weather we'd endured in other seasons.

I sat quietly and listened. It was about 10:30 a.m. The deer were most active in the early morning and in the early evening just before dark. A couple of guys in our party had already claimed their deer, but now at mid-morning the woods were still. I laid my Benelli Black Eagle aside and quietly unwrapped a sandwich.

Troubles at MyPillow were still weighing me down. With our overstock of pillows and only a trickle of sales, I'd laid off hundreds of people. It was one of the hardest things I'd ever had to do. I kept a core staff and told my managers that when we made it out of this slump we were probably going to have to sew and make pillows ourselves, as we had done before the infomercial.

We had tried a couple of one-minute television commercials with paid actors. Both flopped. My finance director, Kim, told me why. "Mike, you need to be in the commercial," she said.

I didn't really want to get in front of a camera again, but she talked me into it. It was basically the same commercial. The only difference was that I did the selling part. We'd started testing it, but didn't have funds to buy a lot of media, so testing was slow and the jury was still out.

At this point, MyPillow's accounts were nearly empty. We had a $2 million payment that was coming from QVC that Monday, but we had already promised it to our creditors, all of whom had been waiting patiently for more than six months.

As I ate I checked my phone periodically. Tom didn't like it when we used our cells during hunts. A hunter might get away with the noise of walking through the woods, but deer have excellent hearing, and no forest creature sounds like a human talking. I wasn't talking though, just checking the same sales graph I'd been checking for years.

You see, I was waiting for my miracle. The fulfillment of my $8.2 million premonition.

It was already early November. If we were going to end 2014 with $8.2 million in the bank, there wasn't much time left. But I had 100 percent faith that everything was going to be okay. I munched on my sandwich, occasionally refreshing the sales metrics page. Then at 10:45, my eyes popped wide open. The graph on my screen was showing a huge spike. It went straight up, leveled out for a bit, then went back down again.

What in the world…?

Without even hesitating, I broke Tom's telephone rule. I phoned my media tracker, Rick Griswold, pointed out the spike, and quoted him the sales figure indicated on the graph.

"That doesn't sound right," he said. "But if it's true, that would be amazing."

"Check the promo code," I said. That would tell us which ads were generating the sales. I held the line until he came back.

"Fox News Channel," he said when he came back on. It was the commercial with me in it, the one Kim had talked me into doing.

I lit up. My heart started thumping. I knew immediately that this was it, the deviation I'd been waiting for. "Find out how much I can buy on Fox if I went all in. I'll call you back in an hour."

Now I had a logistical problem. This was maybe one of the top five pivotal moments in my company's history, and I desperately needed to leave the hunt. But hunting etiquette said I had to stay put until I got my deer so as not to disturb the other hunters. For non-hunters, this might not seem like a big deal. But trust me, you don't want to be the cause of your buddies not getting their deer because you crashed through the woods and scared all the game away.

Meanwhile, I couldn't take just any deer. The state had tag rules as to what kind of deer each hunter could shoot in a given season, and Tom had his own rules on top of those. On this hunt, the only kind of deer I could take was a large doe. I could leave my stand when I got one of those and not before. That meant I'd probably have to wait until dark. With my business hanging in the balance, that seemed like an eternity away.

I picked up my Benelli and was wondering whether God answers hunting prayers when a large doe clip-clopped out of the woods. I'm not kidding you: This happened less than 10 minutes after I had hung up with Rick. I raised my gun and took her down. That brought Tom trotting up the hill toward my stand. Tom was one of those friends who had always stuck by me, even through my addictions. He was anti-drugs like you wouldn't believe, but he always held out hope for me.

Now he looked the doe over. "Wow, nice one!" he said. Apparently, she fit Tom's special rules on size.

"Tom, I'm sorry, but I have to leave," I said. "You won't believe what happened…"

I rattled on for a solid minute about the sales graph and what it meant.

Tom grinned. "Go, go, go!" he said. "We'll take care of your deer."

I got to my truck as quickly as I could and called Rick back to find out how much airtime I could buy right away on Fox News. "Two million dollars' worth," he said.

It was exactly the amount we had coming in from QVC. This was Saturday, November 5. We were supposed to receive the QVC check on Monday, November 7. The ad that caused the spike had brought in six times what it cost us, Rick said.

"I want to buy all $2 million. Give me two hours. I need to make some calls."

In quick succession I called our creditors and explained what was happening. "You've been patient with me for months," I said, "but I'm asking you to hang in there with me a little bit longer. I need you to trust me just one more time."

When every single creditor said yes, I called Rick back and told him to buy it all.

Next, I phoned Kim and Jessica. "When you get the QVC check on Monday, send it to LifeBrands. We're going all in with the commercial on Fox News."

I wasn't buying a political point of view. I was investing in the spike I saw on the graph. You've got to remember, I'd been in a drug-induced cultural coma for over 30 years. I didn't know Fox News from ABC News or MSNBC. But it turned out that Fox's politics actually helped us. The national midterm elections had taken place that Tuesday. The Republicans had retaken Congress, branding it as a reclaiming of America. Fox News watchers were all fired up and really resonated with the new MyPillow commercial we'd been testing—the one with me talking about my invention made in small-town U.S.A.

The Fox News gamble paid off in seven figures. Sales shot off the charts. We were able to rehire many of the people we had laid off. And MyPillow's bank balance at the end of 2014?

$8.19 million.

Net. I'd learned the difference by then.

After that, we never looked back.

CHAPTER

40

Awakening

The following year, 2015, I told my board we'd wind up with $14.4 million in the bank, and we did. This time I was determined to use the money for good. I relaunched the Lindell Foundation, a nonprofit I'd started in 2012. The foundation directed private-sector donations to vetted needs with no administrative costs. We also began offering in-house innovations for MyPillow employees. For example, if we discovered that an employee was struggling with drugs or alcohol, we didn't fire them. Instead, we paid for treatment—and also paid them wages while they were in recovery.

Because I knew programs that emphasized Jesus had a higher success rate, I encouraged employees to try those. But the irony was that Kendra said she didn't think I knew Jesus myself. I had begun seeing Kendra on a regular basis, carrying on a long-distance relationship between Minnesota and Texas. She began accompanying me to events and on trips. We always got separate hotel rooms. It was very different for me. I had never been in a relationship with a woman who was so mature in her Christian faith.

"If you don't have a relationship with Jesus," she'd tell me, "how can you help anyone else?"

"What are you talking about?" I'd say, more than a little offended.

By now, I understood that these premonitions I'd had all my life weren't premonitions at all. They were God whispering to my heart in that still, small voice spoken of in Scripture. How could I be hearing from God if I didn't have a relationship with Him?

I already felt spiritually inferior to Kendra, and also to our new friends Stephen and Kennya Baldwin. I met Stephen, the actor, during a trip to AM 970, a radio station in New York. I'd felt led to visit the station in early 2014, though at the time I wasn't sure why. Now I know it was to meet Stephen, who became like a brother to me. For decades I had been caught up in my own tiny and often chaotic world, like a man trapped in a dysfunctional snow globe. Stephen, Kennya, and Kendra helped me to broaden my outlook on the world.

One day in April 2015, Stephen was changing clothes in a taxicab as we rolled through the middle of midtown Manhattan. (I told you we were like brothers.) We were headed to the Plaza Hotel for an awards gala, and Stephen was putting on a suit. For years he'd been associated with the Federal Enforcement Homeland Security Foundation, a humanitarian organization that assists federal law enforcement officers and their families in times of need. He had nominated me for the 2015 FEHSF Patriot Award because of the work of my foundation. Now, I was about to receive it.

Of course, you know my main concern. "I don't have to talk, do I?" I asked Stephen as he knotted his necktie.

"No, no," he said. "You'll be at a table, and you might have to say a couple of things there. When they give you the award, just stand up and say thanks."

I was becoming more confident in my role as MyPillow CEO and more experienced in public situations. But speaking in front of people still terrified me. And speaking in front of a room full of intelligence and law enforcement agents? Are you kidding me?

"By the way," Stephen said as he put on his suit jacket, "it might be better if you don't mention doing crack."

Check. Don't tell crack stories to law enforcement types.

When we got to the Plaza, I discovered that Stephen had been soft-selling me. One of the first things I had to do was give an acceptance speech. I stood up and blurted out something about MyPillow, thanks for the award, blah blah blah. I don't remember what I said, only that it was probably the most awkward speech in the history of speeches. Afterward, I was seated at a table with 12 people, including a handful who were associated with the CIA, Homeland Security, and the U.S. Marshals. On my right sat a billionaire grocer, and on my left, a guy who said he knew Donald Trump and that I should meet him. Definitely a three-fork crowd.

I was so nervous, more uncomfortable than I'd been in a very long time. Somehow, I managed to small-talk my way through dinner. When dessert came, the wife of one of the homeland security agents spoke up. "Mike, I think I read somewhere that you were an addict at one time." She said this from her seat all the way across the huge round table.

I looked at Stephen. Sighing a little, he gave me a nod: *Oh, go ahead.*

"Yes, I was a crack cocaine addict," I said. "And here's a great Homeland Security story for you."

It happened in 2008, I said, when my crack addiction was at its worst. I was driving across Wisconsin on my way to a home show. My truck bed was filled with pillows that were vacuum-packed, 12 to a bundle, stacked three feet higher than the cab of my pickup truck and secured by bungie cords. It looked like I was carrying a giant marshmallow. Meanwhile, I had brought along a large personal supply of cocaine. After a while, I noticed that a helicopter had been flying behind me for a weirdly long time. Why would a helicopter be following me? I wondered. Maybe I was just paranoid…or was I?

Suddenly, I rounded a bend in the road and saw emergency lights spinning all over the place. It was a roadblock set up just for me. Instead of police officers, the place was swarming with Homeland Security agents. When I came to a stop, agents ordered me out of my truck and conducted a thorough search.

"Of course, all they found were pillows," I told my dinner companions. It was all a misunderstanding, it turned out. Someone had called Homeland Security because they thought my cargo looked suspicious.

One of the Homeland Security guys at the table spoke up. "What did you do with the cocaine?"

I smiled. "Oh, I snorted it all when I saw the helicopter. I've seen *Goodfellas.*"

Everyone at the table cracked up, and the billionaire grocer beside me said, "You're not like any other CEO we've ever seen."

As I learned to navigate this strange, three-fork world Stephen had introduced me to, I also began waking up from my cultural coma. Remember, the only political experience I'd had to this point was looking on as the "beer block" voted for Jesse Ventura. Even up to 2014, I had no idea of the difference between a Republican and a Democrat, or a liberal and a conservative. In 2015, I started asking questions. I didn't really care which side I came down on. After all those years wandering in an addictive desert, I was just thirsty for information.

The month after the Patriot Award gala, I had a very weird, very vivid dream. Donald Trump and I were in some kind of room. It was an office with pictures on the wall behind us, and we were standing next to each other posing for a picture. In the background of this "photo," I could even see the framed memorabilia on the wall.

Why would I be meeting Donald Trump, I wondered? It made no sense. Then a couple of weeks later, he came down that famous escalator and announced he was running for president. Now my dream made even less sense. Why would a presidential candidate meet with an ex-crack addict like me?

CHAPTER

41

Branching Out

Later that year, Stephen, Kennya, Kendra, and I joined Salem Radio on a tour of Israel. On the long plane ride over, I told my friend, radio host Kevin McCullough, about the dream I had. He started telling me more about politics. I still knew almost nothing. I was like a student in elementary school who was just being introduced to an entirely new subject. As Kevin began explaining some of the views on both sides, I found that most of the things I cared about came down on the conservative side. This wasn't a value judgment. It was just the way things fell for me.

The Israel trip, though, wasn't about politics. It was about faith, and in that beautiful country, my faith grew even stronger. There were things I'd wondered about since I was a kid, lying in bed wondering if God lived on the other side of infinity. In Israel, I was able to put tangible evidence to things I had only remembered hearing about in Sunday school or in movies. For example, the Garden Tomb that is thought to be the tomb where Jesus was buried and rose again. The Dead Sea Scrolls and how their discovery confirmed that many Old Testament biblical texts were at least a thousand years older than previously thought. How the scrolls had been passed down through centuries with hardly any change. We visited archaeological digs dating back to the time of Jesus.

One evening, as I stood on the shore of the Sea of Galilee in the glow of the most unbelievable sunset I had ever seen, I could feel God's actual presence. And it wasn't only me. I hadn't thought Kendra's faith could be lifted to another level. But just being in the Holy Land filled her with so much joy, and experiencing it together brought us closer.

During our tour, Stephen, Kevin and some of the pastors would get up and offer sermons or remarks. A couple of times, Kevin said, "Hey, Mike why don't you get up and say a few words?"

I always brushed him off. I had always admired people who could get up, make an unscripted speech and hold an audience's attention. But I knew I could never do anything like that. Besides, it was enough for me just to be in this amazing country and see so much evidence that supported my faith. Israel was to me a beautiful, peaceful place. I had never felt so safe, inside or out.

A few months later, in February 2016, I found myself in a discussion about the direction of the country at the National Prayer Breakfast. Kendra and I had been invited along with Stephen and Kennya. During the Friday night breakout session I met Bob Dees, a retired Air Force general. At first, I was a little starstruck. (Woooow…This guy's a general.) I had met others in the three-fork crowd who definitely had a better-than-you attitude, but Bob turned out to be a pragmatic, down-to-earth guy who put me at ease. I talked with him for over an hour, and he would later join my foundation board.

The next day, Saturday, February 6, was the actual prayer breakfast. I don't know what I had expected, exactly—maybe church on steroids?—but as I listened to President Barack Obama's keynote speech, I knew this wasn't it. I'd never been in the same room as a U.S. president before, and I should've been more impressed. But early in his speech, the president began drawing a comparison between the current epidemic of Islamic jihad that has killed tens of thousands around the world and past abuses of Christianity such as the Crusades. I understood that he was trying to lift up the value of all faiths, and not elevate any one above another. His effect, though, was to take Christians down a peg, to say that Christians ought not get too high and mighty since our history includes violence too. I sat there thinking that you probably don't have a very good argument when you have to go back 500 years to make your point.

After the breakfast, someone came over and told Stephen and me that we had been selected as part of a group of about 12 people who were to gather with

Dr. Ben Carson, who was still running for president at the time. My friendship with Stephen was helping me get over my tendency to be starstruck—after all, how was I going to keep rubbing shoulders with the three-fork crowd if I couldn't get past an actor?—but the idea of being in this small group of strangers turned me into a nervous wreck. When the time came, Stephen and I went to a breakout room where I suddenly found myself surrounded by people talking about God and politics. Even though the Israel trip had strengthened my faith, that didn't mean I was ready to talk about it.

As you already know, this was the complete opposite of Kendra. As our relationship progressed, I had continued to watch her. Kendra seemed in touch with God in a very special way. Of course, sometimes I thought she was a little too in touch with God. I was driving down the road lost one day and she said, "Let's pray about which way to go."

"I'm going to pray the GPS works," I said.

Still, I wanted what she had. Now, I was standing in this breakout room waiting for Ben Carson with what seemed like a whole room full of Kendras. I thought, what am I doing here?

Finally, Dr. Carson walked in. Stephen introduced us and reminded us that Dr. Carson was running for president. Knowing I was nervous, Stephen broke the ice.

"Mike," he said, "what would your slogan be if you ran for president?"

It was a setup for a punchline we'd discussed before, based on the way I pronounce the word "wash" in my commercials. I wasn't sure I should say it, but I did anyway. "Vote for me," I said smiling, "and I'll put the 'R' back in 'Warshington.'"

Dr. Carson cracked up and I breathed a sigh of relief. I could talk now. I could be myself.

The dozen people in the room gathered in a circle and began talking about the critical importance of the 2016 election. We agreed it was going to be a real spiritual turning point for the country. One path could lead us toward national renewal. The other could lead us down a dark path from which there might be no return, a path that had begun with the removal of God from the public square. The discussion opened my eyes to the impact of politics on ordinary people.

Later, we all bowed our heads and prayed for our country. As we prayed, I opened one eye and saw Stephen taking a picture. Then just as quickly, I snapped my eye shut and scolded myself: What are you doing opening your eyes during this prayer thing?

After the prayer, a man stood up and declared, "Two or three of you in this room are going to become great friends, and you will be part of a great change in our nation."

That night Kendra and I visited with the Baldwins in their hotel room. The television was on but muted as we chatted. Suddenly, Kennya nodded toward the TV where a man was speaking to a crowd of at least 50,000 people.

"That's gonna be you, Mike," Kennya said.

No way, I thought. Absolutely not. I shook my head. "Maybe Stephen, but not me," I said.

Kennya smiled at me. "No, Mike, it's you."

I pushed back some more, but was starting to wonder myself. There was the whole "platform" thing, and I did seem to be zeroing in on some kind of calling. Still, I stared at the man on the screen and shook my head again. Whatever my calling was, it wouldn't be public speaking. It would take an act of God to get me to be that guy on TV.

Some time later, a friend of Stephen's invited me to attend the 2016 Republican National Convention and got me a seat in the section where the Trump family was sitting. It was a strange experience. Politically, I still felt as though I'd been living in the woods all my life and suddenly found myself plopped into civilization.

I found myself impressed with Donald Trump's adult kids—Donald, Jr., Ivanka, Eric, and Tiffany. They were well-spoken and convincing. As vice presidential candidate Mike Pence said onstage, "You can't fake good kids." I also resonated with Mr. Trump's convention speech. His vision for America seemed sensible and down-to-earth.

Multiple people at the convention told me they felt I should meet with him, but I still couldn't figure out why, much less how. Someone who had ridden on his plane said Mr. Trump had taken notice of my advertising. When a channel would go to commercial, he would say, "Watch. It's going to be that pillow guy." He'd apparently also noticed that MyPillow was made in the U.S.A.

After the convention I was scheduled to fly to Philadelphia to do a QVC airing, but I missed my flight and had to take a different one. When I walked onto the plane, I heard someone call out, "Mike!"

It was Candy Carson. Sitting next to her in first class was her husband, Dr. Carson. Candy is a bubbly, vivacious woman with a gentle spirit and a genuine heart. She said, "We knew you'd be on this plane." They'd gotten this in prayer two weeks before, she said.

Candy kindly switched seats with me so that I could talk with her husband. During the flight, he told me what it was like to run for president, how he'd known when it was time to drop out, and why he'd backed Donald Trump in the end. "God picked him for this moment in time," he said.

Dr. Carson asked me to call him Ben, and we talked all the way to Philadelphia. When I ran into the Carsons again at baggage claim, he handed me his card. In the space of that plane flight, we'd formed a friendship that would stretch far into the future.

After the QVC segment in Philly I headed back to the airport, stopping in at a bookstore for a magazine to read on the flight home. On the plane, I opened the magazine to an article about Mr. Trump. As I was flipping through the pages my eyes fell on a picture of the candidate in his office at Trump Tower. The wall in the office was the same one I had seen in my dream. A little shaken, I stared at the picture for a few seconds. Then I closed my eyes and prayed: "God, I don't know what's going on here. Please show me."

In the middle of that prayer, my phone pinged. I opened my eyes and looked at the phone. On the screen was a text message with an invitation: Donald Trump wanted to meet me at Trump Tower in New York.

CHAPTER

42

Confirmations

T he text inviting me to Trump Tower floored me. It's hard to explain the
feeling I get when my premonitions come true, but this was beyond
anything I'd ever experienced. The timing of the invitation—occurring
right in the middle of my prayer—was unbelievable. I was excited to meet a
presidential candidate, but this moment wasn't at all about that. What brought
tears to my eyes was the fact that it seemed God had spoken directly to me in
real time. It was surreal. Astonishing. And extremely humbling.

The meeting was set for Monday, August 15, 2016. Kendra and I flew to
New York City on Friday, August 12. She wanted to attend services at Beth Israel
Worship Center, a congregation pastored by the messianic rabbi, Jonathan Cahn.
We had attended one service there with Stephen and Kennya and I had briefly
been introduced to him. I knew Rabbi Cahn was a bestselling author, teacher,

and evangelist who had ministered all over the world. I had read a few of his books and was impressed with the way he compared biblical prophecies with current events.

I was nervous about the Trump Tower meeting, but over and over God seemed to put people in my path to calm me down. Kendra and I drove down to Wayne, New Jersey, to attend the Beth Israel service. Afterward, Rabbi Cahn, who knew nothing about the reason for our visit, walked up and said, "I sense there's something important we need to pray about."

"Yes," I said. "On Monday, I have a meeting with Donald Trump." Rabbi Cahn prayed with us for the next half-hour.

Later, Kendra and I were eating lunch at a restaurant in Wayne when two women, both perfect strangers, stopped at our table. "You have something very important coming up, and we want to pray with you that whatever it is, it goes well."

I looked at Kendra. She looked at me. "Wow," was all we could say, yet again. Those ladies joined us, and we bowed our heads together.

Next, Kendra and I headed back to the city and checked in at the Trump International Hotel. That afternoon, I got a call inviting me to an outdoor evening reception at the Long Island home of an influential businessman and political donor. Mr. Trump was going to be there, the caller said. I could meet him.

I didn't want to go. An outdoor event in the Hamptons was not what I'd seen in my dream. I was supposed to meet Donald Trump in an office—*his* office, if the photo in the magazine had anything to do with anything. I know it sounds crazy, like something about the "space-time continuum" from *Back to the Future*, but I did not want to disrupt whatever was supposed to happen on Monday.

"I'm not coming," I told the guy on the phone and hung up.

I told Kendra about the conversation. "I think you're supposed to go," she said. "There's someone else you're supposed to meet. Maybe more than one person."

Suddenly, I knew she was right. I called the guy back and told him I'd be there.

That late summer evening, I drove through one of the fanciest parts of the Hamptons wondering briefly whether there was maybe something higher than a three-fork crowd. When I arrived at the businessman's impressive estate, I was ushered around back, where I saw a spotless white outdoor canopy set up on a lush green lawn. I was surprised at how few people were there, just a couple dozen mingling over cocktails. The only people I spoke with were Mr. Trump's longtime assistant, Rhona Graff, who was very kind, and Rudy Giuliani, who was funny and engaging.

After a brief wait, the candidate arrived and offered a few remarks from a podium that had been placed beneath the canopy. Afterward, he moved among the guests, signing those famous red MAGA hats and talking cheerfully about the campaign. I kept my distance and watched.

Back at the hotel, Kendra and I had two rooms, both with balconies overlooking Central Park. August is hot in the city, and on the night of the 14th the temperature stayed in the 90s well past dark. The Trump Tower meeting was just hours away and I still couldn't figure out why I'd been invited. It flashed through my head that maybe it was a fundraising thing, but I dismissed that fairly quickly. I just didn't think that was it. In any case, I might never have another chance like this. I decided I wanted to have some thoughts to offer. Kendra and I stayed up late into the night talking about my biggest concerns. Helping addicts was number one, of course, along with revitalizing America's urban centers. I wasn't sure a presidential candidate would be interested in what I had to say about these topics, but I wanted to come prepared to discuss them.

When Kendra went to her own room at around 3:00 a.m., I walked out on the balcony and gazed down at Central Park. What are the odds that a guy like me would wind up meeting with a man who might be the next President of the United States? I thought. I marveled at how I had gotten here. I thought about where I'd come from and all the mistakes I'd made. Cocaine, crack, gambling. The hundreds of thousands of dollars I'd let slip through my fingers. The ways I'd failed as a husband and a father. How does a guy like that get here? I had only one answer: It had to be God.

The past year or so had been like living in a movie. But now it hit me: This is real. And suddenly, I realized that God had a bigger plan for my life than I had ever imagined. Standing there on that balcony, I felt humbled again. A wave of emotion washed over me, followed by an incredible sense of peace. However broken the road I'd traveled, God had meant it for good. The odds were just too incredible for me not to be on the right path.

Four hours later, I awoke in bed to the multiple alarms I'd set, feeling like I'd slept for 10 hours straight. I showered and dressed, debating whether or not to wear a tie. I ended up leaving off the tie and wearing my silver cross necklace outside my shirt collar just like I always did.

Trump Tower was down 5th Avenue, three long blocks away. I decided to walk and arrived early, taking a seat on a bench in the lobby. For a few minutes, I listened to the waterfall sheening down an atrium wall 60-feet high. I had been told by the candidate's handlers that I would not meet with him alone. I had also been told that since Mr. Trump had lost a brother to alcoholism, I shouldn't bring up my past addictions.

Soon, a guy walked out of the elevator and recognized me. He was a fundraising type, I think, and he offered to take me up. We exited the elevator on a floor containing a suite of offices, were cleared by Secret Service agents, and entered a little lobby. There was a bench where I could look down and see Manhattan. I sat down. It was 9:37 a.m.

Sitting in that lobby was very much like sitting at MyPillow. This wasn't a waiting room, but a place where business was happening. People strode back and forth looking busy and efficient. A hallway led off the lobby and I could see a woman sitting at the desk at the end.

About 10 minutes passed. A man walked through the lobby and I realized it was Eric Trump. Again, I thought about my strange journey—the bar days, the crack days, the dreams, the prayer breakfast, the Republican convention, even those ladies who had prayed with Kendra and me the day before. I thought about how, if you pulled out just one piece, I might not be in this moment.

Five more minutes passed and now three campaign guys gathered around me. These were the people who evidently planned to be in the meeting with me, and we made a little small talk. Then, at exactly 10 a.m., a controlled chaos broke out. A woman came running up and told one guy, "Hey, come into my office. You've got to take this call." She pointed at another man and said, "You need to come too." Then the last guy's cell phone rang.

"Hold on, Mike," he said, then walked a few feet away to take the call.

With the minute hand just past 10 a.m., and the last guy deep in conversation on his phone, I saw the woman from the hallway desk walking toward me. It was Rhona Graff, whom I'd met the evening before in the Hamptons.

"Mike, you don't have to wait for him," she said, nodding toward the guy on the phone and taking me by the arm. "Come on in." She led me down the hallway, and we turned right around a partition. "There he is," Rhona said. "Go ahead." She didn't announce me or introduce me, but just walked out.

And there was Donald Trump, in the very office I'd seen in my dream, sitting at his desk alone. He stood and we shook hands. "Hello, Michael," he said. "Thanks for coming."

Right away, his eyes fell on the silver cross at my neck. "In your commercials, I always see you wearing your cross. Are you a Christian?"

I laughed. "Yes I am, and this is a divine appointment for sure."

We took our seats and in spite of what people had told me, I brought up addiction right away—beginning with my own. I wanted to know where Mr. Trump stood on helping addicts, and also on providing hope for people trapped in failing inner cities. He listened graciously and offered what I thought were compassionate solutions.

From that moment on, we talked about everything from advertising to U.S. manufacturing to jobs. Our conversation was detailed and down-to-earth, and not full of campaign-speak. In my old life, I might have been sitting there the whole time thinking how surreal this was. But Mr. Trump was genuine and sincere and seemed to have no particular agenda other than to get one citizen's opinion on things. He was also very focused, and in my opinion, had a lot of practical, businesslike approaches to solving real problems facing our nation.

After about 30 minutes, we wrapped up the meeting and said our goodbyes. I was heading toward the door when Rudy Giuliani walked around the wall partition, singing a song I knew very well:

For the best night's sleep in the whole wide world, visit MyPillow...dot-com!

I had met Mr. Giuliani at the Hamptons event. Laughing, I stood and said, "What? Are you following me?"

Just then, a member of the campaign staff came in and asked if I would like a picture of myself with Mr. Trump. I said yes and gave him my phone.

The staffer had started to frame the photo when Mr. Trump said, "No, let's take it over here," and pointed to the wall of memorabilia near his desk. We stood together while the staffer snapped the picture. When I checked it later, I saw that it was the exact image I'd seen in my dream.

CHAPTER

43

Standing Up

When I walked out of his office, I knew I would support Donald Trump for president, 100 percent. I couldn't wait to tell Kendra about the meeting. On my way back up 5th Avenue, I called her on my cell, but was talking so fast she could barely understand me. I said I didn't think the meeting could have gone any better. When I said Mr. Trump had asked about my cross and whether I was a Christian, she was overjoyed.

During the next few days, Kendra and I had the opportunity to speak with numerous Trump employees, and they all told us the same thing: Donald Trump is a great boss, they said. Most of the people we spoke with said he had gone out of his way to help them personally.

That week, I returned to Minnesota for a MyPillow board meeting. I told my board members about the Trump meeting and about my conversations with his employees. I said I felt the Trump organization had the same kind of one-big-family feeling as MyPillow. But even as I shared my enthusiasm, I felt an aura of skepticism enter the room. Still, I pressed on.

"I'm going all-in to help him get elected," I said. I added that I planned to do a press release about my private conversation with the candidate. The Minnesota press would bombard me as usual, I predicted. Then I could talk about why I thought Donald Trump would make a great president.

My corporate attorney spoke up immediately. "Mike, I strongly advise you against going public with this. It will cost MyPillow dearly."

Suddenly, I felt flushed with annoyance. Of course I was concerned about my company's standing, but there were larger issues here. Not wanting to show the extent of my irritation, I got up and left the boardroom. Jessica Maskovich, now MyPillow's chief marketing officer, followed me out and stopped me in the hall.

She expressed her profound disagreement with my attorney, and said, "Mike, we didn't get this far by you not listening to God."

I looked at Jessica for a moment. Then I turned, walked back into the boardroom, and said, "We didn't get this far by me not listening to God!"

The next day, I did the press release. As MyPillow's profile had grown over the past couple of years, the press had begun reaching out to me on a regular basis, especially when I announced anything new. But this time, my phone never rang. What I got instead were messages from multiple media outlets calling me racist and evil. I was completely taken aback. None of those who sent the messages wanted to know why I met with Mr. Trump or what was said. Not a single media outlet, from radio to TV to print, wanted to know what led me to announce my support. Just the fact that I'd met with Donald Trump had somehow turned me from local-guy-done-good to media enemy overnight.

My emotions went from anger to complete discouragement. This was my first glimpse of how unfair the press can be. Now I faced a choice: I could retreat and go silent in the interest of protecting my business, or I could go all-in, knowing there would be no turning back.

I went all-in.

In 2016, I went to two of the three presidential debates. Stephen and I flew together to the third one, which was held in Las Vegas. Sitting in a window seat, looking down on the city where my first and most serious addiction began, was like flying into a time warp. This was the place where the hook was set. The place where I had turned five silver dollars into thousands, and thought what would turn out to be one of the most misguided and ultimately self-destructive thoughts of my life:

This is the easiest thing in the world.

My life in God was so different now, and as we landed at McCarran Airport, I knew I'd left the past behind forever.

Stephen and I took a car to the University of Nevada and listened as Fox News journalist Chris Wallace moderated the debate between the candidates, Donald Trump and Hillary Clinton. There were cameras everywhere. I must have gotten 27 texts from friends back in Minnesota saying they heard Fox News's Neil Cavuto asking on the air why in the world the "MyPillow guy" was at the debate.

Afterward, I was surprised to be invited, along with Stephen, into the spin room, where the media interviews the candidates' surrogates and gets their analysis of the debate. The room was packed, and Stephen began giving interviews. I thought I'd just be observing until a media handler yelled out, "Does anybody want to talk to the MyPillow guy?"

Several reporters yelled back that they did. The media were crowded behind a rope line and the first reporter to get my attention was Kennedy from Fox Business News. I told her I was there to give my credibility to Donald Trump.

Then a reporter from a national cable news channel called out, "Hey Mike Lindell, you always wear your cross. What do you think of the Access Hollywood video?"

She was referring to the video of Donald Trump and Billy Bush, recorded 11 years earlier, that was being played over and over in the media at the time. Looking back, I think the reporter thought she had a "gotcha" moment. What would a guy wearing a great big cross have to say about the candidate's crass locker room talk about women?

"I was a crack cocaine addict for years," I told her. "Then, by the grace of God, I quit overnight, but I'm still in transformation. Recently I met Donald Trump. He was so different from the man in that video. The guy I met must be in a really amazing transformation, too. And did you know that Phil Robertson recently shared the gospel with him—"

"Never mind," the reporter said, cutting me off. She gestured to her cameraman to stop recording.

Apparently, I wasn't telling her what she wanted to hear. But soon another reporter came along, and I said I thought Donald Trump was going to be the greatest president we'd ever had.

By that time, people in my life had gotten used to me telling them one crazy premonition or another. They had gotten just as used to the fact that if I told them something was going to happen, it did. Right after the third debate I had another visual premonition: Donald Trump was speaking at a rally in Minnesota, and I was speaking there too.

When I told my friends about this, they said, "Mike, Trump's not gonna waste his time here. Minnesota hasn't voted for a Republican presidential candidate since 1972."

That surprised me, then I learned it was true. Even when every other state in the country went for Reagan in 1984, Minnesota voted Democrat. Now, as time ticked toward Election Day, the campaign announced no plans to stop in Minnesota.

Four days before the election, Stephen and I flew to Las Vegas. A group of his friends had invited us to attend the championship welterweight fight between Manny Pacquiao and Jesse Vargas. It turned out that Manny was also a Christian. On fight night, as music thumped in the arena, Stephen and I gathered with Manny and others to pray before the bout. Afterward, my group took seats in the first or second row ringside, and I took a moment to look around.

The seats around me were dotted with celebrities, and I reflected again on my long, wild history with Vegas, a town that had nearly been the end of me. I couldn't count the number of times I'd card-counted here, sitting at the tables hour after hour just to put food on the table and keep MyPillow alive. And it hadn't been so long ago that I would have skipped the fight and headed straight to a craps table, no question. But this night, I had absolutely no desire to gamble, even though I now had the money to do it. I took a moment to feel grateful.

One of the men in our party was a prominent Democrat I'd met at the National Prayer Breakfast, and beneath the pounding hip-hop, he and I had to lean in close to chat. It was November 5, and with Election Day now only three days away, the conversation turned to presidential politics. My friend told me Hillary Clinton was going to win.

"It's not even going to be close," he said.

Smiling, I said I disagreed. Then I proceeded to explain the deviations, all things that had happened to me personally. I told him that, from a "what are the odds?" standpoint, those things could only mean one thing as far as I was concerned.

"Donald Trump is going to win," I said.

Of course, my reasoning didn't square at all with either the electoral college map or the polls. My Democrat friend was genuinely nice about my naïve prediction. I don't remember exactly what he said, but it amounted to, "That's impossible."

He seemed to feel kind of sorry for me and put his hand on my shoulder as if to console me for the crushing blow he was sure was coming my way.

As history shows, Manny won the fight. Afterward, Stephen and I went to

a restaurant with a large group that included Larry Ross, a longtime friend of
Billy Graham's. While we were eating, my phone rang. It was someone from the
Trump campaign.

"Mr. Trump will be making a surprise stop in Minnesota tomorrow," the
caller said. "It should be a big crowd, and we'd like to know if you'd be one of
the speakers."

I didn't even hesitate. "Of course I will," I said.

When I hung up and shared the news with my dinner companions, the
table erupted with excitement. But there was one small problem: Because of the
Pacquiao fight, every flight out of Vegas that night was overbooked. How was I
going to get back to Minnesota in time? Everyone whipped out cell phones and
started searching for flights. There was one red-eye that would get me there, but
it was completely sold out. Also, it was departing in less than an hour. I closed my
eyes and sent up a flare prayer. Suddenly, Larry called out, "Got it!"

There had been a cancellation. A seat on the red-eye had opened up, and we
grabbed it.

"Go! Go! Go!" everyone said. Larry hustled me out of the restaurant, and
we jumped in a car and raced for McCarran.

I flew all night to get home. At 30,000 feet, it hit me that I'd been asked in a
formal way to help elect the next President of the United States. Wow, God,
I thought. I know this is You. But in the rush of excitement, I'd ignored the
obvious problem: I was about to go speak in front of a whole bunch of people.
Fear washed over me. What in the world was I going to say? How long would
I talk? Would I be able to overcome my fear enough to physically speak even a
word? I wrestled with those questions all the way home.

A couple of times, I started to jot a few notes and then stopped. I was no
politician. What could I, a pillow salesman from Chaska, possibly have to say to
these people? I just couldn't put my head around anything. After landing, having
failed to write my speech, I decided to go home and at least get some sleep. At
11 a.m., I woke up and spent 15 minutes stumped on which suit I should wear,
which was ridiculous since I only owned two.

This whole thing had happened so fast that I didn't post the event
on Facebook. I didn't even have time to grab my kids or anybody to come
with me. Only my COO, Kim Rasmussen, would be there since I had called
her the night before. When I pulled up to a private hangar at Minneapolis-
St. Paul Airport, I saw a huge sea of people. I couldn't believe it. The crowd
had to be in the thousands. Fear swamped me again.

Though the candidate wasn't supposed to be there for hours, the lines to get onto the tarmac stretched for literal miles. People had parked their cars in ditches. I saw security lines that didn't seem to end, and I didn't know quite where to go. For a moment, I wondered whether I was supposed to stand in line with everyone else. In the end, I decided to walk up to the front and ask for instructions. Even though I was a speaker, I still felt guilty about cutting in line.

As I passed, people started calling out my name, cheering, and flashing thumbs-up. "Mike! Hey, Mike! Hey, it's the MyPillow guy!"

I'd been recognized before by a few people, but now it was like everyone knew me. It felt so strange. Finally, someone walked up and ushered me into a hangar where a bunch of Minnesota politicians started introducing themselves. My mind was going a million miles a minute:

What—? How—? Why—?

What am I doing here?

Why am I speaking and not one of these professionals?

From that moment on, people kept asking me to pose for pictures. Dozens and dozens of them. Finally, a campaign guy grabbed me and helped me navigate my way back out to the tarmac. Still with no idea what I was going to say, I stood there for a moment all alone, asking God to give me the words.

I must have looked as terrified as I felt, because a slender lady with long dark hair walked up and said, "Mike, I'm Michele Bachmann. You look like we need to pray." Michele represented Minnesota's 6th district in Congress.

Relief flooded me. "Yes, we do," I said. And we prayed right there on the tarmac in front of the whole crowd.

The next thing I knew, I was up on stage. I looked across the massive crowd at the bank of cameras behind them. ABC. CBS. NBC. Then, suddenly, I began, saying something like, "I was born and raised in Minnesota..."

The crowd went crazy.

I don't remember what all I said, just that I probably told my story. That I was a recovered crackhead. That I didn't know anything about politics. That I had experienced a series of little miracles. Each time I paused the tarmac rang with cheers. I do remember one of the last things I said.

I pointed at the media standing behind the people. "They are wrong," I said. "Donald Trump will win the election and he will be the most amazing president this country has ever seen in history!"

CHAPTER

44

Full Surrender

My airport speech ran at the top of every newscast in Minnesota. Okay, that's absolutely false. Despite that bank of television cameras rolling tape the whole time, the media completely ignored my speech. Maybe it was because I said their predictions were wrong, but I suspected that if I had bashed Donald Trump instead of supporting him, my speech would have been replayed on an endless loop. It probably would have gone national.

On election night, Kendra and I attended the Trump watch party at the New York Hilton in midtown Manhattan. It was standing room only as the election results slowly rolled in. Kevin McCullough had told me to watch the returns from certain eastern states—Virginia, for example, which many experts said would go solidly blue. If that happened, Kevin said, it would probably be a good night for Hillary Clinton.

As we watched the news media call the states for one candidate or the other, my confidence started to waver: What if he doesn't win?

Because of what I'd learned about how politics affects our daily lives, the thought scared me. But I pushed it from my mind and my confidence swung back in the other direction. Then, when Virginia returns showed Donald Trump doing very well there, I knew it was the deviation I'd been waiting for. From my front row seat, I turned to the people sitting around me and said, "He's going to win."

When the media called Pennsylvania for Donald Trump, the Hilton ballroom erupted in cheers. People were hugging and high-fiving all around us. Around 3 a.m., the room exploded again when the president-elect and his family walked in. It was a moment for the history books, and I took a photo as they walked past. I was amazed at the level of energy in the room despite the fact that people had been standing and waiting for many, many hours. After Mr. Trump made his victory speech, Kendra and I stayed, soaking in every last moment of this once-in-a-lifetime event.

It was around 5 a.m. when we got back to our hotel. Kendra had gone to her room, but I was too keyed up to sleep and used the TV remote to jump between the news stations that continued to provide election coverage. By 8 a.m., some of those stations were calling my cell, including media outlets from my home state and as far away as Australia.

What did I think of Trump's victory? they wanted to know. I guess they had forgiven me for the Minnesota airport rally when I had pointed at the news cameras and told the crowd the media were all wrong.

A Minnesota television station invited me to appear on a news program the following Sunday. A few days later, I walked into the show's green room to find my counterpart, a college professor who was also there to discuss the election results. He was very kind and polite, but also seemed a little rattled when I began talking about the results in terms of divine intervention.

On the air, host Esme Murphy asked me all kinds of questions, including this one: "What would you say to people who are afraid now that Donald Trump has been elected?"

"Just give it a chance," I said. "God has His hand in this. Change is coming, and it's going to be good change."

The change in my own life had definitely been good. During my strange journey, God had placed in my path people of faith, integrity, and generosity—people with a heart to help others. I began to understand what God might intend for the "platform" He had provided, and that the Lindell Foundation and our focus on helping people might be a vessel for that. Throughout 2016, I had asked myself why a guy like me would be invited to participate in high-profile, nationally watched events. Now I was beginning to think that maybe God had opened those doors in order to expand whatever good the Lindell Foundation might do.

But as much as I believed God's hand was on my life, I knew something was missing. It was like I would get right up to the edge of fully surrendering my life to Him, but just couldn't quite hand over the wheel. I wanted what Kendra had, but didn't know how to get it. In fact, I didn't even know what "it" was.

During my first year-and-a-half with Kendra, I would assure her that I had been saved—born again—but she didn't believe it. I talked a good game, but she didn't see the spiritual fruit in my life. I knew she was right because I saw with painful clarity the person I wasn't. Though free from my addictions, I still had fits of rage and often took my deep-seated anger out on people who didn't deserve it, including Kendra. But she was incredibly patient with me. She wanted the best for me and knew exactly what that "best" was.

At a November meeting of my foundation board, Larry Ross (the guy who got me the red-eye seat from Vegas to Minneapolis and rushed me to airport) told me about a retreat he'd recently attended. It was called Operation Restored Warrior (ORW) and was run by a man named Paul Lavelle, a former Army medic—and a former atheist. I'd actually met Paul at the National Prayer Breakfast in 2016. His ministry has helped hundreds of men—most of them Special Forces and Special Operations—come to a place of freedom by locating primary points of pain in their pasts, and inviting God in to heal them.

Larry had attended an Operation Restored Warrior "Drop Zone" event. Even after 30 years working alongside Billy Graham, Larry said the Drop Zone really enriched his relationship with Jesus.

"I think it would be a good idea for you to go," he told me.

My first instinct was rebellion. Though I knew something was missing in my spiritual life, I didn't like the idea that others might think so too. Was something wrong with me? Was I broken?

After the board meeting, Larry pulled me aside and shared more about his ORW experience. Not many civilians got to attend, so he'd felt very blessed to be invited, he said. As it turned out, Paul and his team had been praying since our National Prayer Breakfast encounter and had felt led to invite me too. Larry had already spoken with Kendra about it, and she was very excited.

But I felt conflicted. On the one hand, it seemed another God-given opportunity. On the other, it meant spending five days in the mountains with perfect strangers. Reluctantly, I said I'd go if a space opened up. But when one did the very next month, I turned it down.

I had a good excuse—in fact, it was a great excuse. Along with Larry Ross, I had been invited to the Philippines to discuss matters related to the Lindell Foundation. There was even the possibility of meeting Philippine President Rodrigo Duterte. But it was still an excuse, and Kendra wasn't happy about it. She insisted we get Paul Lavelle on the phone to reschedule. He found another opening and put me on his calendar: I was to travel to Lake Tahoe for a Drop Zone event in February 2017.

In December 2016, I traveled to the Philippines and got to meet President Duterte. Two months later, on February 16, I got on a plane to meet Jesus.

Or at least I hoped I would meet Him. I had thought I'd still be reluctant to attend the Drop Zone, but now I found myself filled with hope because of a man named Dr. Barry Black. I had just attended the 2017 National Prayer Breakfast where I'd heard Dr. Black, chaplain of the United States Senate, give a powerful, jaw-dropping message. The whole time, I felt he was talking directly to me. After two catastrophic events that happened between the Philippines and the Drop Zone, his message refreshed me with optimism.

As my plane touched down at the Reno-Tahoe Airport, I received a text from my assistant:

> Mike, Paul just told me there are a couple of other Drop Zone guys at the airport right now. They've offered to drive you up to the lodge. That way you don't have to get a rental car.

It was an hour-long drive to the lodge, where ORW was holding the event.

"Absolutely not," I texted my assistant. "I'm not riding with anybody I don't know." It was sad, really. Here I was, 55 years old and still afraid of strangers.

"Get me a rental car," I texted.

When my phone chimed again in my hand, I expected it to be my assistant giving a thumbs-up. Instead, it was a new text:

> Hi, I'm Jason. Paul Lavelle gave me your number. We're headed up to Drop Zone and heard you need a ride. We'll meet you by baggage claim.

Crap. The next thing I knew, here come two guys, both obviously ex-military, one of them walking with a cane. They introduced themselves as Jason and Tim. Hey, how you doin' and all that. Jason, who looked rock-hard even in his 40s, took the lead, and the conversation went something like this:

Jason: Ride up with us. No sense in you driving up alone.
Me: No, that's okay. I've got some work to do. I have to
         make some calls.
Jason: Won't bother us at all.
Me: Well, I wasn't planning on leaving for another hour.
Jason: Not a problem. We'll wait.

Ugh. These guys weren't taking no for an answer. I really did have calls to make. But after an hour, they were still waiting. Resigned, I followed them out to their car. But no small talk, I vowed. As we started down the road, I stared out the window making it very apparent that I wasn't interested in conversation. They probably thought I was a jerk when really I was just paralyzed. But it was more than the fact that I was uncomfortable with strangers. I had other things on my mind. Serious things.

The catastrophes I mentioned earlier had begun on January 2, 2017. I had just completed a 24-hour stint on a Canadian shopping channel that had broken all kinds of records. As I walked out of the last airing and turned my phone back on, it went crazy, buzzing and dinging with messages and notifications. I checked a few of them and found terrible news. The Better Business Bureau (BBB) had dropped MyPillow's rating from an A+ to an F. Not only that, but they'd done a press release about it. I was in complete disbelief.

We'd sold over 25 million pillows by then, and the BBB had received only about 230 complaints—or less than 0.001 percent of sales. I'd resolved most of those personally, just as I had when I drove all over Iowa delivering pillows. As far as I knew, nothing had changed. Now I had three urgent questions. One, why in the world would the BBB trash our rating? Two, why would they do so without contacting me first for a resolution? And three, since when did the BBB issue press releases about a business's rating?

As I gathered my thoughts, I scrambled to the airport while making calls. I learned that the BBB had tanked our rating because MyPillow's "buy one, get one free" ad had been running longer than they thought was appropriate.

So, with customer satisfaction of literally 99.9 percent, the BBB had rated MyPillow an F, then announced it to the media, who were turning it into national news. The thought crossed my mind that this was a political hit job designed to destroy my company's reputation, and I couldn't dismiss that idea.

To fight back, my publicist arranged for reporters to visit my Shakopee factory. Outlet after outlet set up in different offices and when I got back from Canada, I circulated among them, answering the charges in the BBB's press release. The media were stern and skeptical, as though my offering customers two pillows for the price of one were some heinous breech of business ethics. Suddenly, I felt like a fugitive again, the way I had after the 1983 gas station incident. Back then, I had destroyed my own reputation. Now, someone else was destroying it for me.

Unbelievably, the media requests went on and on. Days into the deluge, I was feeling discouraged and beaten down when my sister Marcy called with even more bad news. Our dad had been admitted to the hospital. Marcy ran down the symptoms using medical terms that seemed natural to her because she's a nurse, but made no sense at all to me. I rushed to the hospital, calling my sister Robin on the way. Robin always sees the sunny side of things and when she told me she could hardly stand to see our dad like this, I knew it was bad.

When I arrived in Dad's hospital room, he didn't even recognize me. He was talking to himself, sputtering as he spoke, unable to form full words. One second, he was gripped in extreme agitation. The next, he would lapse into a blank stare that reminded me of a movie I'd seen where a man gets a lobotomy. Seeing my father this way, I just about lost it and dashed into the hall screaming for a doctor. Eventually, the doctors told us they believed there was only a 5-percent chance that my dad would ever come out of this state. When one said we should start looking for a nursing home to put him in, tears welled in my eyes.

"Are you okay?"

The voice that interrupted my thoughts came from the front seat of the rental car, and I realized that the two guys from the Reno-Tahoe Airport had already navigated far up into the mountains.

"Yes," I said. I quickly shook off my reflective state and began engaging with them a bit, asking questions. I learned that both were military veterans, that neither had attended a Drop Zone before and that like me, they weren't sure what to expect. We were all in the same boat.

The one who used a cane shared some things he'd seen in Iraq—things I couldn't even imagine. He was wounded in action, he said. After listening to their stories, I dropped my defenses and found myself opening up. By the time we reached the lake, I had decided that in spite of my resistance, riding with these guys had been another divine appointment. Instead of arriving at the Drop Zone with perfect strangers, I felt like I was arriving with friends.

****

When we arrived at the lodge, it felt like we had driven straight into a Christmas card. Snow-covered grounds led off into the woods in every direction and a ring of white-capped mountains surrounded the crystal blue lake. Inside, I put my bags in one of the many guest rooms and joined the rest of the attendees downstairs for a meet and greet. My nerves ramped up again as I realized I was in for a round of three things I wasn't a fan of: small talk, rules, and expectations. On top of that, I discovered that all of the other men were veterans. I'd had brushes with death myself, guns pointed at me, that machete held to my throat. But that paled in comparison to what these guys had been through. I could tell they were some of the toughest men in America. Intimidating? Absolutely. As soon as I could, I retreated to my room and stayed there.

As I lay in bed that night wondering why I'd come, I remembered a conversation I'd had in May 2015 with a pastor who, along the way, helped me with this book. By that time, I had a long manuscript that was really not a book, but more a collection of stories. I had separated the manuscript into individual stories and lined them up in little stacks on a long table.

"My problem is, I don't know what to leave in and what to leave out," I told the pastor.

By then, he had read many of the stories you've now read. Suddenly, he grabbed a random pile of paper from somewhere in the middle and waved it at me. "You could take any one of these things that happened to you, and any normal person would have surrendered to God right there on the spot." Then he gave me a long, penetrating look. "Mike, God's been chasing you this whole time. Maybe all these things happened to you to get you to Jesus. How much more does He need to do to prove to you that He is real?"

I realized now the pastor was right—and he didn't even know about the incredible events of the past two years. How many one-in-a-million, one-in-a-billion events did I need? As I fell asleep that first night in Tahoe, my hope returned.

The next morning I woke up early and went downstairs. Paul Lavelle walked up and greeted me. "Mike, I've got two things to ask you," he said. "Number one, will you commit to staying off your phone? I know it's glued to your hand and you need it to run your business. But it's really important that you stay off of it here."

I already knew about this requirement and it had been one of the big reasons I didn't want to come. I ran my entire business off my phone. Paul looked at me, waiting for my answer.

"Yes…?" I said. "Okay. Yes."

"Number two, do you know this guy?" Paul reached out and touched my cross. I was wearing it outside my collar like always.

"Yes...?" I said again, knowing he meant Jesus. "I mean, I know Him about as well as anyone could know Him."

"Here's a promise," Paul said. "If you will open your heart while you're here, you're going to be in a completely different place when you leave."

Fairly quickly, I began to see what he meant. Throughout that day, I found myself slowly letting my guard down. Paul encouraged us all to share our stories. He'd had heads of state come through ORW. He'd listened to generals, priests, and Ph.D.s. "Every story matters," he said. "The power of one person's story does not diminish the power and authority of another person's story."

I realized that the group conversations and sharing reminded me of those I'd attended nearly a decade ago at Living Free. It wasn't about your lowest points in life, how many drugs you'd done, who you were, or where you'd been. It's that everyone has emotional wounds and trauma, and that for many people, those wounds leave debilitating scars.

Back in my room that night with time to reflect, I realized that for most of my life I had been playing chicken with God. Each time I faced a one-in-a-million or one-in-a-billion circumstance—each time I'd wondered, "How am I going to get out of this one?"—I somehow always did. That gave me the illusion of control and caused me to keep testing the limits. Now I knew that God hadn't protected me in all those moments for nothing. The platform He had provided was real, and as Kendra had told me many times, how was I going to convince anyone of anything if I hadn't been truly redeemed myself? That night, I resolved to hand over the wheel. I would no longer be the driver of my own life.

A couple of days in, we each had to write down the major experiences in our lives—our "core memories," or primary points of pain—just as we had at Living Free. Paul compared these memories to a spiderweb that sends out poison silk into every area of our lives.

"We don't get through life without taking hits," Paul said. "You have to go back and address these broken places."

The next afternoon, I sat in a room alone with a facilitator and did exactly that. The facilitator asked me to close my eyes and take myself back to those pivotal moments in my life when my heart and spirit were wounded. I was 5 years old again. Then I was 7, then 10, then a teenager, then an adult. It was like watching the first movie of my life all over again, that first reel in the double feature.

With the facilitator's guidance, I didn't just relive events, I was *there*. I could see everything. I could smell and taste and feel. The pain of my past swelled like a river overflowing its banks, and deep, heaving sobs broke from my chest. It was only then I realized I'd spent more than 50 years holding it all in.

"Can you look around?" the facilitator said softly.

"Yes," I said. In the eye of my spirit, I did look around.

"Is there anyone there with you?"

Yes! I could see Him. Jesus was with me!

And suddenly I knew He had been with me through it all. I knew He had been with me through my parents' divorce. He had been with me when I rolled through the fire, and the time I almost died when I wrecked Fred's truck. Jesus had been with me when I made terrible, terrible mistakes. Jesus was with me in the casinos, bars, and crack houses. He was with me when Karen left me, and when I left my kids alone. He was with me when I won fortunes and when I foolishly lost them.

Jesus had been there the whole time, chasing me, running after me the way a father pursues a lost son. I had buried the pain deep, but all my life it had punched through to the surface, like weeds breaking through concrete. I couldn't talk to people, not because I didn't like talking, but because I didn't feel like I was good enough. I felt different, ignored, unworthy. That spirit of unworthiness hung over my entire life like a cloud, and I spent all my time trying to claw through to the clear, clean sky.

All my death-defying stunts? That was 7-year-old Mike waving his arms, yelling at the world, "Hey, I'm here! I. Am. Here."

And when that didn't work, I started to medicate the pain. First gambling. Then alcohol. Then cocaine and crack. And even amid all that, God kept trying to get my attention.

Many times I had prayed the prayer of salvation, asking Jesus to come into my life. But now I had been with Him, and I prayed with a passion I had never known. Right there in that living room in Lake Tahoe, I surrendered.

The sense of release I felt was overwhelming. As I prayed, I felt myself letting go of all the guilt for things I'd done in the past, even that shameful moment at the gas station when I'd broken my own moral code and embarrassed my family. What replaced the guilt was an incredible mixture of joy, love, and peace. So many times before, I'd glimpsed this moment—I'd felt God holding out His hand, but I wasn't ready to relinquish control. Now, finally, I turned it all over to God. All my sins fell away, like a heavy burden I didn't have to carry anymore. I trusted Him completely and had complete faith that He would guide my path. It had taken 55 years, but God finally caught me. I had finally given up my seat behind the wheel.

Five days after I got there, I left Lake Tahoe. But I never came down from that mountain. The next time I spoke with Kendra, she was overjoyed. Even over the telephone, she could tell I had been changed.

It had all become clear. All the close calls, all the impossible coincidences, all the times I asked myself, what are the odds?

That was Jesus, waving His arms and saying, "I. AM. HERE."

March 2008 I had been up for 14 days straight by the time my drug dealers did an intervention and cut off my supply. One of them snapped this photo.

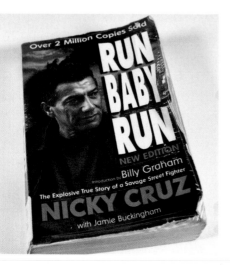

January 19, 2009 After the phrase "run, baby, run" came to me one morning, I learned it was the title of a book by Nicky Cruz, a former gang leader who converted to Christianity. Instead of borrowing the book, I bought it from the local library.

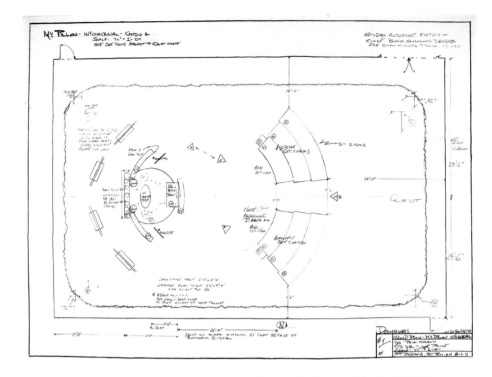

AUGUST 1, 2011 While planning the infomercial that would take MyPillow global, we came up with this sketch for the studio set.

October 2011 Tonja Waring and I appeared in MyPillow's very first infomercial. Soon after its first airing, MyPillow sales skyrocketed and the infomercial became the top infomercial of its kind in the world.

October 27, 2012 After years of trying, MyPillow was finally featured on QVC.

2015 With my son Darren on one of our many hunting trips.

2015 Radio and television personality Don Imus was an early MyPillow endorser. During lean times, his support sometimes single-handedly carried the company.

October 31, 2015 With (left to right) Kennya and Stephen Baldwin, and radio host Kevin McCullough in Israel. At right, Kevin addresses our group on the significance of an ancient site.

With Kendra at the Garden Tomb.

July 22, 2016 After first meeting him in early 2016, I ran into Dr. Ben Carson on a plane. Our conversation on that trip began a long and rewarding friendship.

August 2016 With Kendra and Rabbi Jonathan Cahn.

August 15, 2016 At the conclusion of a meeting with then-candidate Donald Trump in his office at Trump Towers, a staffer snapped this photo.

October 19, 2016
With Stephen Baldwin before entering the "spin room" after the third presidential debate in Las Vegas, Nevada.

November 6, 2016 Left: Preparing to speak at a Trump campaign rally in Minnesota, I took a moment to reflect. Right: The rally was my first time ever speaking before an audience in the thousands, and I was terrified. But I spoke from the heart and somehow made it through.

November 8, 2016 Left: With Kendra at the Trump election night watch party. Right: Celebrating President-elect Donald Trump's victory.

January 3, 2017 With Stuart Varney of *Fox Business News*, discussing my assessment of the Better Business Bureau.

February 20, 2017 With Paul Lavelle of Operation Restored Warrior. Paul leads the ministry that helped me make a full commitment to Christ.

September 10, 2017 An informal reunion with Officer Larry who, in 2008, let me take care of some important MyPillow business and *then* arrested me.

June 10, 2017 Left: My dad, Jim, with my sister Marcy during his seven-month hospital stay. Doctors said he would never recover. Right: Ten days later, through divine intervention, not only did my dad recover, he got well enough to beat me at pool.

July 19, 2017 With President Trump at Made in America, a U.S. manufacturing summit.

April 2018 Rabbi Jonathan Cahn baptized me in the Jordan River.

May 18, 2018
Above: Onstage with PULSE
founder, Nick Hall, at a youth
event held at U.S. Bank Stadium.
Right: It was my first experience
leading public prayer and again,
I was terrified.

October 24, 2018 I was invited to the White House bill-signing ceremony for the bipartisan Overdose Prevention and Patient Safety Act. Having discussed how to help addicts with then-candidate Trump in August 2016, I was elated to see President Trump and Congress working together to take concrete, meaningful steps.

August 21, 2019 Speaking at Liberty University's Convocation. After sharing my story with thousands of young college students, I urged each of them to find and fulfill their individual callings.

EPILOGUE

When I walked out on the stage, all I had was a mic in my hand. There was a podium, but I didn't stand behind it. I had prepared some notes to speak from, but I didn't use them. Without any shield or crutch, I was able to, for the very first time, stand on a stage without fear and deliver a message of hope.

It was August 21, 2019. The venue was Liberty University's Vines Center, a deep amphitheater with rows and rows of seats stretching up toward the rafters. The event was the university's weekly convocation. With more than 13,000 in attendance, and thousands more watching on TV and online, it is North America's largest gathering of Christian students. Past speakers have come from diverse viewpoints and all walks of life, from preachers to presidents and everything in between. As I stood on that same stage and was welcomed by an incredibly gracious crowd, it was a humbling experience.

When I opened my mouth and began to speak, all I did was tell my story. I have come to understand this as my calling—telling about a life spent running from, and then running *to*, the God of second and third and fourth chances. It is the story of a God who is in the business of redeeming sin and failure with love and grace. My own history is proof that none of us should ever give up on our dreams, and that with God all things are possible. My goal is to spend the rest of my life telling people about His awesome redeeming power.

One of the first people to encourage me to be public about my faith was Don Imus. The first time I appeared on his television show and started talking about God, Imus said, "Now don't get crazy on us, Lindell."

For years after that, whenever I appeared on his show I would leave God out. During my final appearance, he asked me to retell the MyPillow story. I got to the part about our first failed mall kiosk, when we sold only a few pillows. It was the time that guy asked for my number in case he wanted his money back, then turned out to be an organizer for the Minneapolis Home and Garden Show.

I was sharing how that phone call had been key to launching my company when Imus interrupted me.

"Why do you think that guy called you?" he said.

"Because he liked the pillow…?" I said hesitantly. I knew Imus didn't want me talking about God.

But he kept asking me over and over: "No, Mike. *Why do you think that guy called you?*"

Finally, I said, "Well, if you want the truth, it was a divine appointment."

"No! I want you to lie to me!" Imus snapped, scolding me on national television. "Of course I want the truth! You don't have to be ashamed of talking about the baby Jesus. There's a big calling on your life. Don't you ever back down!"

Imus is one of many people who helped me along the way. From hundreds of new friends to perfect strangers who reached out when I didn't have the courage, so many people have made a major impact on my life and work.

That was especially true in the case of my ongoing battle with the Better Business Bureau. Remember when the BBB dropped MyPillow's rating from an A+ to an F? Following the group's January 3, 2017 press release, the media attacked, and the onslaught did not let up. Then, on January 11, *Bloomberg News* published an article called, "The Preposterous Success Story of America's Pillow King." Bloomberg had been working on the story for months, and it was a godsend. Not only was it our first major national feature, but it really changed the narrative.

When people all over the country read the article, which was basically a brief version of the story in this book, they launched a counteroffensive on social media and on the BBB website itself. In fact, so many MyPillow supporters bombarded the BBB that one of their executives eventually had to go on TV and endure a reporter's questions about why the organization had slashed our rating from an A+ to an F instead of, for example, a B or a C. The whole incident, which seemed designed to destroy MyPillow, instead raised our profile exponentially. Our sales actually increased and, more importantly, our platform for doing good gained enormous visibility.

Believe it or not, MyPillow's BBB rating is still an F today. I like to tell people that the F stands for "Fantastic!"

On the heels of the BBB episode, in July 2017, I was invited to the White House for a manufacturing summit. I had visited historic places in Washington, D.C., but never 1600 Pennsylvania Avenue. So when I arrived at the famous address, I was as excited as a kid on a junior high field trip.

After jumping through all the security hoops, I walked into the conference room and found the nameplate that indicated my seat. The seat next to me didn't have a nameplate. I got the attention of some official-looking person and asked,

"Who's sitting there?"

"The president," he said.

During the meeting, reporters positioned themselves around the room, snapping photos, cameras rolling. The next thing I knew, there were stills and video plastered all over the news. I started getting texts from my addict friends back home along the lines of, "Wow, Mike! From the crack house to the White House."

More importantly, this crazy circumstance also prompted some serious reflection, people later told me. "That's impossible," these friends thought. "Mike Lindell, an ex-crack addict from Minnesota, is sitting next to the President of the United States. Jesus *must* be real!"

Several of them got sober after that, and I'm not kidding. They had witnessed so many of the improbable things that had happened to me, including my sobriety. Dick VanSloun had been my "hope match," and now I had become theirs.

As I progressed in my recovery, I developed a passion for connecting addicts with effective recovery programs on a large scale, and for helping them rebuild their lives. And how do addicts rebuild? We benefit from the right rehab, yes. But we rebuild by having our hearts restored. Not only do we need to be set free from physical addictions, but from emotional wounds and trauma, which often occur in childhood.

That's all it is. It's that simple. The Lindell Recovery Network, in development for the past two years, will do just that. Through a series of divine connections, God has helped me create a unique plan that will offer addicts the most powerful help available anywhere, and on an unprecedented scale. And because of Donald and Melania Trump's passion for wiping out addiction, the Trump administration is also eliminating many of the bureaucratic roadblocks that prevent help from reaching the people who need it. With God's help, my goal is to help millions of addicts and to create thousands of jobs. I can hardly believe God has put me in a position to put this plan into action.

Two months after the manufacturing summit, in September 2017, MyPillow entered a float in the annual Steamboat Days parade in Carver, Minnesota. Visiting Carver was very meaningful for me. I'd spent more than two-thirds of my life in the town, and so much had happened here. So many bad decisions, but some good ones, too. So many wrong turns, but also some right ones. Now, I was going to ride this parade float and toss out MyPillows to kids along the route. I was already aboard and ready to go when a police cruiser pulled up next to us and stopped. The car door opened and a uniform got out. It was Officer Larry.

I laughed. "Just like the old days, isn't it Larry? You pulling me over."

Larry was the Carver police officer who pulled me over on a warrant, but then let me get those important papers to Corey instead of arresting me instantly. I jumped off the float and we caught up for a few moments.

"Hey, am I in that book you're writing?" Larry said.

"You sure are! Do you remember what I said to you back then?"

I'd told Larry I knew he had an arrest warrant for me, but that if I didn't get those papers to Corey, MyPillow was finished. That the "platform," which had something to do with God, would be gone. That it would change history.

"Of course I remember," Larry said.

"Why did you believe me, Larry?" It was a question I'd wondered about for years.

Larry said, "Mike, you were so passionate. I just believed that *you* believed what you were saying." Bottom line: Like so many others, he took a chance on me—and probably changed the course of my life.

Larry and I said our goodbyes. I climbed back onto the float and the parade began. Riding through Carver felt like a homecoming. As I tossed out pillows to kids along the route, I saw so many familiar faces. People I'd grown up with. Some Regulars from Schmitty's. City leaders. Old friends and new ones. It was like a rewind of all the seasons of my life, and I thought I could see in their faces that they had forgiven me. And finally, I had forgiven myself.

Kendra has taught me so much about forgiveness. About grace and redemption. As we navigate life together, we continue to grow closer, building our relationship with God as our firm foundation. Along the way, many people ushered me toward Jesus, but she is the one who led me home. Since our first meeting, she has stood by me and behind me with love and prayer.

Maybe more than anything, prayer is the thing my newfound relationship with Jesus has impacted most. It was January 2017 when I found out my dad was in the hospital, trapped in the nightmare of delirium. Doctors said he would never escape. Dad spent the next seven months in three different hospitals. During that time, my siblings and I never gave up. Marcy spent almost every day next to his bed while the rest of us prayed fervently for his recovery. Before I met Jesus, I was reactive in prayer, asking God to get me out of one scrape or another. But after the Drop Zone, I became proactive in prayer, seeking God's will and praying according to His word in Scripture.

That's where we were with my dad. We told the doctors, "We don't believe you." Our father had entered the hospital pushing a walker. "He's going to walk out of here carrying that walker over his head," we said.

In prayer, God revealed to us that there was a medication that was keeping our dad in what seemed like a medically induced lobotomized state. Over and over, we pleaded with the doctors to take him off it. Finally, we asked for just a chance. Take him off for a week, we said.

"Alright," one physician said. "You've got seven days."

Seven days later, Dad woke up. He literally just came to, suddenly himself again. A few days later, he walked out of the hospital carrying his walker over his head. Three weeks later, I played him in pool and he beat me. Utterly and completely healed, Dad has never looked back.

Maybe that kind of attitude is in my genes. Everything I tried in life, I dove into it with a passion. If something happened where I had to change course, it would often knock me for a loop. But I look back now and realize those things had to happen. I wasn't *just* an addict. I was an addict *and* an entrepreneur. I was an addict *and* a child of God. My life was just like any other—full of trials. Crack cocaine took everything: my marriage, my relationship with my kids, Schmitty's, and my company. But each time I fell, by God's grace I got back up again.

Now, standing on the Vines Center stage at Liberty University, I looked out at the crowd and remembered the premonition I'd had at that home show in Des Moines, when I'd seen those thousands of empty seats in that arena and realized that someday I'd have to face my worst fear. Not only had God now brought that to fruition, but He had also taken away my fear. There is no feeling like the knowledge that you are exactly where you are supposed to be, doing exactly what God would have you do, and that is what I felt that day at Liberty.

As I wrapped up my Convocation speech, I emphasized that each person in that audience also had a calling and that they should never give up their quest to fulfill it. When I took my seat at stage left, it hit me again: the awesome and unimaginable plans God has for each of us.

Honestly, I don't know where this ends. Just when I think God can't bless me any more, He does. Sitting there on that wildly unlikely platform, I asked my favorite question: What are the odds?

What are the odds that an ex-crack addict, drinker, and gambling addict would be invited to address this group of young people?

One in a million? One in a billion? Impossible?

Let's call it what it is: a miracle.

TO BE CONTINUED…

Trust in the Lord with all your heart,
and lean not on your own understanding;
In all your ways acknowledge Him,
and He shall direct your paths.

Proverbs 3: 5-6